KIDNAPPED FROM GOD:

The Call to Come Home

KIDNAPPED FROM GOD:

The Call to Come Home

How Wars, Politics and Personal Agendas of
Influential People Shaped the Faith of Believers Today

By Andrew Gabriel Roth

"I am the light of the world. He who follows me will

not walk in darkness, but he will find the light of life for

his soul." (John 8:12)

DEDICATIONS

This book is dedicated to our Heavenly Father, YHWH, Who inspired our quest for wisdom and truth and allowed us, my wife Jaye and I, through the guidance of His Holy Spirit, to write this book. He has led the way for this book, directing every aspect from what needs to be researched and included to how it should be presented. Glory be to Him and to His Only-Begotten Son, our Messiah and Savior, Yeshua (Jesus) of Nazareth. And glory also to his Set-Apart Apostles for showing us the way to a life of truth and salvation.

I am profoundly grateful to you, Jaye, for not only encouraging and helping me through your own divinely inspired research, writing and editing to produce a coherent narrative about this book's hopeful message, but also for your particular gifting in being able to take this immense and majestic story and distill it down to its essence. Your role in making this work what it is today cannot be overstated. Thank you for being my wife and co-laborer.

To many of you who have been with us for a long time, encouraged and supported this work, we also humbly dedicate this book. A special thanks to our friends, especially in the USA, UK, Ireland, New Zealand, Switzerland, Israel, South Africa and Swaziland. Our deepest gratitude also to Terrie Gerakines, for your precious time to help edit this book and for your feedback and to Judah Gabriel Himango, for your technical expertise and support over the years. May all of you and your descendants be blessed for your service to Him.

Lastly, to the remnant God Almighty knows He can trust, who have labored in obscurity, we thank you for your service.

Andrew Gabriel Roth

Table of Contents

Oh that my ways may be established to guard Your statutes! Then I shall not be ashamed when I look upon all Your commandments. I shall give thanks to You with uprightness of heart, when I learn Your righteous judgments. I shall keep Your statutes.

Do not completely abandon me!

(Psalm 119:5-8)

INTRODUCTION

Something exceedingly precious and irreplaceable has been stolen from you! It is called *the Truth*. While clearly a nefarious crime from the deep past, this indispensable thing you have lost must be urgently recovered at all costs.

For centuries, we have walked around, *kidnapped from God*, unaware of how much our environment has influenced our thoughts and God given ability to discern the truth from falsehood. The tragedy is, while He has always preserved a remnant to pass down the wisdom of the ages to His beloved people, we have chosen to go through the broad gate, after our common, perceived history that is often subject to what is popular or comfortable.

God Almighty is now pulling back the curtains to reveal what has been hidden and is giving you the choice – come home to Him or stay with your captors. No more will He allow you to be lukewarm regarding Him (Revelation 3:16).

God had to test Abraham to make sure that he truly loved Him and that he could be trusted with the great gift he was about to receive. Likewise, He wants to see if you are worthy of His gift of Salvation and so a delusion was sent to confound the unsuspecting.

When we have nothing but void where the truth should be; our enemy is always eager to fill in that void with lies and deception, chaos and confusion. He prowls around like a roaring lion, seeking out whom he can devour (1 Peter 5:8), and the end result is that the truth was stolen from you when you were *kidnapped from God*.

Our captivity began in the early decades of the faith, when the original message of the Bible and the Good News became diluted in favor of political correctness, the quest for unbridled power and expediency. Paul warned us against such men who will pervert the Gospel of Messiah and create confusion (Galatians 1:7). It was their attempt to outwit God, to usurp His power and authority, as if that were even possible.

The question is, are you ready to know the Messiah as his original followers did? He stands at your door and knocks. Salvation is one thing but, walking intimately with him in covenant is quite another, and that is your path home to our Heavenly Father.

Whether you realize it or not, you have a deeper identity beyond your individual church denomination and are instead members of *the Way* who first heard the call of the Apostles. Your destiny is inextricably linked, not just to the salvation of the Messiah, but to the First Covenant promises all the way back to Genesis.

Unfortunately, wars, politics and personal agendas have consistently blocked your path, while a counterfeit vision was put in its place to keep you in exile. We need to recognize that Scripture is the ultimate change agent, not just in our individual lives but in the destiny of nations. The bottom line is we often don't have the will because we don't know His will.

This book will uncover, step by step, that the best evidence we have for this bait and switch is revealed through Scripture and the writings of the Early Church Fathers.

Join us as we journey into the past and unveil how it all began to prepare ourselves for Messiah's return!

SECTION ONE

The Call to the Nations

And it will be that all who call on the name of Master YHWH will be saved. (Acts 2:21)

Have you ever stopped for a moment and considered having a DNA test to find out more about your family lineage? It has fascinated us for many centuries to discover all we can about who we are and those who came before us, but it has only been in recent years with the rise of the internet and the advances in science that we now have the opportunity to fulfill our deep yearning, insatiable curiosity and desire to answer the ultimate question of "Who am I?"

Likewise, have you ever wondered, secretly or openly, which church or Messianic assembly today is truly following the mandates of our King and Savior? Have you, as a believer in our Messiah, ever wondered who you are among the 41,000 versions of Christianity or among the various sects of the Messianic or Hebrew Roots movements? We all claim that we love our Savior

11

yet, we are not breaking down the walls that divide us as believers. Why is this?

If there are times you feel disconnected from your brothers and sisters in other churches or the Torah-observant believers of Messiah and the Jewish roots of our faith, please know that this is not what the Scripture intended to happen.

The Renewed Covenant gives us a few clues. When the Apostles were preaching to non-Aramaic or non-Hebrew speaking Gentiles, the new believers were called "Kristianay" (1 Peter 4:16), a word derived from the Greek *christos*, referring to "the Anointed One" (the Messiah).

But in many of the Aramaic-speaking places that the Apostles went to, the Gentile believers would not have been called by the Greek term, Kristianay. We are not told if the Gentile believers were called anything except that they were followers of *The Way*, which is why, when Paul is being questioned by Jewish and Roman authorities he says:

But this I admit to you, that according to the Way which they call a sect I do serve the God of our fathers, believing everything that is in accordance with the Law and that is written in the Prophets." (Acts 24:14 NAU)

Hence, we have two groups who are bound together by one God and one Messiah as clearly stated below:

Or is God the God of Jews only? Is He not the God of Gentiles also? Yes, of Gentiles also, since indeed God who will justify the circumcised by faith and the uncircumcised through faith is one. (Romans 3:29-30 NAU)

While the Renewed Covenant is clear on Christians having a covenantal role, what sometimes gets overlooked is that their role did not start with the Messiah but is deeply embedded in the overall story of the First Covenant, all the way back to Genesis.

In fact, for the first nineteen generations of people, there were no ethnic distinctions given at all. Though there clearly were people from different places or nations, the Scripture only discriminated between whether they were righteous or wicked, not if they were Jewish or Gentile, for neither classification even existed at that time.

After the Flood, ten generations pass until we get to Abraham, and it was Abraham's faith, not his lineage or ethnicity, that set him apart for the Almighty's great purpose, and in turn, blessed the world. However, did you know that Abraham, the father of the Hebrew people, was himself born a Gentile? He literally went to bed a Babylonian and woke up a *Hebrew*. Derived from the word *abar*, to be a *Hebrew* means "to cross over," and so our hero Abraham crossed over from ignorance of the one true God to obedience and allegiance to His will (Genesis 22:15-17).

The problem for us today is that trying to understand Messiah without looking at four millennia of Scripture background before he was born is like trying to study for a history test by ignoring 75% of the history book. Perhaps that is why the first thing Matthew tells us is that Yeshua is the son of David and the son of Abraham. But what can that possibly mean to believers today and how does that relate to him also being the Son of God?

Alternatively, for those of you that took the less common path of professional Bible study, did your Bible college or seminary teachers tell you that you are a believer in a Jewish Messiah named Yeshua and that there was no such thing as the New Testament when Yeshua (Jesus) was preaching?

He is called Yeshua, meaning "YAH saves," and everything that he and his Apostles were teaching was either based on or from the Tanakh (First Covenant a.k.a. Old Testament). That is because the New Testament did not exist and would not even be written until many years after Yeshua's death and resurrection. Matthew was completed around 45 CE and Revelation in about 96 CE. These books in turn agreed with Paul who said he believed "everything" that is *written* in the Law (Torah) and the prophets. The written word or Scripture, however, is not to be confused with the *oral law* of customs and traditions.

Having said that, how do you think the first generations of Christians would relate to Christianity today—as something familiar or foreign? Ask yourself, who was our Savior before he performed the miracles? What were the traditions of his family and did he follow them? What was his childhood like? Perhaps you have considered asking your pastor, church or congregational leaders questions like these or sadly, you have become conditioned to not asking questions for fear of isolation or worse. One thing we know for sure is that he was not put into a time machine as a child and then magically popped out as a man performing miracles.

Also, what about our Savior's Heavenly Father? Why is it important to know His Name and more importantly, how do we call on His Name if we don't know it? How do we honor Him in the way He desires and commands us to if we don't obey His instructions? Does this affect our blessings – of wisdom, discernment, peace, prosperity and so on? Why and how did some of our early Church Fathers also separate us from the Truth and cause us to fail?

Or, looking at your own lineage, could your ancestors have belonged to one of the 12 tribes that strayed away from God Almighty during Solomon's and Jeroboam's reign and are part of the lost tribes, dispersed subsequently to foreign lands?

If you are like most people we have met, you probably never really gave these questions any serious thought, but instead followed what you believed or were taught.

These questions, and many more like them, are often unanswered in the sweep of later Christian tradition. However, if your heart yearns for more truth, then please read on and rediscover some of our early history and the reasons for the divisions that occurred.

Abraham, and later Messiah Yeshua himself, is literally the path and passport for the nations to come home to the One True God. It only remains for His people who are now scattered across the world to find their *spiritual DNA* and begin their journey home to the original covenantal role the Scriptures intended for them all along.

This book is dedicated to sharing that Scripture message and showing how it plays out both in history and in our collective prophetic future. It has been written for a time such as this, at the prompting of the Holy Spirit, to let you know God Almighty is pulling down strongholds that have held our nations and churches in bondage in anticipation of the Messiah's return and the need to prepare ourselves.

You will read about the struggles of God's people, the lessons learned and not learned, and about having His Mercy and Grace. We hope your time with us will be both enlightening and thought provoking. There is no offense intended to any one group of people, nor excuses made for others, although we do seek to challenge you and give you hope for a better future, so that you can become the best version of yourself and get closer to your Creator, putting your trust in Him instead of man.

For it is foretold that, in the End of Days, when the nations of the world unite according to the prophecies of Micah and Isaiah, we will stream into the future Temple like gushing rivers all pouring into the ocean, being compelled to His Holy House, to receive the Source of His divine light and life. And so it will come to be, as the Apostle John wrote:

After these things I looked, and behold, a great multitude which no one could count, from every nation and all tribes and peoples and tongues, standing before the throne and before the Lamb, clothed in white robes, and palm branches were in their hands; and they cry out with a loud voice, saying, "Salvation to our God who sits on the throne, and to the Lamb." And all the angels were standing around the throne and around the elders and the four living creatures; and they fell on their faces before the throne and worshiped God, saying, "Amen, blessing and glory and wisdom and thanksgiving and honor and power and might, be to our God forever and ever. Amen."

(Revelation 7:9-12 NAU)

OUR CREATOR'S NAME

*Sing to God, sing praises to His name; extol Him who rides on
the clouds, by His name YAH, and rejoice before Him.
(Psalm 68:4 - NKJV)*

Many of us have grown up hearing uplifting hymns proclaiming
"Hallelujah." However, here is the first truth revealed: The letter
"J" was not invented before 1600 CE and so the proper spelling
"Halleluyah" comes from the Hebrew phrase "Hallel-u-YAH"
which actually means "Praise you YAH." It does not mean "Praise
the LORD," because LORD is His title in English, while YAH is
the simplified form of His Name. The longer name, pronounced
Yahweh, means "YAH Who exists" or "YAH He who exists."

As for the Messiah, he said that his name was the same as His
Father's (John 17:11), because he was called *Yeshua*, a Hebrew
name meaning "YAH is salvation" or "YAH saves," and now you
have another truth. The correct translation of Luke 2:21 should
read as follows:

And when eight days had passed, before his circumcision, his name was then called Yeshua, the name given by the angel before he was conceived in the womb.

The English term "Jesus" comes to us from the Greek *Iesous* and later in Latin as *Ihsous*. In the early 17th century when the letter "J" was introduced, his name became *Jihsous* in Latin which later became Jesus in English. Since Messiah's actual name then contains the promise of God's salvation, we have opted to use it throughout this book.

At the same time, and to be helpful to our Christian readers, we have also retained the more common English designations for Deity such as "LORD," "God," "the Creator" and "the Almighty," into which we will intersperse His actual Name, instead of frequently using the Hebrew term *Elohim*, which means "God." Alternatively, out of respect for His Set-Apart Name and our Jewish readers, we will almost always show His Name as "YHWH" rather than fully vocalize it.

Lastly, are you aware that early church leaders knew the Name of our Heavenly Father but decided in the last few centuries to hide it or avoid using it? The photos, courtesy of the Charles Payette collection, appearing on pages 20 and 21, show the 1611 King James Bible and the 1607 Geneva Bible with the Name of YHWH prominently displayed.

'For I know the plans that I have for you,' declares YHWH, 'plans for complete peace and not for misery, to give you a future and a hope. Then you will call upon Me and come and pray to Me, and I will listen to you. You will seek Me and find Me when you search for Me with all your heart (Jeremiah 29:11-13)

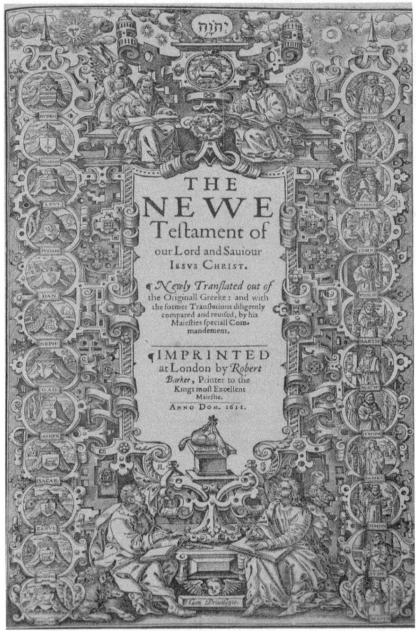

Image from the 1611 King James Bible – Name of Almighty God, YHWH, at the top in Hebrew

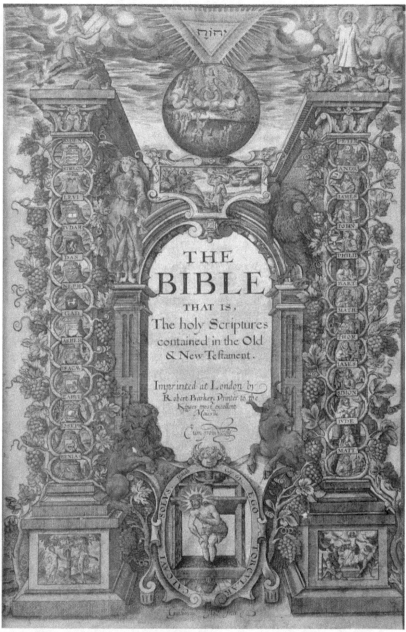

Image from the 1607 Geneva Bible - Name of Almighty God, YHWH, at the top in Hebrew

HEAVENLY FATHER

WE PRAISE YOU, BLESS YOU

AND SANCTIFY YOUR SET-APART NAME

AND GIVE YOU ALL THE THANKS AND PRAISE AND
GLORY.

WE THANK YOU FOR ALL YOUR BLESSINGS

YOUR PROTECTION AND GUIDANCE

BUT MOST OF ALL WE THANK YOU FOR SENDING US

YOUR ONLY BEGOTTEN SON

THROUGH WHOM YOU GAVE US SALVATION AND
WHO TAUGHT US

HOW TO LIVE AND WALK

ACCORDING TO YOUR WORD

SO THAT WE TOO MAY BE PLEASING TO YOU.

WE PRAY THAT YOU WILL ROLL BACK THE
DARKNESS OF THIS AGE

AND TILL THE GARDEN OF OUR HEARTS

SO THAT IT MAY PRODUCE GOOD FRUIT.

MAY YOUR KINGDOM OF HEAVEN SPREAD ACROSS
THE EARTH

AND TAKE GROUND FOR YOUR GLORY.

AMEN, AMEN.

SECTION TWO

YHWH and His Remnant

*Mercy and peace in love be multiplied to you. My beloved, while
I take all pains to write to you of our common life, it is needful
for me to write to you, encouraging you to maintain a conflict for
the faith which was once delivered to the Set Apart believers.
(Jude 1:2-3)*

We have always had the freedom to choose tradition, family and community over history and truth, but is that what our Heavenly Father and His Son would want for us? And is that not why He sent His Only Begotten Son to teach us so that we may have eternal life?

Most of the stories that have come down to us from the ancient world deal with extraordinary people who, through great courage, wisdom or the assistance of their deities, win an important battle or surmount a tremendous obstacle.

Sometimes, like with the Trojan War, the deities take sides against each other; in other tales, such as Jason and the Argonauts or the Twelve Labors of Hercules, the individual's nearly superhuman status shines through their efforts to bring great victory. However, when it comes to the Bible, we find it stands nearly alone and in complete defiance to these other kinds of stories.

It is not so much that we do not have our own biblical paragons of tremendous physical strength (Samson) or leaders celebrated for their amazing wisdom and cunning (Solomon), for clearly we do. However, what sets the biblical great men and women apart from any other ancient literature is that, but for the intervention of the Almighty, they would be weak and ordinary.

Therefore, we must ask ourselves: Why does our Creator so often choose the disadvantaged or the undistinguished among us to be His greatest representatives? Why choose the second son so frequently when clearly tradition always favored the eldest? How does a stutterer and fugitive from justice like Moses end up leading two million people out of bondage from the greatest empire on the planet at that time? How does a humble shepherd boy—the youngest of eight sons—rise to become King David?

In all these cases and so many others, what made these biblical heroes special has to do with their faith in Elohim (God) and their willingness to follow His commandments. In fact, ever since one tribal leader named Abraham was humble and worthy enough to hear His voice, he has been a continuous blessing to the rest of the world (Genesis 12:3, Acts 3:25, Romans 4:16).

When dealing with the First Covenant Scriptures (Old Testament) in particular, the few things that all these great men and women have in common are the key attributes of hearing from God, obeying His words and having courage with humility to carry out their individual mission. Additionally, in the Apostolic

24

Writings (New Testament) we find, according to Yeshua, that faith and obedience are inextricably bound to each other in a profound way:

Then a man said to him, "Behold, your mother and your brothers are standing outside and desire to speak with you." But he answered and said to him that had spoken to him, "Who is my mother? And who are they who are my brothers?" And he stretched forth His hand towards his disciples and said, "Behold my mother and my brothers. For anyone who does the will of my Father who is in heaven, is my brother, and my sister, and my mother." (Matthew 12:47-50)

Likewise, in the Parable of the Vineyard, Yeshua made the point that the obedient son was the one who was most valued and esteemed by his father (Matthew 21:28-41).

As such, the original faith and personal beliefs of our individual Scripture heroes really matters, because that was what got them called—whether patriarch, prophet or apostle—to Father YHWH's great purpose in the first place. These great men and women literally became *the remnant of Yahweh.*

Despite the fact that millennia separate us as the believers of today from all of our spiritual ancestors, Paul was eager to point out that Abraham is the father of us all (Romans 4:16), while Yeshua said that the true sons of Abraham must do the deeds of Abraham (John 8:39-40).

What happens, then, when our own modernity stands in the way of understanding the beliefs and actions of our spiritual ancestors? What happens when we instead sacrifice those timeless righteous precepts on a false altar of personal agendas and political correctness? In that case, my friends, as we struggle with conflicting priorities, the answer must be it is *we* who have been *kidnapped from God,* and we, if we are to be His remnant, desperately need to return home to our Heavenly Father!

But for many believers today, the way back seems either unclear or impossibly distant. In other cases, the true history of what the patriarchs, Messiah, his Apostles, and even early leaders in the church actually believed has been either ignored or deliberately covered up.

For example, did you know that some of the earliest leaders in the Catholic Church, people who were directly trained by the apostles, were Torah observant, adhering to the Saturday Sabbath and the Feasts of YHWH? Or about the righteous bishop who was warned in Rome to disregard the instructions he got directly from the Apostles in favor of the later traditions of that same church?

Did you know that the first fifteen bishops of Jerusalem were "Hebrews of the circumcision" and praised for their righteousness and piety in Catholic records? Or that when these same bishops were exiled from their homeland, they were replaced by others who disregarded what their predecessors originally believed?

If any of these examples—and there are plenty of others that this book will reveal to you—sound surprising, it is because of our own cultural core assumptions. Please read on to see how where we originally came from has a direct bearing on where we will all be going in these years leading up to the return of the Messiah.

YHWH and His Word

For the earth shall be filled with the knowledge of the glory of YHWH as the waters cover the sea. (Habakkuk 2:14)

The Bible as we know it today is not really a "book." It is an ancient library, an archive of our God speaking and intervening in human history. In all of what is conventionally counted as sixty-six books, from Genesis to Revelation, the Word is constantly being issued and re-issued to humanity so that we might "choose life" and declare, as Joshua did, "As for me and my house, we will serve Master YHWH."

Our hope for all of you is that it becomes clear how history and politics have interfered with our ability to see that original biblical vision. In saying this though we are not trying to assert preeminence of one denomination over another, but, rather, we are attempting to give back the history that has been lost or even suppressed to the average English-speaking believer, you. We want you take control of your beliefs once more.

The purpose of this book is to relate this history to believers around the world, to strengthen their faith and to give them back what they have lost. Nearly all aspects of faith traditions agree on the basics and yet, for whatever reason, no longer teach or emphasize the wider history.

From the Oral Traditions of the Jews to the Catechism of the Catholics and the writings of Luther, Calvin and so many others, each tradition only has a piece of the tapestry that makes up the story of God's people. We will try and gather those threads without judging which one is superior to all others, find common ground, and then attempt to recover the overall truth as objectively as possible. We are not here as an ambassador or an apologist for a particular point of view.

While most historians strive for objectivity, telling a grand story from one's point of view with regard to culture and faith traditions has its challenges. Even in our modern age, when we have actual podcasts or films of historical events, we still see this tension play out.

We might think that having a camera or microphone record of events would take the subjectivity out of the equation, but we would be wrong. Pictures can be doctored, images cropped, and videos edited to tell a story vastly different than the one that actually unfolded. How many court cases have we seen that show videos which seem "airtight" and which were later proven to not tell the complete story? How much more problematic for things from the distant past, where history often unfolds through the pen of a single individual?

Even so, for the learned elite who did leave behind their histories, there existed back in times past (at least in theory) a way to check their work: Across the Middle East and into Asia Minor great libraries existed, where almost anyone could borrow books and make sure certain sources were quoted accurately.

The Apostle Paul's hometown of Tarsus boasted one of the finest libraries in the world, as did Alexandria, Egypt, which were familiar to the Jewish historians Philo and Josephus.

While it may have required great effort and expense to verify sources in times past, we know today that the threat of being investigated kept most ancient historians honest. Furthermore, in the light of modern analysis, it is easy to prove that learned men like Paul, his biographer Luke, Josephus and Philo strived to maintain the highest standard of credibility possible during their age.

Our point is simple: Today's historians stand on the shoulders of the giants who came before them, and it is, therefore, our job to accurately explain their legacy and continue the work that they began in earnest. We cannot know where we are going without understanding from where we came. While we know this to be true by understanding secular history, it is even more critical to understand the history of the people in the Bible and the ancestry of our faith.

We hope at a later time to write a book about the history of the Bible itself, from the time the Word was given to its current iterations. Accordingly, we will seek to tell you, not just the twists and turns that occurred to bring the biblical text into our hands today, but to also relate the stories of the people who lived these events, as well as the people who put the text into the manuscripts and translations that we currently possess.

This includes telling the stories of less than stellar people who were involved and thus demonstrate our Heavenly Father's ability to work with even the worst of people if they can play a role in preserving His Word!

Moreover, we believe, when this story is told in the correct order, many previously obscure biblical and historical facts will clearly and convincingly come to light. May the truth set us free indeed.

The Role of our Earliest Ancestors

"Your descendants will also be like the dust of the earth, and you will spread out to the west and to the east and to the north and to the south; and in you and in your descendants shall all the families of the earth be blessed. "Behold, I am with you and will keep you wherever you go, and will bring you back to this land; for I will not leave you until I have done what I have promised you." (Genesis 28:14-15 NAU)

From the moment Adam was created, struggle, conflict and challenges became part of the human condition. While it was clear Adam and Eve loved each other, conflict came again in the form of a serpent tempting Eve to eat the forbidden fruit. After she had done so, she persuaded Adam to do the same and so incurred the wrath of God.

Their subsequent expulsion from Paradise earned them a much harder life and even greater challenges, culminating with their elder son Cain killing their younger son Abel. Cain was then forced to flee from their presence, never to be seen again.

As hard as these trials were, Adam and Eve overcame their grief, and had another son, Seth. In him hope was renewed once more. Also, Adam's very long lifespan of 930 years allowed him to do more than merely improve himself, but also affect the lives of his descendants.

In Enoch's case, whose name means "dedicated and trained," Adam's life lessons seem to have been really taken to heart, resulting in a man so righteous that he was said to have literally walked with his God flawlessly for 300 years! At the end of that dedicated walk, he was taken by God up to heaven while still alive, just as Elijah would be later, them being the only two to receive such a rare and prestigious honor.

Noah, whose name means "peace and comfort," found favor with YHWH and was granted the right of survival from the Flood. But his world gets turned upside down in the greatest disaster of all time because of the hardship and grief he witnessed, as he watched the extinction of the human race from the window of his crowded ark. After the rain stopped, he had to face the devastation all around him. Even though everything that was human in Noah probably felt great hopelessness, Noah's faith in his God and obedience to His commands kept him and his family together through the worst trials imaginable. When it was all over, everyone Noah protected survived, left the ark and went on to repopulate the human race.

Ten generations later God's next great leader, Abraham, arose. Abraham showed time and time again how to prosper by simply following his Master's voice and treating everyone around him with dignity and respect. While he is blessed and gains favor and fortune, he has to constantly face struggles.

Whether it be dealing with the Pharaoh and the people of the land he entered, accommodating his wife Sarah by expelling Ishmael or settling a dispute with his nephew Lot that threatened to tear the family apart, Abraham's faith helped him prevail.

On the occasions where Abraham's faith was lacking, such as in doubting the promise that he and Sarah would have a son in their old age, the obedience with which he was credited was only justified when he attempted to sacrifice Isaac (James 2:20). Abraham's righteousness was described by God this way: "Abraham kept My divine instructions, My statutes, My regulations and My laws (Torah)" (Genesis 26:5). And, because of him, his descendants throughout all the nations would also be blessed (Genesis 22:16-18).

Yet, even with all that Abraham knew and would have passed on to his grandson, Jacob exploited his brother's hunger to gain his inheritance. He was crafty in getting the blessing due to Esau and was not concerned about the morality of it but, rather, with being caught.

As a result, he was forced to leave his home and learn a few hard lessons while living with an even more shrewd uncle for 20 years. Laban used his daughters in a complicated chess game to keep Jacob bound in servitude. But because of the promise of Father YHWH to Abraham and Isaac, Jacob prospered before he returned home to be reunited with his brother Esau and successfully lead his family.

However, later, Abraham's great-grandson Joseph, due to his boastful arrogance and conceit, endured family betrayal and slavery before he learned humility along with how to use his gifts. He rose to second in command to Pharaoh and saved Egypt and Israel from famine. The point is, in every generation and crisis, Father YHWH sent great leaders to take care of their families, help the wider world around them and keep His commandments as their binding tie to stay together.

Walking with the Almighty

And many people shall go and say, Come and let us go up to the mountain of YHWH, to the house of the Mighty One of Jacob; and He will teach us of His ways, and we will walk in his paths! For out of Zion shall go forth the Torah and the Word of YHWH from Jerusalem. (Isaiah 2:3)

When Solomon was asked by the Almighty what he wanted for his future rule, the young prince famously asked for wisdom, saying that his father David had *walked* before Him "in truth and righteousness and in the uprightness of his heart" (1 Kings 3:6).

As it turns out, *walking*, in the spiritual sense, is an extremely important concept that helps us understand the earliest origins of the Bible. It means to agree to spend time with and go in the same direction as another person; and in this case, that other one is the Almighty Himself! We learn, for example, that Adam and Eve walked with the Creator in Genesis 3. Subsequently, the next time this walking happens is with Enoch, and, in that case, he is so good at pleasing his Creator, that he is taken up bodily to heaven while still alive.

Noah, we are told, walked with the Almighty and was blameless (Genesis 6:9). Then Abraham was called to the same walk (Genesis 17:1) and completed it successfully (Genesis 26:5). The same process applied to Isaac, Jacob and Joseph (Genesis 24:40, 48:15; Psalm 80:1). Later on, we would all be commanded to also walk with the Creator (Isaiah 2:3).

As the prophet Amos (3:3) points out, two cannot walk together unless they first have a meeting, and this is what our Creator wishes to do with all of His people. He desires to *meet* with us, give us instructions and then have us walk with Him.

Since at the heart of "walking" is an agreement or covenant with our Creator, it stands to reason that those blessed men and women in Genesis maintained their covenant by hearing His Voice and acting in agreement with it.

As a result, this oral chain of transmission is easily understood in the context of the long lives of the patriarchs. Adam, after all of his experiences with God, passed that understanding down to his son Seth. Both Adam and Seth, in their turn, lived more than 900 years each. Since Enoch was born 622 years after Adam was created and 492 years after Seth was born, this gave Adam more than 300 years to educate Enoch with the help of his son Seth.

Before Enoch gets taken up to heaven, he had 300 years to train his son Methuselah and 113 years to train his grandson Lamech, along with Adam and Seth while they were still alive. Both Methuselah and Lamech, the 7th and 8th generation from Adam lived with Noah about 600 years before the Flood came and they died, leaving Noah with the benefit of generations of knowledge.

Noah, however, survives the Flood and in the subsequent 350 years of his life, the oral transmission of the Word of God is passed on to his son Shem and everyone else, all the way down to Terah, Abraham's father. Because Shem lives more than 500 years, he is still alive well after Abraham's son Isaac is born. The great wisdom and experience these people must have had over their multi-century long lives in hearing Father YHWH's voice, obeying it and passing it down the generations must have been both amazing and exceptional.

Each generation thereafter informs the one following it, from Isaac to Jacob and then from Jacob to Joseph. However, nearly a century and a half after Joseph dies, an even greater challenge was looming large on the horizon. As Israel continued to multiply in Egypt, the natives viewed them with increasing suspicion.

When a new king who did not know of Joseph's good deeds took over, he very quickly enslaved Joseph's descendants until their Exodus from Egypt. It would then fall to Moses to hear the entire testimony about Father YHWH's people and write it all down, so that the ancestry of our faith is finally recorded for posterity. But as it turns out, Moses' path to power would be far from easy.

We have seen up to this point how Man has walked with the Almighty by hearing and obeying Him. However, if we are going to truly understand why so many of us today, starting with the Hebrew or Jewish people, have truly been *kidnapped from God*, we need to go deeper into the story of their struggles to keep the covenant in biblical times. Their faith would be sorely tested with the manifold temptations of the paganism around them. Their journey is one where they fall into sin and are severely punished, before God brings salvation to His lost sheep and calls them home. In so doing, their story is very much connected to the story of the church today.

SECTION THREE

The Struggle of the Hebrew People – Freedom to Captivity

"I will put My Spirit within you and cause you to walk in My statutes, and you will be careful to observe My ordinances. You will live in the land that I gave to your forefathers; so you will be My people, and I will be your God." (Ezekiel 36:27-28 NAU)

During the reign of an evil Egyptian king who began murdering male Hebrew infants, Moses was born. However, 80 years would go by before the Israelites see their deliverance from bondage. Moses, as most of you know, led two million people out of Egypt and into the uncertainty of a wilderness trek, fraught with danger. Coming out of a pagan nation after such an extended captivity helped plant seeds for Israel's later rebellion and idolatry, such as the worshipping of the Golden Calf.

Moses spent the next four decades dealing with the task of teaching God's Laws to his stiff-necked people, who had constant complaints, lack of faith and disrespect towards his leadership. On occasions his own siblings, and even others he worked closely with for years, plotted against him.

Israel also courted and barely escaped complete destruction several times, all because petty grievances became more important to them than being united in covenant under God. But Moses' steadfastness in recording and teaching these laws becomes the enduring legacy of his people that is still blessing the world even today.

The point is these struggles are just as relevant for modern believers as they were back in Moses' day. The cycle of coming together in covenant, only to be pulled away from it due to sin and temptation, is a tension and problem that has yet to be overcome. When we then consider the challenges of remaining pure in our culture and faith, the example that Moses left behind in humility, patience, grace, along with a willingness to be obedient to God, comes forward today with even greater force than it first did.

Under the leadership of Moses' chosen successor Joshua, Israel finally experiences what it is like to be united under the covenantal laws of their Creator. Joshua takes this dejected and confused lot and soon turns them into an obedient and effective war machine. With almost unchecked progress and very few defeats, Israel under Joshua surged forward to claim their land which was promised to Abraham yet delayed due to the wickedness of the previous generation. Joshua dies about a half century later with his people united, but with significant territory remaining for them to conquer without him. As it turns out, that task will prove to be far from either easy or quick.

After Joshua died, followed by other elders who had been trained by him, the chaotic period of the Judges began, with Israel once again abandoning God's divine laws. As a result of their flagrant rebellion and lapse back into paganism, when God withdrew His protection, Israel was unable to conquer their remaining territory.

Now the enemies that were promised to be wiped out, namely Canaanites, Sidonians and Philistines, instead grew into an even greater threat against Israel. Opposing them were sometimes brilliant and righteous judges and generals like Deborah and Barak, followed by inspired leaders like Gideon who were faithful in covenant during war but unfaithful to the Divine Law in peace.

Still other times Israel came under the direct yoke of pagans or became so apostate themselves that it was impossible to tell the difference between them and the nations around them. Judges even records one occasion where a civil war broke out amongst the tribes with horrific results. The lesson is clear: Keep the Commandments of the Almighty and live or disregard them and die.

And yet, for all that turmoil, a righteous remnant continued in their midst as well. The priesthood remained intact and the central shrine and altar had been set up at Shiloh, along with the Ark of the Covenant. Those therefore who did not go astray had a proper place to pray, do their sacrifices and keep the Torah. Their example endured as a shining light, just enough to ensure the nation's survival, at least for a while.

However, not all was right even amongst these people at Shiloh. Slowly a corrupt line emerged under the high priesthood of Eli when his two sons, Hophni and Phinehas, engaged in illicit sex and theft while performing their duties. Samuel, a little boy being raised in Eli's home, was then given the unenviable task of proclaiming God's judgment against Eli's entire family line.

A decade or so later, Eli and his wicked sons were dead, while the Ark was taken by the Philistines as a spoil of war. Forced to leave their home region of Crete probably due to a volcanic eruption, the Philistines left in ships and came to the Israelite side of the Mediterranean Sea, camping in territory that Israel had yet to claim for themselves.

In short order, the Philistines had built five fortified cities in the region and brought to it a sophisticated military and technological presence that included smelting iron, which was a huge feat for that time. Now they were armed and ready for war, striking from a position of strength, with Israel's most sacred relic firmly in their possession.

But Samuel, by this time a fully grown and charismatic young man, rallied his people. Using the theft of the Ark as a battle cry, Samuel brought his people to tears with his fiery rhetoric and drove them to their knees with a national prayer of repentance.

God immediately reinstated His protection and sent plagues on the Philistines, forcing them to urgently return what they had stolen and attempted to display before their idols.

His people now secure, Samuel continued to reign with peace and justice, but even then, challenges remained as his two sons became just as corrupt as Eli's had been. This then sparked a crisis, as Israelite clan leaders worried Samuel was growing too old to continue and his sons were not worthy successors. In the end there was only one solution: Samuel had to give them a king.

On the other hand, would Saul the son of Kish be the right man to lead his people as Samuel had done for so long? Would he, like Samuel before him, inspire his people in righteous covenant keeping or cause them to descend into apostasy yet again?

As Saul begins his reign, the Philistines and other enemies surround him on every side. By all conventional measure, these enemies greatly surpass him in military might and battle experience, but Saul has a powerful secret weapon in the form of the prophet and high priest Samuel.

As long as Saul follows Samuel's counsel, the nation is victorious against her enemies and prosperous as it expands her borders. But Saul is battling his own demons. Fear and self-doubt are just waiting to emerge in a public and disgraceful way to the shame of all.

Hence, when the giant Philistine Goliath of Gath mocks Israel and her God, King Saul has no answer for him. He will neither bring a single champion against the giant to gain victory, as was a common custom of the time, nor will he send his full armies against the enemy camp. Instead, Saul simply marinates in his own self-pity day after day. He does nothing while his people look on helplessly, wondering if their king will defend their nation, or even their faith. With all the resources at Saul's command, it is his own lack of confidence that keeps him, and his army, paralyzed.

Fortunately for Israel, not everyone in Saul's kingdom was so complacent. A simple shepherd boy, David the son of Jesse, becomes enraged at Goliath's vicious taunts against their covenantal pact with the Almighty, and he yearns for these threats to be answered with righteous bravery. David is not scared of being small in stature or lacking combat experience. He had used his lowly position to learn how to protect his sheep from wolves, bears and lions, armed with nothing more than his slingshot.

With enduring faith in his God to help him kill the greatest soldier in the Philistine army, David convinces Saul to allow him to confront Goliath. David's mindset is critical here. He _knows_ that the one true God, YHWH, fights for them when they honor Him. As a result, it is a forgone conclusion to David that Goliath is doomed, and a single well aimed stone is all that is needed to bring that outcome to fruition. David's courage in turn sets the standard for how a warrior can literally use his faith as a weapon. How did David have such a _knowing_ that his God will stand by him? Was it his life of obedience that gave him such faith?

Interestingly enough David's wondrous victory over Goliath also had many unintended consequences that ultimately lead to the destruction of Saul's reign. David, who had already won the admiration of the crown prince Jonathan and Saul's daughter, Michal, David's future first wife, now adds to his supporters many of the common people.

Their frequent and loud exultations of, _Saul has slain thousands of Philistines, but David has slain tens of thousands_ rang in Saul's ears and only fed his fear that all he had built was under threat. In the end it was not Saul's frequent attempts against David's life that brought him down.

His descent actually began with his doubts and fears getting magnified on an international stage. No longer are the clear pronouncements of God through Samuel getting the faithful performance from Saul they once did. Saul is feeling he can rationalize those commands to go from destroying an enemy army as he was instructed to do, to leaving it alive and negotiating a treaty with their king. Saul also uses the hunger of his troops as an excuse to do sacrifices that were only permitted for priests to perform, usurping Samuel's God-given authority.

Then, in a final debasing act, after Samuel's death, Saul breaks his own righteous law and hires the witch of Endor to raise Samuel's spirit. Saul's hope, that Samuel will, from the grave, give him good counsel to survive a battle, are dashed when he hears he is doomed to abandonment and death, and the prophecy is fulfilled to the letter. Saul's bad decisions, all done in full public view, sent a terrifying message to his people that Covenant protection was situational, not absolute.

However, for David, his previous hero status did nothing to help transition him into a popular and effective king. Saul, despite his many flaws, remained popular with the majority of Israel. Even though Saul the man was gone, he still had sons who were eager to reclaim the throne from the upstart shepherd of Bethlehem.

In fact, it is not until David has ruled 8 years, with Jerusalem now the center of his nation's life and faith, that his people completely accepted him. David has fulfilled the goal first given to Abraham to conquer that place for his God and make it the sacred center of His kingdom on earth. The final goal, that of a permanent Temple where YHWH would dwell directly and presently with His people, at last seemed within reach.

Unfortunately, David became a victim of his own success which had devastating consequences for himself, his entire family and, of course, the nation. Almighty God had honored every single promise He made to David. He gave him victory on all sides from his enemies and multiplied his wealth and power. David was even told more could be given to him if he just asked for it, but none of that made him above the law. Adultery, covetousness, murder and later idolatry were crouching at his door.

David could not take that which rightfully belonged to another man without consequence. When he first lays eyes on the beautiful Bathsheba, it matters very little that she is married to Uriah the Hittite, one of his more faithful soldiers. But when Bathsheba becomes pregnant at a time when her soldier-husband is away from her bed, the scandal threatens to totally unravel David's kingdom.

He attempts to cover up the liaison by clumsily trying to get Uriah and Bathsheba together so he can deny the child is his. But Uriah is literally too loyal for his own good, refusing the privilege of a carnal visit while his men have been offered no such favor. Even when David gets Uriah drunk the alcohol does nothing to dislodge Uriah's personal sense of honor, so David concludes he needs to get him killed in battle.

What he could not have imagined however, is that God would communicate the details of this scandal directly to the royal prophet Nathan, along with a special plan to force David to confront his sin. Nathan begins by telling the story of a poor man who was greatly wronged by a rich and cruel man, knowing that David would react angrily by calling for the rich man's death. Nathan then responds by saying that David is in fact that rich man who took Uriah's precious wife from him and then abandoned him to his death. Prostrate now with regret and grief, David immediately admits his faults, but this is only enough to prevent his early death, not absolve him from all sin.

He will pay the final cost of that sin when he is forever disqualified from building the Temple he has already designed, after he shed family blood and went to war. While David will eventually be forgiven after he endures these hardships, in many ways he never recovers. He also fails to recognize the growing influence of paganism in his court wrought by his other foreign wives, which will then bring disastrous consequences on his son and successor, Solomon.

Solomon comes to the throne as a marked contrast to his father David. While David was 30 years old when taking the throne, Solomon is barely a teenager. So, David, just before his death, counseled his son to be strong, show himself to be a man and keep the charge of YHWH his God, according to what is written in the Divine Law (Torah).

David emphasized this righteousness so that Solomon would succeed in all that he did and wherever he turned because God had promised David, "**IF** your sons are careful of their way, to walk before Me in truth with all their heart and with all their soul, you shall not lack a man on the throne of Israel" (1 Kings 2:2-4).

While his father was famous as a warrior, Solomon was made famous for his great riches and wisdom, and all but avoided war except for brief incidents at the start and end of his reign. Even Solomon's name, meaning "peaceful," was meant to showcase how different his reign would be from his father's. Nowhere would this contrast be truer than with Solomon being able to finally build the one Temple for the One Almighty God in Jerusalem.

In a mere eleven years, Solomon completely reorganizes government for the better, expands Israel's borders and regional influence, brings in unprecedented wealth and prosperity and finishes the Temple. The fact that Solomon is still a fairly young man at this point must surely have given many great justifications to celebrate the glorious future he seemed certain to bring. Sadly however, it was not to be.

The one area where Solomon did far worse than his father David was with his nearly 1,000 wives and concubines. Solomon's particular taste for foreign queens soon became an obsession as he directed his great mind to understanding and performing nearly every possible variety of pagan belief in his midst.

His wives had turned his heart away from YHWH to their mighty ones. Solomon even went so far as to follow after Ashtoreth, the goddess of the Sidonians and Milkom, the detestable god of the Ammonites. He built high places for Kemosh, the abomination of Moab and for Molech, a horrific god that required child sacrifices. He built these many shrines and high places throughout the country, to burn incense and offer animal sacrifices to their mighty ones (1 Kings 11:4-9).

By doing this, Solomon enticed Israel to abandon Master YHWH, the God of Israel, not even a decade after he finished building the Temple. What a devastating example that must have set for the faithful! It was also a flagrant violation of Deuteronomy 20:17-18 where Moses commanded that the paganism in their midst be destroyed and to not intermarry with their pagan sons and daughters, for they would lead Israel to do all their abominations and sin against YHWH their God. With the establishment of *ungodly soul ties* created through these relationships and idolatry, the stage was now set for a fearsome judgment, with God promising civil war and the dissolution of the united monarchy coming in the next generation.

For the sake of His chosen place of Jerusalem where He placed His Name, only Judah, Benjamin and the priesthood would be given to Solomon's descendants, while the rest would be torn away from the throne because of Solomon's sin. In fact, the only reason why David's kingdom was allowed to endure in spite of these persistent lapses into paganism was because David's line had to be preserved to eventually bring us Messiah Yeshua.

Meanwhile, there was a brave soldier in Solomon's army by the name of Jeroboam, who got noticed by the king for his great work ethic. Solomon promptly promoted him to supervise one of the largest divisions of laborers working on construction projects in and around Jerusalem. For a time, all was well.

Then one day, when Jeroboam was on his way out of Jerusalem, he was confronted by the prophet Ahijah. The prophet told him that God had chosen him to take ten tribes away from Solomon to punish the king for his flagrant idolatry and allowing paganism to dominate the last twenty years of his reign. When Solomon became aware that Jeroboam was plotting against him, he tried to kill him, but Jeroboam fled to the court of Pharaoh Shishak I in Egypt and remained there, biding his time.

During this period, however, the very fabric of Israel's monarchy was about to be torn apart. After King Solomon died in 931 BCE, his son Rehoboam assumed the throne. Solomon had gifted to his son a kingdom of great wealth and power, but because of his idolatry now everything the king had built was at grave risk.

Under Solomon's rulership, the only persistent complaints he seems to have received were with regards to higher taxes to support his massive building projects. Many workers on those projects did not like the way they were forced from their homes to perform that labor. However, because almost everyone in the country was reaping financial benefits from those same projects and now had a beautiful new Temple to worship in, those complaints did not become serious enough to threaten his rule.

Rehoboam however was very different. He was everything his father was not. He was neither wise nor gentle nor in any way a people person like Solomon. In only five years he managed to provoke nearly every powerful leader or special interest group in Israel to frustration. He spurned repeatedly the good advice of elders who prospered under Solomon and raised punishing new taxes on the working poor that had none of the offsetting benefits they had when building up Jerusalem and the Temple just two decades earlier.

If any of this feels like déjà vu, perhaps we need to remember that, while the broad strokes of history tend to repeat themselves, the details of each iteration are different. For example, if our own leaders today are not willing to listen to the wise counsel of the experts that were given to them, can we truly expect them to have different and better results than Rehoboam did? Can our nation live up to its fullest potential?

In order to fulfill what He spoke to Jeroboam through the prophet Ahijah, YHWH hardened the heart of the king like the

Pharaoh of the Exodus that Moses confronted. This was designed to set the foundation for the fall of his kingdom. So, after Solomon died, reports of Rehoboam's offenses made their way to Jeroboam, who was still in Egypt.

The Pharaoh, Shishak I, recognized Rehoboam's weakness and invaded his kingdom five years later (926 BCE), exacting massive tribute from this impotent ruler in return for not burning Jerusalem to the ground. It is truly remarkable that we actually have a record of Shishak's campaign on his own tomb walls. As for Rehoboam, he took Temple treasures to pay Shishak, convinced that Almighty God would not come to his defense since he was not righteous. What a tragic contrast this was to his grandfather David who stood up to Goliath _knowing_ God was with him.

At the same time, Jeroboam had returned and was inciting an insurrection in Jerusalem. Unable to fight on two fronts, Rehoboam had no choice but to accept the division of his country as the ten tribes decided to set Jeroboam up as their king.

The Israel formerly under Solomon is now divided: The northern kingdom under Jeroboam is now called Israel and the southern kingdom under Rehoboam is called Judah, the latter named after the largest tribe remaining in and around Jerusalem.

Rehoboam had led Judah astray by doing evil in the sight of YHWH. He, following the pattern of his father Solomon, had Judah build high places and sacred pillars and Asherim on every high hill. Rehoboam also encouraged the return of the cult prostitutes that were removed when the pagans were forced out of the land. These prostitutes were dedicated to the fertility goddess Asherah and her husband Baal.

The belief was that to have sexual relations with them would also join them to their gods and so the people engaged in all the detestable practices of the nations which God drove out before the sons of Israel. As a result, God brought down judgment on Rehoboam and in the end, he will die in disgrace.

Meanwhile, Jeroboam fulfills his charge and takes the ten tribes with him northwards, making the city of Samaria his new capital and establishing the northern kingdom of Israel. It is important to remember that, at this moment, Jeroboam is acting in accordance with God's will and instructions, while Solomon and Rehoboam had forsaken Him and did not walk in His ways.

Jeroboam, however, is cautioned in 1 Kings 11:38, "And it shall be, **IF** you obey all that I command you, and shall walk in My ways, and do what is right in My eyes, to guard My laws and My commandments, as My servant David did, then I shall be with you and build for you a steadfast house, as I built for David, and shall give Israel to you."

For the most part, Jeroboam was an effective and popular ruler for 22 years. His people however were pining for the Temple and yearning for the Feast times in and around Jerusalem and would, during these Set-Apart holy times, return there with offerings and sacrifices. This did not please Jeroboam, because their monies were going south rather than into his coffers and draining his economy.

As a *spirit of fear* touches his heart that the kingdom will return to the house of David, he combats this trend by building two golden calves and saying to the people, "It is too much for you to go up to Jerusalem; behold your gods, O Israel, that brought you up from the land of Egypt" (1 Kings 12:28 NAU), appealing to their need to connect with the history of their ancestors.

He sets these calves up at rival shrines in Dan and Bethel, the archaeological remnants of which are still in those places today. Also, since these two cities in his realm have a rich biblical history and strong links back to the patriarchs in Genesis, Jeroboam is hoping his people will forgo Jerusalem in favor of worshipping these idols at his shrines.

So, as the people of Israel went to worship before these gods as far as Dan, they fell into sin. Unsatisfied, Jeroboam takes things a step further, and this is where the king descends further into evil. He ordains a new priesthood not derived from the sons of Aaron, invents a brand-new holiday on the full moon of the 8th month, and makes offerings of animal sacrifices at these high places. Sometime later, Jeroboam and his people are participating fully in the pagan cults of the region, abandoning their covenantal faith almost completely.

Some of the lessons I hope we can take away from what we have read so far are that, regardless of persons, God Almighty, YHWH, will not be put second to any other form of worship. The people of Israel cannot use the excuse, as the Nazis did at the Nuremberg trials, that they were only following orders.

Let us pause for a moment now and reflect on our current situation—individually and as a nation. Which leaders of our government and religious organizations are we using as an excuse to justify our actions? And are money, power, fame, sex, food, or the latest tech toys, to name a few, our idols? Are capitalism and democracy the names of our altars—where we sacrifice all that is good in God's eyes? Think about it, folks! Just like Israel, we have been programmed and re-trained to sin against our God.

Due to the sins of the house of Jeroboam which culminated in making Israel sin, God sent word though Ahijah the prophet saying, "Thus says YHWH God of Israel, Because I exalted you from among the people and made you ruler over My people Israel, and tore the kingdom away from the house of David and gave it to you, but you have not been like My servant David, who kept My commandments and who followed Me with all his heart, to do only that which was right in My sight; you also have done more evil than all who were before you, and have gone and made for yourself other gods and molten images to provoke Me to anger, and have cast Me behind your back. Therefore behold, I am bringing calamity on the house of Jeroboam, and will cut off from Jeroboam every man, both slave and free in Israel, and I will make a clean sweep of the house of Jeroboam, as one sweeps away dung until it is all gone. Anyone belonging to Jeroboam who dies in the city the dogs will eat. And he who dies in the field the birds of the heavens will eat; for YHWH has spoken it" (1 Kings 14:7-11). Thus, God Almighty has judged Jeroboam.

There are a couple of things we would like to point out here. The first is that God's judgment does not always manifest itself immediately. He is patient and merciful, so sometimes we get the false impression that what we are doing is acceptable or will be overlooked. But, as you will see, the full force of that judgment may only come down hundreds of years later, affecting the descendants of those who sinned. Secondly, during times of political turmoil, people of all walks of life make decisions, including seemingly minor ones, that can have a ripple effect with huge repercussions—like wars and division.

In Rehoboam's case, after a few years of war, which does nothing to heal the rift between the tribes, he dies and is succeeded by his son Abijam. As king of Judah, he too "walked in all the sins of his father" and was just as wicked and ineffective. Abijam dies after only three years on the throne and is succeeded by his son Asa.

However, unlike his father and grandfather, King Asa destroys the pagan shrines, removes the cult prostitutes and single-handedly stabilizes the Judahite monarchy during his prosperous and righteous 41-year long reign. But while Scripture says that Asa's heart overall was perfect before God all of his life, we note that he did not remove the high places where people still sacrificed animals to their gods. Asa also took Temple treasure to bribe the king of Aram to help him in battle against the king of Israel, Ba'asha.

Jehoshaphat, the son of King Asa, is generally regarded as another righteous king of Judah who walked in the ways of his father, removing Asherah shrines and the cult prostitutes from the land. As he also raised up many righteous judges (2 Chronicles 19:1-7), his reforms will pave the way for later kings like Hezekiah and Josiah.

Then again, like his father, the high places were not removed, thus allowing for pagan rituals of burning incense and animal sacrifices to their gods to continue. The encroachment of paganism into Judah accelerated when Jehoshaphat agreed to a strategic alliance with Ahab, now the king of Israel. While he may not have intended to do so, by declaring peace with Ahab, Jehoshaphat's covenant with him opened the door to sin by creating *soul ties* with Ahab's house.

We know this since he said to Ahab, and later to Ahab's son, "I am as you are, my people as your people, my horses as your horses" and because he allowed his son Jehoram to marry the daughter of Ahab and Jezebel. Like some of his forefathers, King Jehoram also walked in the ways of the king of Israel and did evil in the eyes of God, as the house of Ahab had done. His son, Ahaziah, who married Ahab's granddaughter, was just as evil.

It seems, sometimes, Almighty God preserves mediocre kings who have some merit because He knows greater kings will come from their loins.

As for Ahab, he comes down from a long line of wicked kings going back to Jeroboam. He is simply one example of a series of competing royal houses to rule the ten tribes of Israel, each one set up by God, but ultimately wiped out due to disobedience. In his case, Ahab was so wicked that Scripture says he did more to provoke YHWH the God of Israel, than all of the kings of Israel who came before him.

One of the chief reasons behind much of Ahab's evil comes from his marriage to Jezebel, who is one of the deadliest persecutors of God's people. She killed all of His prophets except for the hundred that the prophet Obadiah managed to hide in caves.

When the prophet Elijah predicted three years of drought and famine, saying that no rain would come except by God Almighty's command, he gets Ahab to call the 850 prophets of Baal and Asherah to Mount Carmel for a showdown in front of all the people of Israel. Elijah begins by challenging the people, saying, "How long will you be hopping between two opinions? If YHWH is God, follow Him and if it is Baal follow him" (1 Kings 18:21).

But the people were silent, so Elijah urged the pagan prophets to have their god consume a sacrifice. When Baal's prophets failed to do so, Elijah taunted them, mocking their god, saying, "Shout louder! Surely, he is a god. Perhaps he is busy or meditating or he is on a journey, or it could be he is asleep and needs to wake up!"

Of course, Ahab's prophets were unsuccessful and when it was Elijah's turn, one short request to YHWH was all he needed for fire from heaven to consume the sacrifices and even burn the drenched wood.

After Elijah completely humiliated their gods in front of all Israel, the people fell on their faces and turned to YHWH as their God. The miracle of Elijah got the people who were sitting on the fence to return back to YHWH, at least for a little while. Elijah then told them to seize all of the pagan prophets and kill them. Seeing this, Jezebel sought revenge and tried to kill Elijah, but he escaped.

Ahab, nevertheless, in spite of his evil ways, is sometimes favored by the Almighty in battle (1 Kings 20:28). But, when he allows Jezebel to kill Naboth for his vineyard, Ahab receives a devastating prophetic rebuke through Elijah. This causes the king to greatly repent, humble himself and receive a reprieve from immediate destruction (1 Kings 21:20-29).

However, a few years later, Ahab's doom comes to fruition when he uses false prophets to enlist the help of king Jehoshaphat of Judah to attack the king of Aram. Because of this, God allowed a *spirit of falsehood* into the prophets and also to entice Ahab to think he will win in battle by disguising himself. However, the Arameans kill him and while his blood was still on the chariot, the dogs licked it up, just as it was prophesied.

We are told in Deuteronomy 18:20, "the prophet who speaks a word presumptuously in My name which I have not commanded him to speak, or which he speaks in the name of other gods, that prophet shall die." Consequently, later because of this rebuke, the false prophets of Ahab and Jezebel are killed. Also, as prophesied by Elijah, Jezebel is killed when she was thrown down from her balcony and the dogs devour her remains while the rest of their sons and household were killed, thus ending their royal line because of disobedience to God.

For those of us who claim to have prophetic gifts or a prophetic word, let us take this lesson to heart. Let us remember also that this lesson is confirmed by Yeshua when he says, "Therefore I say to you, any sin and blasphemy shall be forgiven people, but blasphemy against the Spirit shall not be forgiven. Whoever speaks a word against the Son of Man, it shall be forgiven him; but whoever speaks against the Holy Spirit, it shall not be forgiven him, either in this age or in the age to come" (Matthew 12:31-32).

For a very long time now, the function of the Holy Spirit has been misunderstood and its role in sanctification misapplied. Most importantly, for all of us who believe we can get direct revelation from the Holy Spirit, the Holy Spirit never contradicts the Word of God, because God is both the Spirit and the Word. When we act inappropriately, we are denigrating our Heavenly Father and misdirecting the majesty that belongs to Him.

The northern kingdom of Israel also showcases a very important pattern. It is a series of half a dozen royal families, rather than the unified line of David in Judah. Starting with Jeroboam, each house begins with the blessing of God, but each one fails to live up to their end of the bargain, resulting in them being replaced.

Jeroboam's rapid and deep descent into sin was grave enough to ensure that only his son Nadab would succeed him. YHWH then rose up Ba'asha to replace Jeroboam's house, but the same thing happened there as well, with only his son Elah ruling before that house was replaced. Then came king Zimri, who only ruled for a week because the people of Israel decided Omri was the better choice for them.

It is Omri who fathered Ahab, and when Ahab met his end only his two sons followed him to the throne before their whole house was destroyed at the hands of Jehu, who will subsequently give birth to the most stable of all the northern dynasties. Jehu's royal lineage, in spite of persistent wickedness, will yield a total of five kings reigning over a period of 108 years. However, once the last king of that dynasty (Zakharyah) is deposed after only 6 months on the throne, lesser rulers will dominate Israel.

The judgment against Israel was so severe, that the northern kingdom was attacked by Assyria in 722 BCE and they were taken into captivity. There is no evidence that a significant righteous remnant maintained the covenant after being forcibly deported.

The only thing we do know, according to the Jewish historian Josephus, is that the lost tribes of Israel were still there intact during the eight centuries that elapsed between that event and his time in the 1st century CE.

Meanwhile, in the land that was once occupied by the ten tribes, the Assyrians re-settled thousands of their own Aramaic-speaking people. These Assyrians would eventually inter-breed with the few remaining Israelites there, giving rise to the people we now call the Samaritans.

The story of the kings of Israel very much demonstrates in action what Almighty God spoke to Moses when He gave him the Ten Commandments. He declares that He will visit the iniquity of the fathers unto the children to the third and fourth generation of those that hate Him but show loving kindness (mercy) to the thousandth generation of those who love Him and keep His commandments. We see over and over again that He desires even those who have done evil to turn back to Him, because He is compassionate and patient, forgiving iniquity, transgression and sin.

At this point in our story, we are also starting to see the migration of God's people away from the land He had promised their forefathers. Over centuries and millennia, they will move from place to place, country to country, marry foreigners and forget their true heritage. Is it any surprise then that many today are discovering a Jewish component in their DNA?

All in all, Judah and Israel would exist as separate kingdoms for a total of 209 years. These two nations sometimes cooperated with each other and other times threatened to fight each other. While Judah also suffered frequent bouts with paganism, going between righteousness, rebellion and back to righteousness, Israel was never able to remain loyal to Father YHWH and His Covenant.

Judah, in spite of her wicked tendencies, always managed to get back to Covenant because she had far more righteous kings than the northern kingdom of Israel. Judah was also supported by the true priesthood of Aaron and the Temple with the Ark of the Covenant, unlike the kingdom of Israel. Therefore, the righteous remnant from both kingdoms had powerful incentives to make sure they emigrated to or stayed in close proximity to Jerusalem. Judah may have been frequently chastised by the prophets of YHWH, but it was clear the Covenant would remain with her and not Israel, just as before when it descended through Isaac and not Ishmael.

After Solomon's apostasy which dominated the last 20 years of his reign, we saw how a combination of paganism and arrogance tore the ten tribes of Israel away from his son Rehoboam. His son Abijam was also evil and died after only three years as king. Fortunately for Judah, however, righteousness and prosperity would continue under the next two kings, Asa and Jehoshaphat, for the next 65 years.

Unfortunately, things got much worse after Jehoshaphat died and his wicked son Jehoram took over for 8 years, emulating and admiring the evil of the northern kingdom. Jehoram then was succeeded by Ahaziah who also married the granddaughter of Ahab and reigned for only a year. In the wake of his death, Athaliah, the daughter of King Ahab of Israel, became the only queen of Judah and she attempted to assassinate the rest of the royal house. But, after 6 years of terror, she was killed and replaced by Jehoash, son of Ahaziah, who was saved.

Although he was only seven when he became king, Jehoash is remembered as a righteous ruler who, like Asa before him, gave a full generation of Judah a peaceful 40-year long reign. However, like Asa, he and his next three successors of Amaziah, Uzziah and Jotham, while generally walking in the ways of righteousness, never destroyed the high places, thereby allowing pagan worship to continue in Judah.

These kings also came under rebuke for their propensity to use sacred Temple treasure to bribe or pay off foreign kings when they felt threatened and when they tried to take upon themselves what only the priests are permitted to do. We saw this with Saul earlier and we are told Uzziah got leprosy for trying to burn incense at the Temple (2 Chronicles 26:17-19).

Then under King Ahaz, son of Jotham, Judah comes under threat from both Aram and Israel. The *spirit of fear* enters the heart of Ahaz and his people, so Isaiah the prophet is sent to meet the king. Through Isaiah, God reassures Ahaz by saying, "Take heed, and be calm. Do not fear or be fainthearted." But, instead of putting his faith in the Almighty, Ahaz decides to bribe the king of Assyria using Temple treasure while building a slaughter place for pagan rituals. After 16 years, King Ahaz dies, and his son Hezekiah assumes the throne.

King Hezekiah, unlike everyone who was before him, put his trust completely in YHWH and clung to Him with all his heart. He completely destroyed the high places and other centers of pagan worship that so many of his predecessors had left in place. Even the bronze serpent that Moses made after the Exodus, Hezekiah destroyed when it became an object of pagan veneration. Scripture tells us that God was with him and that wherever he went he acted wisely.

But 22 years after Assyria conquered the northern kingdom, they turned their attention to Judah in the south (700 BCE). Hezekiah however, whose faith was strong, rebelled against the king of Assyria and would not serve him. Consequently, the Assyrian general Sennacherib sends an overwhelmingly large army to Jerusalem, along with a delegation to the king, taunting

Hezekiah by saying that his Mighty One will not be able to save Jerusalem.

However, when King Hezekiah gets the surrender letter, he tears his clothes as a sign of mourning, covers himself in sackcloth and takes the letter into the Holy of Holies. He spreads it out on the showbread table directly facing the Ark of the Covenant and prays to Father YHWH for deliverance. God answered him through the prophet Isaiah who accurately predicted to Hezekiah the victory he would have, and while the king slept, an angel of God came and struck and killed 185,000 soldiers in the camp of the Assyrians. This miracle would turn out to be a high point for the kingdom of Judah.

Also, because Hezekiah was deathly ill at this moment of deliverance, Isaiah also blesses him with the news that his illness is now cured and he will live another 15 years, reigning for a total of 29 years in all. Little did anyone expect at that time that Judah's next king, Hezekiah's son Manasseh, would turn out to be the most dangerous and wicked king of either kingdom.

Manasseh reigned 55 years beginning at age 12, and he did all he could in his long reign to persecute and attempt to destroy the worship of the One True God in Jerusalem. All the pagan high places that his father Hezekiah destroyed and all the wickedness that he removed, Manasseh immediately and completely rebuilt and reinstated. He even made his own sons pass through the fire and they practiced all manner of magic, witchcraft and consulted with spiritists and mediums.

Priests and holy men were slaughtered in such numbers that the Scripture says Jerusalem was defiled with the innocent blood from one end of the city to the other. Manasseh even placed an idol in the inner sanctum of the Holy of Holies, defiling the place where the Ark was supposed to be.

In short, he led his entire nation astray and was said to have done more evil than all the Amorites who did detestable practices, including child sacrifices. It was a very dark time and the very faith of the children of Abraham was in real danger of becoming extinct forever.

But then, after 52 years of unrighteousness, something completely unexpected happens. The king of Babylon invades Manasseh's kingdom, not to target Jerusalem or her Temple or her people, but only for Manasseh personally, and the king is led away in chains to Babylon. Once there, he repents of his sins and begs God to give him a second chance.

While Father YHWH does not forgive Manasseh completely and will in fact hold on to his offenses as a reason to destroy Jerusalem later (2 Kings 21:13-14), He does allow Manasseh to return to power in Jerusalem.

For his part, Manasseh, now grateful for this kindness and favor, tells his entire nation how wrong he was to go against the One True God of Israel. He then ends his final years by rebuilding the city and restoring the Temple he had once defiled. However, even after all these events, the death of Manasseh was far from the death of apostasy from within the kingdom of Judah.

Amon, Manasseh's son, came to the throne and continued the wicked ways of his father. Once again, a king was actively involved in trying to restore a pagan cult to Judah, but fortunately, in this case, Amon only ruled two years before he was assassinated by his own servants. This act cleared the way for his 8-year old son Josiah to become king.

During the next 18 years, this young king is sequestered and educated by disciplined and expert advisors, and the Scripture records almost nothing about what happened in Jerusalem during those years. But, when Josiah turns 26, the high priest Hilkiah discovers a Torah scroll that had been hidden in the Temple walls for safekeeping during Manasseh's reign of terror, but which now had come to light during reconstruction efforts to restore it to its former glory.

When Josiah hears the words of the Torah for the first time, he is immediately transformed. He loved YHWH and humbled himself, prostrate with grief. But Josiah, beloved by God as he is, unfortunately cannot save Jerusalem from destruction. A prophetess tells him that the final judgment against Judah will come after he dies, with the only mercy being he will not see everything fall with his own eyes.

Josiah becomes a warrior for change and launches the greatest religious reforms Judah would ever see. High places and pagan altars were obliterated from the land while Torah, once again, becomes the law of the nation. Josiah caps off his efforts with holding what is now known as the Great Passover. It was a transformative national moment that the Scripture says had not been done since the days of Samuel, nor did the northern kingdom ever have a Great Feast like it.

Nonetheless, for reasons that remain mysterious to this day, Josiah will soon die in battle at the hand of Pharaoh Neco of Egypt. This is tragic because Scripture also tells us he had every opportunity to escape this fate, but deliberately chose not to. Nevertheless, Josiah is justifiably looked upon as the most righteous king either royal line ever produced, with his great-grandfather Hezekiah qualifying for a close second place. Josiah's 31 years on the throne will never be equaled in Judah again before Messiah comes.

Then, after the death of Josiah, only four more kings (Jehoahaz, Jehoiakim, Jehoiachin and Zedekiah), all of whom were wicked, would reign in Judah during the final 22 years prior to its destruction and exile of her people. Rising, though, to protect both the throne and the people of Judah was the prophet Jeremiah.

Born a priest, Jeremiah knew King Josiah very well while growing up and was therefore devastated by that king's untimely demise and wrote a eulogy to memorialize his righteous life (2 Chronicles 35:25-26). Later, after being called by the Almighty to be a prophet, Jeremiah did all he could do, if not to prevent Judah's destruction, to at least delay it as long as possible. What Jeremiah did not know was that international events hundreds of miles away from his home were shaping the instrument of wrath that would be used to execute God's judgment on the weakened southern kingdom.

The Struggle of the Hebrew People – A Second Chance

It is He who changes the times and the epochs; He removes kings and establishes kings; He gives wisdom to wise men and knowledge to men of understanding. (Daniel 2:21)

Nebuchadnezzar, the future first emperor of the New Babylonian Empire, began his career as a humble soldier in the Assyrian army and soon arose to the rank of general due to his ability to immediately adjust to changing battle conditions and gain victory through unconventional tactics. In 606 BCE, Nebuchadnezzar mounted a successful rebellion against his Assyrian overlords and assumed rulership over their lands, while relocating their capital to Babylon, the ancient city of his ancestors that had by this time been abandoned for many centuries.

60

Now fully in power, Nebuchadnezzar sought to turn Babylon into a showplace of the region while rapidly rebuilding it and populating her with the best and brightest people he could find throughout his newly conquered lands. To that end, he invades Judah twice to deport her finest people to his new city.

The first time, in 603 BCE, he takes thousands of people from Jerusalem, including the royal family along with the prophet Daniel, the Temple treasures and those of the king. In the invasion six years later, in 597 BCE, the prophet Ezekiel is part of the group deported to Babylon.

A short time later, with King Jehoiachin now a captive servant in the Babylonian court, Nebuchadnezzar installed Zedekiah to Judah's throne. Sadly, Zedekiah will prove to be a stubborn and rebellious king, and his 11-year reign will be the last Judah will have before being destroyed. He provokes Nebuchadnezzar to anger by refusing to swear allegiance to him and when Jeremiah came to him in good faith, begging him to turn back to God, it was all in vain. Not only did Zedekiah completely disrespect both the word and the prophet who gave it, but so did the priests and the people who were defiling the Temple.

YHWH, Who had compassion for His people and His dwelling place, sent His messengers and prophets in one last attempt to bring them to repentance. Regrettably, they mocked them and despised His words until His anger arose against His people and there was no turning back. Nebuchadnezzar had the Temple of YHWH burnt (2 Kings 9), but we can see from the Book of Isaiah that all this was foretold.

Some years later, Nebuchadnezzar gives yet another stern warning to Zedekiah by invading his country and laying Jerusalem to siege and famine. But, after another year and half without any submission to prophets, priests or Nebuchadnezzar, Zedekiah's intransigence costs him his city and his life. Jerusalem has now been reduced to little more than a pile of rubble and ash, with her people now almost completely deported to Babylon, in July of 586 BCE.

In the end then, only Jeremiah and a very small remnant of Judah is left in the land. But Nebuchadnezzar is not completely heartless. He offers some hope to those not exiled by assigning a righteous man from their own people, Gedaliah, to be their governor reporting directly back to him. Jeremiah, as a leading priest and prophet of that time, is also left to help Gedaliah.

However, Jeremiah had long before this moment known the terrible truth from the Almighty, that Judah will be captive in Babylon for 70 years. Those still in Judah very quickly lose hope and become jealous over the appointment of Gedaliah, conspiring to assassinate him and his leading ministers. The insurrection is successful, but Jeremiah once again is spared.

When Nebuchadnezzar hears of these rebellions, he is furious and eager to punish Judah once more. Meanwhile, back in Jerusalem, the leadership of the remnant left behind is trying to get everyone there to go to Egypt for protection, against the prophetic utterances by Jeremiah. Not only do the people ignore all warnings once again and go to Egypt, but they also take an elderly Jeremiah with them by force. Nebuchadnezzar pursues the rebels in Egypt and inflicts very heavy casualties on them before withdrawing, while Jeremiah dies in exile a few years later.

The bottom line from these events is that now Judah is almost completely without her people who have either died, fled to Egypt or are in exile in Babylon. If, then, a righteous remnant of God's covenant people was to somehow survive and reconstitute itself, it would have to come from Babylon when the judgment concludes.

During the Persian, Greek and Roman periods which followed Babylon, God's people are once again scattered into foreign lands, marrying foreigners and settling wherever they went until He calls them home to Him at a future date, fulfilling the prophecy that Jews and Gentiles would come to Jerusalem from the east and the west.

Shifting our focus back again to Babylon and Nebuchadnezzar's first invasion of Judah in 603 BCE, Daniel and his three friends, Hananiah, Mishael and Azariah, suddenly found themselves in the king's court. The goal was to educate them for a further three years to be able to enter his royal service. The long-term objective of Nebuchadnezzar was to groom these men to eventually become leaders of their people, much in the same way that Gedaliah was appointed back in Judah. But while the king was very gracious to Daniel and his three friends, danger would soon come to them from a very unexpected place.

It happened when Nebuchadnezzar had a terrifying dream which he could neither remember nor interpret. He only knew that it was of supreme importance to understand it, and that it very likely had to with his future on the throne. He called an emergency meeting with his contingent of astrologers and soothsayers, asking them to decode the mystery.

While Babylon was well known for this kind of esoteric tradition, the king's mystics were powerless to interpret the dream without knowing its content. Enraged, Nebuchadnezzar locked all of them up and vowed to kill them if an answer to his dream could not be found. The edict could also affect Daniel and his friends since they too were counted as "wise men of Babylon."

After some heartfelt prayer, Daniel had the courage to face the king directly about this matter, even at the risk of his own life. Daniel's courage came from the fact that he *knew* this was an opportunity to prove to Nebuchadnezzar that his God was supreme in all the land. He *knew* the king would recognize that knowledge like this could only come from divine revelation.

Ironically it was the king's own soothsayers that prepared the way for this eventual understanding by declaring: "The thing the king asks for is difficult and there is no one else who can declare it to the king except from the gods, whose dwelling place is not with mortal flesh" (Daniel 2:11).

Daniel, now face to face with Nebuchadnezzar, gives a remarkable yet compact statement about Master YHWH as the One True God and then says that what he is about to say comes straight out of His mouth for such a time as this. What is remarkable here is that Daniel, unlike Joseph who was given a full vision of Pharaoh's dream many centuries earlier, literally has nothing to go on.

And yet he was not only able to relate the vision in full, he was also able to *see* what the king did in bed and what he thought before going to sleep! Daniel, being a seer and a prophet, explains that the king saw a massive statue. Its head was made of gold, its torso and arms silver, its belly and thighs of bronze and its legs of iron, with some of the toes being iron while others were clay.

Daniel states plainly that while Nebuchadnezzar will never be challenged in his lifetime, these different materials in the statue each represent an empire that will come after his days.

Daniel's vision is both detailed and precise and history will prove him right. As was prophesied, we now know that the head of gold is Babylon which will endure a short time after Nebuchadnezzar's death, with the silver chest and arms representing the Medes and the Persians who will conquer Babylon. The bronze stomach and thighs are about the Greeks who followed, and the iron legs are the Romans after them. The fact that some of the toes on the Roman feet are clay while others remain iron also means some parts of the Roman Empire will be stronger than others.

Realizing that Daniel completely kept his promise, Nebuchadnezzar freed the imprisoned soothsayers and made Daniel the head of their order. Daniel also received a major promotion in status in the royal court, while his three other friends were also given higher positions as administrators of the province of Babylon. Daniel's position is important to remember when it comes time for the Messiah to be born, as you will see later.

Although Nebuchadnezzar had greater respect for the powers of the God of Israel through the miracles of Daniel, this reverence did not translate into him turning away from his own pagan faith. In short order, under the influence of some wicked advisers who hated the Jews, the king built a colossal golden statue of himself and ordered everyone in Babylon to bow down to it.

While Daniel himself is somehow not forced into this heresy, his three other friends who refused to worship it were thrown into the furnace to see if their God would deliver them. To the king's complete astonishment, however, a fourth figure appeared in the furnace and protected Daniel's friends. Humbled once more, Nebuchadnezzar gives honor to the God of Daniel's friends and the mysterious angel their God sent to save them, but the king will have to learn this lesson all over again one final time before he dies.

About a decade later, Nebuchadnezzar finds himself on the rooftop of his palace. Forgetting that Daniel told him years before that he only rules at the pleasure of Almighty God, Nebuchadnezzar claims aloud that the magnificent city he sees would not exist but for his power (Daniel 4:30). The arrogant words were not even out of the king's mouth when an angel chastised him, condemning him to an animalistic existence for the next seven years. Just as quickly as it happened, at the very moment the seven years expired, Nebuchadnezzar regains his faculties and returns to rule Babylon in peace for the rest of his life, dying in 562 BCE.

It is remarkable that Nebuchadnezzar's grip on power was so absolute, that even when he left the palace for years, no one dared to seize the throne from him, for such was also prophesied by Daniel himself (Daniel 2:37-38).

After the death of Nebuchadnezzar, the Babylonian throne was for a time up for grabs as several contenders fought to be the next king. Eventually though, Belshazzar, one of Nebuchadnezzar's grandsons, ascended to the throne and, for quite some years, all seemed well with his rule.

However, while Daniel's original "statue" prophecy regarding Nebuchadnezzar's dream did not specifically state when Babylon would be conquered, Belshazzar's arrogance and dismissiveness towards the God of Israel certainly did not help matters, as forces outside of Babylon were slowly gathering strength to destroy her.

In 539 BCE, Belshazzar makes the critical mistake of holding a feast to his gods while using golden cups and plates that were taken from the Temple in Jerusalem. YHWH is enraged, and shocks everyone at the feast with a vision of His disembodied hand, writing a cryptic message on the wall in Aramaic: MENE, MENE TEKEL UPARSHIN.

When Daniel arrives he interprets the warning as MENE, your days are numbered, with the second occurrence of that word confirming the judgment; TEKEL, your deeds have been weighed and you have been found lacking; and UPARSHIN, your kingdom will now be divided and given to the Persians and the Medes.

Accordingly, before sunset, Darius the Mede arrives with his massive army right on schedule and takes over the city, killing Belshazzar exactly as Daniel predicted. Then King Darius, much like Nebuchadnezzar before him, hearing of Daniel's righteousness and wisdom, immediately seeks him out.

Most of us know the story of how Daniel was thrown into a den of lions. What is important to note however is that because of the supernatural deliverance Daniel received when God's messengers "shut the lions' mouths," King Darius made a decree that the God of Israel "Is to be feared and that He is faithful forever. He reigns over all until the end of time. He delivers and rescues and He works wonders in the heavens and on earth" (Daniel 6:26). As Daniel excelled in Darius' court, the king's decree also gains the Jewish people much favor, even though they are still in captivity.

In 536 BCE, King Cyrus, who is now in charge of both Persia and Babylon, issues a decree that any Jews who wished to return home to Jerusalem to rebuild her have his permission to do so (Ezra 1:2-7). The first wave of returning exiles will be led by Zerubbabel, but he is only a civilian ruler. In order for the entire kingdom of Judah to be rebuilt, he would need help from prophets and priests alike. Zerubbabel gets this necessary help from the high priest Joshua, son of Jehozadak, who is from the unbroken line of Aaron. Zerubbabel will also receive much needed insight and support from the two most important prophets of the day: Haggai and Zechariah.

Haggai's message is one of great rebuking mixed in with the hope of a better future. On the one hand, he proclaims that the entire nation, including the priesthood, has been and is currently defiled (2:14), while, on the other, he comforts those same people by saying that the glory of the Second Temple will actually exceed that of the former house Solomon built (2:8). Haggai also has some choice words of counsel for Zerubbabel and what he needs to do to reestablish Judah in righteousness (2:21-23).

In the same year (520 BCE), Haggai's colleague Zechariah begins a much longer and more detailed account of what awaits Judah's future until His kingdom is manifested on earth. Zechariah's visons are more than just verbal utterances and instructions as Haggai's were, but are instead full of great signs and miracles happening in and around Jerusalem as her new Temple nears completion.

Then, finally, in February of 516 BCE, the Second Temple is finished. Sacrifices resume once more, but the overall job of restoring Jerusalem completely is still far from being finished. In fact, it will take nearly another half a century before another great leader emerges with a significant number of newly released exiles, ready to usher in the next great phase in Judah's transformation.

While Daniel dies in Babylon and the exiles from Babylon and Persia begin returning home over the subsequently two decades, the mammoth and painstakingly slow process of rebuilding Judah from the ground up begins in earnest. According to King Cyrus of Persia's decree, the Jewish people will be led back home by their governor Zerubbabel who is also a direct descendant of King David (1 Chronicles 3:9-19, Matthew 1:12-13, Luke 3:27-31). He was also the grandson of King Jehoiachin who was taken into captivity from Judah. This is important, because even though the captivity in Babylon lasted nearly two generations, the line of David through the Judahite kings was preserved up to the birth of Yeshua the Messiah, who sits on David's throne forever as King of Kings (Isaiah 9:7, Jeremiah 33:17, Luke 1:32).

However, one of the most vexing challenges the returning Jews will face concerns the issue of intermarriage. At the start of the captivity, Jeremiah wrote a letter to the exiles to encourage them to build a life and prosper in Babylon (Jeremiah 29:1-6). When he talked of taking wives though, he meant they could marry Gentile women there if the women renounced their paganism and became faithful to YHWH (Ruth 1:16-17, 4:10-11). Since the Hebrew text tells us these women remained pagan, Ezra was forced subsequently to declare thousands of marriages illegitimate in Judah.

The priests, in particular, were told they could never serve in the new Temple if such divorces did not happen for them as well (Ezra 10). As a result, when the Jews back in Babylon heard about the mass divorces and considered how that related to their own family life, the thought of abandoning their families and starting over in a place that was foreign to them, never having lived there like their ancestors.

But this was only one of several dramas and challenges going on over the course of nearly a century after the Jews were first allowed to return. Everything, from administrative corruption to hate-based politics and bureaucratic inefficiencies became a depressing quagmire that never seemed to get resolved. Furthermore, by the time everything was settled, the Jews had been comfortable in exile for nearly four generations. They had built houses and businesses, had families and a life that was good, so we can understand why the majority preferred to stay in Babylon and even in Persia.

The Jewish community that was left behind grew exponentially and Babylon became the most populated Jewish area outside of Israel. Its location, over 600 miles away from Jerusalem, also guaranteed that community's independence from Judah. That is the reason Peter went to Babylon when he was sent to the circumcised outside of Israel (Galatians 2:8-9, 1 Peter 5:13).

We know about the huge Jewish community there because we have writings from Josephus that Babylon is "stuffed with Jews." Philo says the same thing—they sent massive treasures to the Temple that indicated they had a huge exile population and there were records of what each person gave according to the dictates of Scripture. In terms of today's money, these Jews were able to send billions of dollars to the Temple.

Moreover, Babylon had one of the most prestigious learning academies in the history of Judaism and became a great haven of Jewish scholars. The great rabbi Hillel the Elder was born in Babylon, and legend says that after he became learned there, he simply walked all the way to Jerusalem to learn more. Did you know that the Talmud and the translations of the original Hebrew Old Testament into Aramaic were done by the Jews in Babylon over the next thousand years?

Even today, Babylonian traditions are popular within mainline Judaism. For example, the practice of Jews reading the Torah over the course of a single year originated in Babylon and has now been adopted by nearly all of Judaism today. Most of the evidence, if not all that we have points to the Jews having thrived in Babylon even more than they did in Persia.

The prophet Ezra, son of Seraiah, was born in Babylon where he eventually rose to the rank of chief priest and scribe for their Jewish community. For reasons still unknown to us, Ezra tarried in Babylon until a third king, Artaxerxes I, gave a clarified and expanded decree allowing specifically for Jerusalem also to be rebuilt. The king tapped Ezra to directly bring this decree back to Jerusalem and complete the project. Unfortunately, when Ezra began this task in the fall of 458 BCE, Judah's enemies who were previously appointed to govern the region, refused to honor the emperor's wishes. As a result, construction for the city ground to a standstill for more than a decade until another great leader, Nehemiah, rose to finish the job.

In 445 BCE, Nehemiah was the trusted servant and wine taster to the same king who sent Ezra to Jerusalem. Nehemiah, who is from the Persian capital of Susa, has been tracking the progress, or rather the lack thereof, of the entire rebuilding effort and when it saddened him greatly, the king noticed this, expressed concern and inquired as to the reason. Nehemiah informed him that the king's previous decree has been ignored by his officials in and around Jerusalem, thus bringing the rebuilding of the city to a halt.

Artaxerxes immediately acts upon it. He writes up documentation, backed by his personal royal seal, confirming the right of the Jews to rebuild all of Jerusalem, and appoints Nehemiah to oversee the project. Nehemiah will, from that day to his death, be the governor of Judah reporting directly to the King of Persia.

Nevertheless, other local Persian officials, such as Sanballat of Samaria and Tobiah the Ammonite, prove to be constant thorns in Nehemiah's side, lobbing baseless accusations and complaints to slow the work down. Though he is clearly frustrated, he manages to soldier on, literally completing one wall at a time and one street at a time, in spite of the resistance.

In the end, though, Jerusalem will need more than an urban facelift to complete her full restoration as God intended for her. Nehemiah will eventually reintroduce the joy of the feasts to the people, with Ezra leading the nation in a massive Feast of Tabernacles celebration. Ezra reads from the Hebrew Torah all morning and translates it into Aramaic for the benefit of the recently returned. Nehemiah then follows this event up with a national prayer of repentance, and sweeping reforms in both civil and religious law, to make sure the Commandments of YHWH are once again reigning supreme over His people.

After that, the entire infrastructure of the society, from the roads and protective walls that guarded Jerusalem, to the total transformation of how Scripture would be read, studied and transmitted to the next generation, had to be firmly established and implemented. It would also be at this important juncture that the remainder of the Hebrew Bible (OT) would be written.

While Jerusalem had its kings David and Solomon write books like Psalms, Proverbs and Ecclesiastes, the last books of Ezra, Nehemiah, Haggai and Malachi would finish off the original corpus as it would be preserved in Israel. Then, with the death of the last prophet Malachi in around 400 BCE, the time of the Hebrew prophets comes to an end—that is, until the Gospels pick up the revelation story all over again four centuries later.

The Struggle of the Hebrew People – Lost Without Divine Guidance

"Then watch yourself, that you do not forget YHWH who brought you from the land of Egypt, out of the house of slavery. You shall have awe only for YHWH your Elohim; and you shall worship Him and swear by His name." (Deuteronomy 6:12-13)

After the death of Malachi around 400 BCE, the restored kingdom of Judah and her people continued to prosper in what is now known as the Persian Period. The Persians were generally tolerant and patient rulers, preferring to rule at a distance with governors who respected the local traditions of their subjects. That is why Esther 1:1 tells us that Persia ruled from India to Ethiopia, with 127 provinces in all.

However, this is also a period of time in biblical history where we know comparatively little. Our history, instead, comes in the form of occasional milestones and guideposts that signal the general direction of change, with not much in between them. For example, why was Malachi the last of the Hebrew Old Testament prophets?

The only thing we can say with any certainty is that, after about two generations of no new prophets arising, the elite leaders in Judah began considering another option called the Great Assembly. In essence, the Great Assembly was a precursor to what eventually became the Sanhedrin, or Jewish High Council. The very best sages, rabbis and scholars were brought together to debate and vote on the most pressing spiritual matters of the day, following a pattern first described by Moses' father in law, Jethro, in Exodus 18.

The question that arose earlier on was this: If the judges in Exodus 18 were intended to take a large portion of the judging burden away off Moses' shoulders, whose job then would it be to play the role of Moses to make the final call? The answer was to invent another office, that of the *Nasi*. Derived from a Hebrew word that means "prince," the *nasi* functioned more like a president does today. His job was to literally preside over all the proceedings, direct the course of all legal discussions, and guide the council as a whole to a majority consensus that he would then officially sign into law.

The challenge though was to find the right man for this critical position. The chosen leader would have to be very much in the mold of a latter-day Samuel, a man whose integrity and honesty would never be questioned by dissenting parties. In the end a humble teacher, Simon the Righteous I, was given the honor of the presidency.

Yet, even at this point, we are lacking some significant details. Except for a few fragments purported to come from his mouth, almost nothing that Simon the Righteous said or did has survived in the Jewish traditions known today as the Talmud and Mishnah.

However, we are on stronger historical ground for what happened after this first president died, in around 300 BCE. Sometime over the next few decades, the Great Assembly ruled that, after more than 1,100 years of usage, the true Name of God (Yahweh) should be banned from public recitation in the synagogues.

Later generations would extend the ban on the Name even to the Temple, except by priests in her inner sanctum or on other very special and rare occasions. Today most Reform and Conservative Jews don't say the Name at all, while the Orthodox will only utter it at the Wailing Wall in Jerusalem on the morning of the Day of Atonement (Yom Kippur).

Meanwhile, far away from Judah, after the death of Alexander the Great in June of 323 BCE, the decision was made for his four greatest generals to divide and rule his empire, which by this time also included vast areas formerly controlled by the Persians. In any case, one of Alexander's former generals, a man named Ptolemy I, was given Egypt and he began the last dynasty of the Pharaohs.

In return for this great honor, Ptolemy built a magnificent new port city and named it Alexandria, after his old master. Then, over the next four decades, both Ptolemy and his son Philadelphus envisioned building there the greatest library in the world. It would boast nearly all of the classic works known at that time, with its crowning edition being a Greek translation of the Five Books of Moses.

This work, now known as the Septuagint, was begun in 280 BCE and completed twenty-four years later by 70 scribes brought in from Jerusalem. This was also because after the destruction of Solomon's Temple, a significant Jewish population grew to exist in Egypt.

While the nature, history and impact of the Septuagint is a topic for discussion at a later time in another book, one important aspect we would like to discuss here is that it showed the first clear evidence of the ban on the Name being in full effect. For example, according to our very earliest Hebrew witnesses (Dead Sea Scrolls, Samaritan Pentateuch), Leviticus 24:16 originally read, "He who *curses* in the Name of YHWH, shall surely be put to death." However, by 256 BCE when the Greek Torah or Septuagint was finished, it was altered to read, "He who names the Name of the LORD, let him die the death."

Another significant change that took place is that even though His Name was clearly seen and understood in the Hebrew and Aramaic Old Testament, because of the ban, the Jewish people will read it as "Hashem" or "Adonai," especially when they vocalize it.

It is probably because of this practice that the Bibles today, translated from Greek, use the word "LORD," derived from *kurios*, where His Name was supposed to be. Unfortunately, without His Name being taught, many believers today don't know their God. Just like you cannot get personal with someone without knowing his or her name, you cannot get intimate with your God without knowing His Name.

The funny thing is, there are many in Africa, such as in Kenya and Nigeria, whom we know of that sing worship songs having His Name. We have also seen videos with school children during their morning assembly sing songs with His Name before they start their classes. The Native Americans are also familiar with His Name. In spite of the ban, He has preserved His Name in many places outside of the Jewish community.

In the last few years, I have been given the honor and privilege to teach internationally on His Name against the wishes of some in the rabbinic circle. However, we feel led to proclaim His Name from the rooftops, so more of you will know your God and be able to call on Almighty YHWH in your prayers.

But getting back to the Great Assembly, they, along with the priesthood in Jerusalem, were able to completely and independently govern themselves with regards to spiritual matters, while still under Persian rule. Unfortunately, though, such autonomy would not last forever.

The problems began after another former general of Alexander the Great was granted rule in Syria. Seleucus Nicator I was a friend and ally to Pharaoh Ptolemy I, and that alliance proved very helpful to getting Seleucus the eastern part of Alexander's old empire, including Judah. Over the next century and a half, the Jews once again prospered under foreign rule by balancing carefully their religious needs with the necessary tributes they owed their Gentile overlords. But later, with the rise of a Syrian-Greek king named Antiochus IV, the Jews were now put in grave danger.

Judah at this time was a small kingdom struggling to maintain its cultural distinctiveness in an unprecedented time of Greek cultural dominance. Alexander the Great began this trend, which we now call *Hellenization*, by introducing popular entertainment in the form of Greek plays and dances throughout his empire. Alexander also spread participation in the Olympics to nations who had previously never even heard of the competition. Starting in 776 BCE, the Olympic games would be held once every four years, at which time wars between nations would often be postponed.

While many focused on Alexander's achievements as a great general, he was also the greatest franchise marketer of Greek culture of all time, packaging its most appealing aspects the way we might package Coca Cola today while selling endless varieties of that culture across his vast empire.

For the rest of the Mediterranean and wider Aegean world, the Olympics represented one of the most important institutions for nations coming together to compete athletically rather than on the battlefield. But, for the Jewish youth who wanted to participate in those games, they became a snare against their ancestral faith to the God of Israel. The *Olympics* are games dedicated to the Greek pantheon of gods that are said to live on Mount *Olympus* and this would have been frowned upon in Jewish culture who believed only in the One True God.

Additionally, because the games were played in the nude, Jews would face immediate ridicule when stripping themselves bare. The unfortunate ramification of that was the development of a medical procedure known as an *epispasm*, which reversed the appearance of a circumcision.

Antiochus IV, unlike both his predecessors and successors, had a ferocious hatred for the Jews and plotted against them from the time he came to power in 175 BCE. In 167 BCE, he defiled the Temple altar and prohibited worship there. That horrible act then sparked outrage from the Jews, and a wealthy group known as the Maccabees rose up in rebellion. Two years after Antiochus IV defiled the Temple, the Maccabees defeated him, restored and rededicated the Temple, and instituted the feast known as Hanukkah (165 BCE). Their independence came in large measure because the Syrian Greeks who started the war eventually repented of their behavior and gave Judah autonomy.

As for the Maccabees themselves, they later become known as the Hasmoneans, the last independent Jewish kingdom. But complications arose due to the Hasmoneans desiring to rule the priesthood as well as the throne. Being of Levitical stock, they should not be kings according to Torah and because they were not direct descendants of Aaron, or *Kohenim*, they could not be priests or high priests either. They tried to get around this issue by suggesting they were stewards, or holders of the throne, until the Messiah came.

While not ideal, these rulers provided necessary stability for the Jewish people for about a hundred years, during which time the people were generally pretty good at keeping Torah. In spite of this, two religious groups, the Pharisees and Sadducees, started fighting one another for dominance.

In 140 BCE, a very powerful and popular ruler named Simon the Hasmonean became high priest and made sure his subordinate priests were personally loyal to him. Simon expelled the priests of Zadok who had faithfully served since David's time. To escape Simon, most of them later fled into the desert to join another rebel group known as the Essenes. Together these two groups would eventually write what became known as the Dead Sea Scrolls.

Others from the Zadokite group lingered on in the cities where they amassed wealth and power. The Sadducees took the name of their order from "Zadok," a name that means "righteousness." Their rivals, the Pharisees, would become the majority religious party. A delicate and detailed power sharing arrangement would subsequently be drawn up between them, where the Sadducees would dominate the priesthood and Sanhedrin, provided they kept the rules and procedures of the Pharisees.

It would be an arrangement very helpful in local politics, but not good in terms of staying pure and righteous. This is why nearly a century later, Messiah confronts them and calls them hypocrites, because with their oral laws, customs and traditions, they were creating stumbling blocks for God's people. It is also why he says:

But woe to you, scribes and Pharisees, hypocrites, because you shut off the kingdom of heaven from people; for you do not enter in yourselves, nor do you allow those who are entering to go in. (Matthew 23:13 NAU)

Many of you have probably read the Gospel of Matthew several times, but have you ever stopped to consider who these modern-day Pharisees and Sadducees might be? Who would Yeshua say these same words to if he was here with us today? Consider each verse from Matthew 23:14 to the end as you think about these questions. Perhaps then you will understand what may also dictate his return as we see in the translation from Aramaic below:

I say to you that you will not see me from now on until you say, 'Blessed is he who comes in the name of Master YHWH. (Matthew 23:39)

Unfortunately, because modern-day Greek-based translations use the word "LORD" or "Lord," we are not calling on God by His Name and furthermore it is sometimes confusing whether Lord is referring to our Creator or to His Son. Compare these two translations below with the one above:

For I say to you, from now on you will not see Me until you say, 'BLESSED IS HE WHO COMES IN THE NAME OF THE LORD!' (Matthew 23:39 NAU)

For I tell you, you will not see me again until you say, 'Blessed is he who comes in the name of the Lord.' (Matthew 23:39 NIV)

If you don't know His Name, how are you going to get close to our Heavenly Father who sent us His Only-Begotten Son? From this point, you need to decide how important all this information is to you and your loved ones. Pray on it and ask the Holy Spirit to guide you. We need to learn from the lessons of the past and apply them to our lives and the times we are living in, for all the blessings our Creator has in store for us. It is most important what God Almighty thinks of us and not what others think of us. If you are reading this book, consider the possibility that you are one of the *lost sheep* hearing His Call!

Now let's get back to our history of events. In 63 BCE, a Roman general named Pompey the Great conquers the land and calls it "Judea," now a tax paying province of Rome. Working with the local leadership, Pompey and later Julius Caesar who succeeded him, created a relatively peaceable environment for the Jewish people, except for one regrettable incident when Pompey defiled the Temple. As long as Rome is a Republic, that is to say a representational democracy, these kinds of partnerships are relatively easy to do and gave some flexibility in the governance for both parties. Rome only needed to deal with the Great Assembly, now known as the Sanhedrin, and whoever the nominal Jewish king is from the Hasmoneans. Conversely, Judean leadership merely needed to report to the Roman Senate for their needs.

In Rome, however, a crisis was brewing in their Senate. When Pompey is assassinated in Egypt, power shifts to Julius Caesar, who was by far the stronger of the two leaders. When a group of barbarian hordes is discovered to be massing just outside Rome, Julius Caesar and his battle-tested and privately funded army is called home to secure the city. Caesar agrees to defend Rome, but only on the condition that they make him "dictator for life."

The Senate agreed to this condition on their naïve hopes that Julius Caesar would not enforce their agreement, but he did. For this reason, in March of 44 BCE, Julius Caesar is famously stabbed to death by these same senators who made him dictator and so it looked like stability had returned to the Roman Republic. Democracy seemed saved, and it was, for a short while.

One of the last things Julius Caesar did before he was killed was have a scandalous affair with the Queen of Egypt, Cleopatra VII. Their child, named Caesarion, was feared to someday become a clear and present danger to Rome. With Caesar now dead, the Roman Senate sent one of their finest generals, Marc Antony, to try to stabilize matters once more in that region.

Unfortunately for them, Marc Antony fell in love with Cleopatra too and it would take more than a decade of strife and civil war, culminating at a battle called Actium, to finally stop the Egyptian separatists. Also the much-feared heir apparent, Caesarion, was murdered before he could avenge the deaths of both of his parents.

Meanwhile, back in Judea, after the ascension of the Hasmonean king Antigonus, an unexpected upstart and rival was emerging to take his throne and start a brand-new independent dynasty.

A politically savvy Arab leader, Herod the Great, began currying favor with Rome by backing both sides in their civil war. He expanded a fortress overlooking the Jerusalem Temple and named it Antonia, after his friend Marc Antony, while simultaneously sending great amounts of money and support to Antony's rival Octavian.

To be fair, both Herod and Antigonus hatched international plots to assassinate the other, but Herod was gaining ground with the Roman Senate, and they eventually declared him king of the Judeans in 40 BCE. It would not be until three years later that Herod solidified his right to rule by convincing Marc Antony to murder the last Hasmonean king, thus ensuring there would be no one left in Judea to oppose him. The stage is now set to tell the story of Messiah Yeshua, who is about to be born into this tumultuous and dangerous time.

As we saw earlier, there has always been tension between the mission of the Jewish people to teach the Divine Law they inherited to the nations, and their desire to keep it amongst themselves and stay apart to maintain their culture and remain in complete compliance with God. However, while this is somewhat understandable given their great hardships and suffering, this isolation has also in some ways made them more vulnerable.

Everyone from Haman to Hitler wanted to eliminate the Jewish culture along with the Jewish people. It is therefore not surprising that some thought there was a zero-sum relationship between keeping traditions intact and sharing "the oracles of God" (Romans 3:1-2) with the rest of the world. This is also why Paul wanted the Gentiles to turn to those same divine principles as a way to make the Jews jealous, and get back to their covenantal function (Romans 11:11-27).

The Hebrew people had been *kidnapped from God* with severe and frightening consequences. Disobedience was the name of their kidnappers and through their blindfolds and the lies told to them, they could not see their way home. This constant cycle of rebellion, punishment, repentance and restoration continues to echo down the millennia.

David and Daniel had an unshakable faith in their God and as a result had a *knowing* that He would be with them and His people in times of need. They knew God Almighty would fight for them if they obeyed Him and walked the righteous path. With Jeroboam, however, although he started off with Divine Sanction to take the 10 tribes away from Solomon's son, he allowed the *spirit of fear* to enter him and walked away from righteousness with the big lie

– that Israel would still be blessed by worshiping the two golden calves he built, led by the false priesthood he ordained, who enabled him, and observing a brand-new feast day he invented. This deception did not happen in a day. This lie would have been perpetuated over time before all of Israel fell into sin.

When we stray from the path of obedience, the enemy is given license to instill a *spirit of fear* as he also did with King Ahaz in spite of God's reassurances through Isaiah, "Do not fear or be fainthearted." Likewise, unrighteous behavior also allows for the enemy to take a hold of peoples' lives, including those of false prophets through a *spirit of falsehood*. When Ahab uses his prophets to enlist the help of king Jehoshaphat, Scripture informs us of this dialog between God and the enemy:

"And a spirit came forward and stood before YHWH, and said, Let me entice him' "And YHWH said to him, 'In what way?' And he said, 'I shall go out and be a spirit of falsehood in the mouth of all his prophets.' And He said, 'Entice him and also prevail. Go out and do so.' (1 Kings22:21-22)

The journey of the Hebrews also showcased their separation from the truth of Scripture through the elevation of their oral laws having equal authority with the Law of Moses (Torah). To remedy this, our Creator sent His Only Begotten Son, Messiah Yeshua, to bring His lost sheep back to Him. Unfortunately, many of them rejected this call to come home when it was offered to them. On the other hand, you will see in the chapters to follow that even though salvation was also extended to the Gentiles, they too suffer many problems and hardships from only getting part of the kingdom message. This next section aims to show how well-meaning Christians too got separated from the truth, but now are hearing the call to come home. Their story, however, is still unfolding.

Wherefore, also, Elohim has highly exalted him and given him a name which is more excellent than all names; that at the name of Yeshua every knee should bow, of (beings) in heaven and on earth and under the earth; and that every tongue should confess that Master YHWH is Yeshua the Mashiyach to the glory of Elohim his Father.

(Philippians 2:9-11)

Translated from the original Aramaic

SECTION FOUR

Our Salvation Arrives

Ask, and it will be given to you; seek, and you will find; knock, and it will be opened to you. For everyone who asks receives, and he who seeks finds, and to him who knocks it will be opened.
(Matthew 7:7-8)

Throughout the four-decade long reign of Herod the Great, Judea had seen some great triumphs, such as the expansion and rebuilding of the Temple complex, and also a series of unnecessary wars, political scandals and assassinations. King Herod may have been so paranoid as to kill his wife and sons based on mere rumors of sedition, but that in no way weakened his overall intellect or political resolve.

As the Gospels open, Herod has subdued virtually all of his enemies, both religious and political, with one exception. Herod was caught preparing to war against an enemy Emperor Augustus forbad him to fight. Infuriated, the Emperor now forced the king to pay taxes and order a census that will bring a certain carpenter and his pregnant wife to Bethlehem.

These events also bring the Magi, Zoroastrian astronomer-priests, from Babylon. Their intimate knowledge of Jewish affairs may have come from their ancestors having been trained by Daniel while he was in Babylon. This would have been after Daniel, being the only one able to interpret Nebuchadnezzar's dream (Daniel 4:8-9), was elevated in status as a prophet in the royal court.

For his part, King Herod almost certainly recognized the Magi as high government officials representing the Parthian Empire and was therefore greatly disturbed that they were calling a baby, and not himself, "King of the Jews" (Matthew 2:2), all based on a star they had been tracking for two whole years (Matthew 2:16).

Hoping perhaps to downplay the significance of this child's birth, Herod inquires of his Torah scholars to shed more light. They, however, told him this rival king was predicted by the prophet Micah to be born in Bethlehem. Hence, from the moment Messiah took his first breath, he had a target on his back and will spend the next few years avoiding assassination in Egypt before Herod's death allows him and his family to return to Galilee.

As Yeshua grows up in the small village of Nazareth, his life there is far from the idyllic and quiet pastoral setting many have imagined over the centuries. His earthly father Joseph may have rightly perceived that it was better to be ruled by Herod Antipas in Galilee rather than by Archelaus in Judea (Matthew 2:21-23), but that only addressed part of the problem, as both of them, even though they were sons of Herod the Great, had to also answer to their Roman masters.

Nazareth was a poor suburb attached to the major city of Sephorris, which was only four miles away and what's more, it became a hotbed of rebellious activity against both religious and civilian authorities, making it a dangerous place.

In 6 CE, when Yeshua would have probably been around ten years old, a major tax rebellion broke out under a man named Judas. As he and his rebels took shelter in Sephorris, Rome burned that city to the ground and crucified thousands, leaving them to rot possibly within sight of Yeshua's home.

Such is what real history can reveal to us about part of Messiah's childhood and it also goes a long way to explaining why the issue of taxes is one of the most consistent flashpoints of conflict throughout the Gospels. Even though the Gospels themselves don't explain any of that background, it is incumbent on us, two millennia later, to do so. If we desire to understand the Bible better, we need to know the circumstances of the first generation of believers who lived during the times of Yeshua and his disciples.

Another level of difficulty for recovering the original message lies in the fact that many of the things which people in the First Century took for granted no longer exist for us to explore today. The Jerusalem Yeshua knew lays in ruins more than seven feet underneath the modern city. The Temple is gone and so is the priesthood.

Besides, even if we were somehow able to make the time and bear the expense for a proper pilgrimage to the Holy Land, much of what we expect to see is actually not in the places where we are told they exist. Tradition in many cases has overwritten much of what history and the archaeological record are revealing to us now.

So, where the Renewed Covenant writers left off, the historical record of eyewitness testimony comes in to pick up and fill in these gaps. What was basic and common knowledge in Paul's day, for example, can only be partially understood with great effort today.

Paul never lived to see the Temple destroyed or he would not have said, in describing the Most Holy Place, "but there is no time to speak particularly of each of the things that were so arranged (Hebrews 9:5)." He would have most probably, in his usual manner of writing, gone into much needed details about the Temple, priesthood and every feast connected with it and the people. Although other witnesses like the historians Josephus and Philo tell us a lot more about the Jerusalem that is now gone, it takes time and effort to bring all that back to our modern understanding.

History and geography forces us to ask the question: Who was Yeshua the person and who were his Apostles before they started preaching the Good News? Also, how does what Scripture tell us about them relate to the wider cultural, historical and theological background they all came from? Many folks of course believe they know the answers since they have been reading the Bible all their lives. And yet nuances of Jewish law and tradition, hard or obscure sayings of Messiah from his Aramaic dialect, along with our own distance from these places and events, continue to frustrate our understanding.

Take for example Yeshua's very famous saying "I am the light of the world" in John 8:12. The backdrop of when he says this is in connection with the Feast of Tabernacles (Sukkot). Yeshua is basically saying that if they thought that the spectacular celebration with light and fire was impressive, his light will overwhelm them beyond measure!

In fact, the word he uses for "world" also means "universe" and "eternity" in Aramaic, so Yeshua is also saying, "I am the light beyond your world, encompassing the Universe and all the ages," which is a much deeper message embedded in the text.

Is it possible then that what we think we know about Messiah, while factual, is nevertheless only at a preliminary level? One of the purposes of this book is to answer that question by encouraging everyone to check these facts and sources for themselves and empower their own personal faith-based investigation. Meanwhile, to help get that process started, here are five surprising facts about Yeshua and his Apostles that are usually not taught today:

#1-Messiah came to proclaim his Father's Name, His Father's great Mercy and for him to be a sacrifice for our sins.

Rabbinic tradition, at this point in time, has called it blasphemy to say the Name of our Heavenly Father and this is reflected in all our Scripture from the Old Testament to the New Testament. Many translators chose to use His title "God" or "LORD," instead of His Name, YHWH or Master YAH, in bibles today. And yet, the most famous Christian Bible ever done in English, the 1611 King James New Testament cover page boldly showed His Name in Hebrew.

The entire pages of the 1611 King James Bible and the 1607 Geneva Bibles that have the Name of our God, YHWH, was shown on pages 20 and 21 but a close up is on the next page.

So, why did the Name of our Creator seemingly vanish from our Bibles? Is it possible that we have lost some of His Blessings and Protection, Guidance and Provision because of not knowing Him intimately and not being able to call out to Him by Name in our prayers, in our time of need or cry for help?

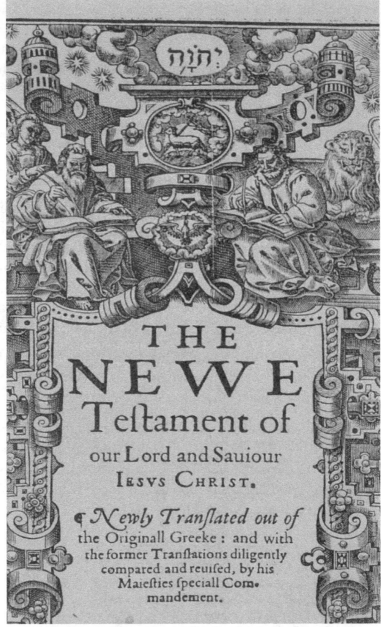

A closeup of part of the original 1611 first print run of the King James Bible showing the name of YHWH, in Hebrew, at the top

Full page (above) and close up (below) of images of Moses beholding the glory of the Divine Name (YHWH) from the 1560 First Edition of the Geneva Bible, page 77, while the people worship the golden calf at the base of the mountain.

Our thanks to Charles Payette who unwittingly inspired this book from the moment we had the privilege of seeing his collection of first edition Bibles going back to the 1500s. When we especially saw the 1611 King James Bible, the 1560 and 1607 Geneva Bibles that had the Name of our God, YHWH, in their first editions, we knew we had to share this information with the believers of Yeshua, many of whom had no knowledge that at one point His Name was known to them. These photos are used with permission from the Charles Payette private collection.

Being brought up in the Jewish culture, I too would not speak His Name aloud until long after I came to be a believer in the Messiah, because traditions are hard to break. His Name, YHWH, is derived from the Hebrew verb "to be" and parses out as "YAH Who Exists," with that same eternal existence being passed on to His Son (John 16:28). In the Apostolic Writings written in Aramaic, the language spoken by Yeshua and his Apostles, they would refer to Him as MarYAH, meaning Master YAH. This is because Aramaic was the main language for the Jews throughout the Middle East following their captivities in Assyria and Babylon.

In Hebrew, Isaiah 42:8 reads, "I am YHWH, that is My name; I will not give My glory to another, nor My praise to graven images" and Exodus 20:1-3 reads, "Then Elohim (God) spoke all these words, saying, 'I am YHWH your Elohim, who brought you out of the land of Egypt, out of the house of slavery. You shall have no other gods before Me.'"

His Name, being extremely sacred, has power and should be used with utmost reverence in prayer. It was never meant to be banned or forgotten altogether and never to be used as a curse (Leviticus 24:16), bringing shame to His Name through our casual, careless or sinful behavior. At the same time, every time you say the word "Halleluyah," you are saying "Praise you YAH" and He needs to be praised!

We know that Yeshua the Messiah taught his disciples the Name of his Father because in John 17:6 Yeshua prays to his Father and says literally "I have revealed Your Name to the men whom You gave me." So what was hidden before by Jewish tradition Messiah reveals directly. Then in 17:11 Messiah says, "Father protect them by Your Name, the same name you have given me," which was also proclaimed as the great promise to the world by the angel Gabriel at his birth (Matthew 1:21). The shortened form of the Father's Name, YAH (Psalm 68:4), is in Messiah's name of *Yeshua*, which means "YAH is salvation." And finally, in John 17:26 we read, "I have made Your Name known to them and I will confess it." Yeshua's willingness to die for us is the ultimate act of love and service.

Having said that, some of Messiah's last dying words have likewise been both mistranslated and misunderstood over the centuries. Yeshua knew he was doing his Father's will by suffering and dying by crucifixion and that is why he said:

For a little while longer I am with you, then I go to Him who sent Me. (John 7:33 NAU)

So, when he said "*Eli, Eli, lama sabachthani?*" that was not, "MY GOD, MY GOD, WHY HAVE YOU FORSAKEN ME?" Contrary to most translations, in his original Aramaic, the message was much closer to, "MY GOD, MY GOD, WHY ARE YOU SPARING ME?" It is a way of saying to His Father that he, Yeshua, was not going to change his mind about taking on the sins of their people by keeping him alive longer.

The Aramaic phrase *shbakthani* (put in Greek as *sabacthani*) has a general meaning of "set aside," but in other situations, it can also refer to being "abandoned" or "forsaken." However, YHWH cannot abandon His Son who is a part of Himself, for that would mean He too would die and God cannot die. In other words,

93

Messiah is only asking his Father to end *his* six hours of suffering so that *he* can die and fulfill his mission to bring eternal life. Immediately after making the request, His Father grants it to him since we are told, "and he gave up his spirit" (Matthew 27:50).

#2-Messiah's goal was to raise up disciples to his truth, not denominations with different opinions about the truth.

On the last night of his life as recorded in John 17, Yeshua said that as he and his Father were one, that he also sought oneness with his disciples, and between the disciples, each with the other. There was never a hint of a divided body with tens of thousands of named denominations as there are today. Calling his disciples brothers to each other, this literally meant they were all now in one spiritual family with one spiritual head, namely Yeshua himself. So, Matthew shouldn't argue with John or Peter with Thomas, for they are all the branches to Yeshua, the one Vine with the one Word by which they will be nourished (John 15:1-4).

Unfortunately, within thirty years of Yeshua giving that message, Paul was complaining of divisions arising from allegiance to charismatic leaders and not about the one truth Messiah came and died for, saying simply:

I plead with you my brothers by the Name of Yeshua the Messiah that there may be no divisions among you but that you may become perfectly of one mind and one way of thinking. (1 Corinthians 1:10)

One modern example of a worst-case scenario of leader-worship was in a Jim Jones or David Koresh style situation, where hundreds of followers committed suicide in the service of a man, not the message of the Messiah. This happens when the timeless and authoritative Word is ignored in favor of hero worship.

Another example is when we don't, deep down in our heart and soul, believe that our Almighty God is the One who heals or saves us, provides for all our needs, and pray accordingly every day. These trends can end up with many chasing after charismatic leaders because of their need for:

- *One prophetic word after another.* This happens many times because of an insatiable need for these prophetic proclamations when the receiver feels unsatisfied or does not like the message. Then they will tend to seek after a more agreeable word from someone else rather than consult the Scripture.
- *Prayers that end up with them being "slain in the Spirit."* Seeking a more intimate connection with the Holy Spirit is both admirable and kosher, but, as one pastor aptly put it, those who look for prayer of this kind should not be too eager to fall down in the Spirit without being willing to get back up as a better person.
- *Spiritual deliverance so that they don't have to do the work of repentance and positive change in order to remain free.* As a seasoned deliverance minister once explained to us, some of these people look at them as a McDonald's drive-thru, where they keep coming back, over and over, for a quick fix.
- *Teachings on what they want to hear only.* They search out pastors, rabbis, teachers and apostles who simply tell them what they want to hear rather than what they need to know from the Word. So, what gets lost is Messiah Yeshua's original full kingdom message that ranges back to Adam and forwards to our deep and ultimate spiritual destiny.

Ultimately, the fruits of the Spirit can only come about from rightly dividing the Word of Truth *through* the Holy Spirit, who never contradicts the Word of God:

For our gospel did not come to you in word only, but also in power and in the Holy Spirit and with full conviction; just as you

know what kind of men we proved to be among you for your sake.
(1 Thessalonians 1:5 NAU)

#3-The Apostles were to give the same Word to everyone, not establish churches that were in opposition to those established by other Apostles.

When Yeshua gives what is now famously called the Great Commission (Matthew 28:18-20, Mark 16:15-20), it is worth noting that the term for "Good News" or "Gospel" is always in the singular. So when Messiah proclaimed simply, *Repent and believe* <u>*THE GOOD NEWS*</u> (Mark 1:15), what exactly was that Good News?

Paul gives a compact yet powerful description of it when he says:

One Master (YHWH), one faith, one immersion, one God and Father of all Who is over all and through all and in all, but to each one of us grace is given according to the measure of the gift of the Messiah. (Ephesians 4:5-7)

In contrast to that one message then, the churches and other religious institutions today are manifesting thousands of different variations on everything from how leadership is structured, to how to view Scripture (or what books it should be), or even how to describe the nature of the Messiah, but they cannot all be right. Moreover, if they all got the same unified message from the Apostles, they should not be in conflict with one another, that is, if the message had not become divided or confused as it was predicted to happen (2 Thessalonians 2:7).

Aside from the Protestant Reformation and all of its modern denominations, anciently speaking there were many important assemblies that have roots going back to the Apostles while theologically different today. These include Jerusalem, Caesarea, Syrian Antioch, every place Paul wrote to, and the assemblies

96

mentioned at the start of Revelation. Others are mentioned by Peter in his travels, such as Pontius, Cappadocia, Bithynia and more. Their direct mention in Scripture proves that Rome, while a very early and important spiritual hub, was not the only game in town, but rather, part of an extended family of churches with their own apostolic pedigree and history of succession.

On the other hand, if there was any place mentioned in the Scripture that functioned as a governing body for everyone, it was Jerusalem, not Rome. Only Jerusalem was supervised directly under the tutelage of the "pillars"—Peter, James and John—which is why even Paul knew he had to go there first to get permission to preach (Galatians 1:18-19, 2:9-10). As a result, Protestantism, which emerged from the Roman rite, not only has to correct Catholic excesses, but also has to look at what other ancient assemblies did properly according to Scripture and make positive progress towards that paradigm.

#4-Yeshua first came to put Judah back to their covenantal responsibilities which included bringing the Gentiles into their midst, united in love and righteousness and in kosher spiritual processes.

Moses was first told in Deuteronomy 4:6 to "keep and do [the Commandments], for that is your wisdom and your understanding in the sight of the peoples who will hear all these statutes and say: Surely this nation is a wise and discerning people." As a result, Israel was supposed to have first learned these precepts well and then passed that understanding on to the rest of the world. This is why Yeshua also said: "Have I not been sent except to the sheep, which went astray from the house of Israel?" (Matthew 15:24)

Unfortunately, they did not accept that charge but rather applied the Divine Instructions only to themselves and even then not universally. And so, in the course of time, Yeshua came to set that matter straight. This is why he reminded them that his Set-apart

97

family was delineated not by blood but by obedience, "for he who does the will of my Heavenly Father is my brother and my sister and my mother" (Matthew 12:50). Also, because the leadership were wedded to the traditions of men that sometimes nullified the Scripture, Yeshua came to correct them.

Not all Pharisees did this, which is why when Yeshua saw them doing things correctly he would say "You are not far from the kingdom of God" (Mark 12:28-34). Keep in mind, though, that not all tradition is bad per se. It only becomes bad when it attempts to supersede the Word, contradict it or claim equal authority with it.

If the Jewish tradition at times sidestepped the Word, why should Christians think it is okay to follow that example and set up institutions or traditions that were also never sanctioned in Scripture? You will see how some of these took form later in this book.

The Christians, who embraced Messiah as the Son of YHWH, did they fully carry forward Yeshua's message of Torah observance in the early churches or did they ignore his words spoken in Matthew 5:17-20? This is what he says:

"Do not think that I've come to loosen Torah or the Prophets. I have not come to loosen but to fill them full with proper understanding. For truly I say to you that until heaven and earth pass away not one Yodh or one stroke will pass from Torah until everything happens. All who loosen [break] one (of) these small commandments and teach thus to the sons of man, will be called inferior in the Kingdom of Heaven, but all who do and teach this will be called great in the Kingdom of Heaven. For I say to you that unless your righteousness exceeds that of the scribes and the Pharisees, you will not enter the Kingdom of Heaven." (See also Mark 12:28-34, Luke 16:17, and John 5:45-47, 7:19)

Exactly 40 years after Yeshua's resurrection, the Second Temple is destroyed by Rome and a long and painful exile of the

Jews from the land of Judea begins. The Christians also go on a long exile from the original biblical truth as church traditions overwhelm real history. Within a century, both Judaism and Christianity have completely split from one another and are now on separate journeys of exile and restoration, either physically from their lands or spiritually from Divine Truth.

Jews and Christians are simply two parts to the same mission and message that Messiah came to give the world. In spite of this, as the centuries dragged on, hostility increased between the two groups who were supposed to work together. Ultimately that hostility also made it extremely difficult for the Jews to teach Christians the Torah which their Messiah kept and for the Christians who did not keep Torah to make the Jews jealous.

I say then, they did not stumble so as to fall, did they? May it never be! But by their transgression salvation has come to the Gentiles, to make them jealous. (Romans 11:11 NAU)

It also prevented the Christians from teaching the Jews how Yeshua fulfilled more than 300 biblical prophecies to let the world know he was the way, the truth and the life. They were at crossroads, and so we wait in our times for the truth to come out and set everyone free.

#5-The confusion of the original message of Messiah and his Apostles was predicted by them to become corrupted.

Though the messaging problem actually began in Apostolic Times, only Scripture can restore the truth that emerging Jewish and Gentile tradition tried to take away. Nearly every major leader in the Renewed Covenant lends his voice to the problem of heretics and false teachers impersonating as apostles.

Paul for example complains of multiplying false teachers who will turn their ears away from the truth and go after fables (2 Timothy 4:3-4) and "deceitful workmen" masquerading as apostles (2 Corinthians 11:13). He cautions us against anyone who tries to deceive us. Then in similar fashion Jude laments of wicked men perverting the grace of God (Jude 1:4).

But perhaps the most stinging indictment against the "antichrists" comes from the apostle John who simply explains that they will come to lead us astray and destroy us. John wanted us to know that, because these antichrists had left them to go off on their own, their teachings were not from the apostles (1 John 2:18-19, 4:3).

Yeshua also cautions us against the Antichrist and false prophets who will perform great signs and miracles (Matthew 24:24), and Peter warns us against false prophets and false teachers who will introduce destructive heresies and even deny Yeshua and God (2 Peter 2:1).

To paraphrase from Matthew once more, we need to be vigilant against all those who would "come to you in sheep's clothing but inwardly are ravenous wolves." Today, many use the same or similar terminology to refer to their beliefs or faith, but if you listen and watch them closely, the way they define those terminologies are quite different.

Often today there is an emphasis on restoring the history of the original Jewish followers of Yeshua the Messiah. While such an endeavor is both noble and necessary, there is a second story just as important that often gets ignored. It is the wider story that emerged after Biblical times.

Early Church History and Church Fathers

Do you not believe that I am in the Father, and the Father is in Me? The words that I say to you I do not speak on My own

initiative, but the Father abiding in Me does His works.
(John 14:10 NAU)

If you keep My commandments, you will abide in My love; just as
I have kept My Father's commandments and abide in His love.
(John 15:10 NAU)

Today it is tempting to believe in a simple linear history of Christians coalescing behind the Roman Catholic Church exceedingly early on and submitting to their leadership under the popes. However, we see throughout Acts that all major theological and corporate decisions that were binding on all believers, including the Apostles, came directly out of Jerusalem, so that wherever they travelled, they were unified in their teachings with Peter, James and John as her "three pillars."

After Jerusalem was destroyed in 70 CE, power did not immediately shift to Rome or to the Catholic Church. There was no "mother church" that followed Jerusalem. The real history is actually much more complex and is derived from the Apostolic Writings directly. We find that the disciples were first called Christians, not in Rome, but in Syrian Antioch and that Peter was always far from Rome, hundreds of miles away from her, visiting other churches and writing from Babylon instead (1 Peter 5:13).

A church like the one in Syrian Antioch had a completely distinct leadership, liturgy and theological outlook from that of Rome, and even what Rome initially believed was subject to revision. It was, in other words, not the homogenized and seamless linear progression that many have been led to believe.

These churches were neither unified nor were they even begrudgingly beholden to a central authority. This is not to say, that Rome was not an important and early assembly, but rather that she was far from the only theological powerhouse that her tradition would otherwise lead us to believe.

While the first person we know of to use the term "Catholic Church" did so in the early 2nd century (Ignatius of Antioch, Letter to the Smynreans, Chapter 8), that term is completely divorced from the exclusive Roman branding these assemblies are generally classified as today. The term "catholic" was originally meant to simply mean "universal" and not as under the leadership of Rome. Likewise the "Roman Catholic Church," as it is known today, did not exist under this name until the 3rd century.

Through the limited historical documentation that we have from the late 1st century to middle 2nd century, we can see evidence of a rivalry going on between Rome in the west and other churches in the east. For example, we find that the chief bishop of Rome, Anicetus, is frustrated with the chief bishop of Smyrna (Polycarp), because they had to agree to disagree about Passover. Surely if Polycarp was subservient to Anicetus of Rome and considered him his "spiritual father," the controversy never would have happened.

Churches like the ones in Syrian Antioch, Rome, Smyrna, Hierapolis, Ephesus and many others each had separate lines of succession in terms of chief bishops after being established by the original Apostles. That is to say, there was not one papal line ruling all areas. Moreover, it was another very powerful assembly, Alexandria Egypt, that is to be credited with being the first to use the term "pope" for their chief bishop after he died in the 3rd century. Rome did not call their chief bishop a "Pope" until centuries later.

Besides which, the great diversity and autonomy of faith models in these original assemblies cannot be overstated. There were some places that took a very mystical, almost Gnostic, view of the world, and devoted themselves to monastic isolation and prayer. There were others that geared themselves to preach the Gospel to pagan groups, showing how their myths were leading to the Messiah, while Jewish or Torah-centered groups who were keeping Sabbath and the Feasts have already been mentioned.

Did Messiah have only one nature or two? Was he truly human or only a divine agent who took on the appearance of flesh? Even questions about seemingly basic ideas and terms like "resurrection" and "salvation" were hotly debated between assemblies and, often within each individual assembly. And, perhaps most shocking of all, they didn't even always agree on what Bible books should be canonized.

Sometimes, when one chief bishop died, his successor would take his flock in a completely different theological direction. As a result, because no one had authority or control over the new bishop, the best that these rival leaders could do was to have a conference of equals and make very gentle suggestions that had no binding force whatsoever at this early time.

On the other hand, it is a true statement to say that certain very powerful assemblies did attempt to unify all the others under them, but there was also a very clear spiritual demarcation and border line between east and west, where one group was not able to cross over and dominate the other. It is therefore important to understand the true state of variety within these earliest bodies before we can proceed to how traditions began to alter that true picture.

There are certain truths about Scripture and Messiah that the church properly received and rightly preserved, including that he was prophesied to be the Savior of the world, born of a virgin, was the Only Begotten Son of God Almighty made flesh and rose from the dead, among other important tenets.

Having said that, as Christianity continued her consistent and widespread separation from Judaism, traditions arose on the western-Catholic side that resulted in an anti-Torah and sometimes anti-Semitic viewpoint.

As that same tradition grew and spread throughout the western Roman Empire before it fell in the mid-5th century, the leadership of the Roman Church attempted to rewrite their own. Fortunately for us however, these revisionists were overruled by other Catholic leaders who opted to preserve their history although, at the same time, these leaders ignored much of what it said to keep their power intact.

It is from those earliest Catholic resources that this history comes back to you, since what they rightly preserved can now shine a light on the contradictions between what it says and what later Catholic leaders taught.

Most modern church leaders have been taught and trained, or at least have some working knowledge, of the writings of the Early Church Fathers. What they haven't been taught, and therefore don't preach, is what we are going to share with you now.

Clement of Rome

The Renewed Covenant mentions two of the earliest chief bishops of Rome by name. The first is Linus, who is referenced by Paul in 2 Timothy 4:21. The second is Clement, in Philippians 4:3. Paul knew both men, but Clement, also knew the Apostle John while he was living in Patmos.

Clement of Rome was the highest-ranking authority in the Roman Church as chief bishop, since there were no popes in those days. According to some lists, Clement was the second head of the Roman Church to lead them, while others put him as the fourth from 88-99 CE, but all agree he lived and died in the 1st century.

104

There is also vast consensus among both Catholic and other scholars that one authentic letter of their chief bishop Clement has survived. It is called the *Letter to the Corinthians*, and the dates given for its composition range from 66-99 CE. If so, this means Clement wrote his letter before the Apostle John finished the book of Revelation.

Other scholars and experts, including the former Pope Benedict the 16th (Joseph Ratzinger), believe the references to the Jerusalem Temple in the present tense necessitate viewing Clement as the second chief bishop of Rome. If that's the case, then the letter was written just before the Temple was destroyed.

In any case, if a recent pope has been willing to publicly proclaim the *Letter of Corinthians* as a legitimate document written by Clement in the 1st century, I can hardly be viewed as being biased against the Catholic Church in believing that what Clement said was true! Therefore, whichever part of the 1st century this letter is from, it must be viewed as both factual and authentic. Who better than the "pope" to comment on the Roman Church he knew back then?

We see in Philippians 4:3 that Clement, who knew the apostles and was discipled by John, is also held in high esteem by Paul:

I also plead with you, my true burden bearer that you assist those women who worked hard with me in the Good News; together with Clement and with the rest of my helpers whose names are written in the book of life.

Clement writes to the Corinthians in response to their request for counsel because of some challenges they were facing. His letter is clear, his words are articulate and one that is worthy of being read. He praises them about many things including their hospitality, humility, virtuous and religious life, and that they walked in the commandments of God, "carefully attending to His

105

words," being "inwardly filled with His doctrine" and "did all things in the fear of God." He is also pleased and says, "the commandments and ordinances of the Lord were written on the tablets of (their) hearts." High praise indeed!

He then talks about how envy and jealousy are creating strife in their church. Clement states that in ancient times these traits caused Cain to rise up against Abel, made Jacob flee from his brother Esau, and Joseph to be persecuted and to come into bondage. Envy compelled Moses to flee from the face of Pharaoh, and he adds that "through envy and jealousy, the greatest and most righteous pillars [of the church] have been persecuted and put to death," including Peter and Paul. Many men and women had to endure indignities and tortures and that envy and strife has also "overthrown great cities and rooted out mighty nations."

So why is this important to us? Because he is addressing the Church:

"These things, beloved, we write unto you, not merely to admonish you of your duty, but also to remind ourselves. For we are struggling on the same arena, and the same conflict is assigned to both of us…Let us turn to every age that has passed, and learn that, from generation to generation, the Lord has granted a place of repentance to all such as would be converted unto Him." (Chapter 7)

Envy, jealousy and pride my friends, is a sin in opposition to humility, and therefore we need to repent to get closer to God. Rome was having strife within her church not having learned from the past, and obviously this was troubling him. With this in mind, let us take a careful look at what else he has to say:

"It is right and holy therefore, men and brethren, rather to obey God than to follow those who, through pride and sedition, have become the leaders of a detestable emulation." (Chapter 14)

"Let us cleave, therefore, to those who cultivate peace with godliness, <u>and not to those who hypocritically confess to desire it</u>. For [the Scripture] says in a certain place, 'This people honor Me with their lips, but their heart is far from Me.'" (Chapter 15)

"Let your children be partakers of <u>true</u> Christian training...For He is a Searcher of the thoughts and desires [of the heart]: His breath is in us and when He pleases, He will take it away." (Chapter 21)

"When and as He pleases He will do all things, and <u>none</u> of the things determined by Him shall pass away." (Chapter 27)

"Let us draw near to Him with holiness of spirit...loving our gracious and merciful Father, Who has <u>made us partakers in His blessings of His elect</u>...His people Jacob became the portion of the Lord, and Israel the lot of His inheritance." (Chapter 29)

"Let us cleave then to His blessing and consider what are the means of possessing it. <u>Let us think over the things which have taken place from the beginning</u>." (Chapter 31)

"So, from him [Jacob] have sprung up the priests and all the Levites who minister at the altar of God. From him also [was descended] our Lord Jesus Christ according to the flesh. From him [arose] kings, princes and rulers of the race of Judah. Nor are his other tribes in small glory, inasmuch as God had promised, 'Thy seed shall be as the stars of heaven'...And we, too, being called by His will in Jesus Christ, are not justified by ourselves, nor by our own wisdom, or understanding, or godliness, or works which we have wrought in holiness of heart; <u>but by that faith through which, from the beginning, Almighty God has justified all men</u>." (Chapter 32)

"Above all, with His holy and undefiled hands He formed man, the most excellent [of His creatures] ...<u>the express likeness of His own image</u>." (Chapter 33)

"Let us therefore earnestly strive to be found in the number of those that wait for Him, in order that we may <u>share</u> in His promised gifts." (Chapter 35)

Again, I would not feel nearly as confident about linking the Clement mentioned by Paul in Philippians 4:3 with the one who is listed as the second or fourth chief bishop of Rome, were it not for the early church fathers who lived between the 2nd and 5th centuries, doing it first:

Origen identifies Pope Clement with St. Paul's fellow-laborer (Philippians 4:3), and so do Eusebius, Epiphanius, and Jerome. - Catholic Encyclopedia

This is not to say that every Catholic authority, ancient or modern, accepted that idea uncritically. Rather, the point is that this list of ancient witnesses which favored the identification of Clement as the one mentioned in Philippians 4:3 forms an authentic historical core around the traditions that sprung up later.

I have also confirmed these facts directly from my own research. Clement served the Philippian assembly but then went to aid Paul during his imprisonment in Rome towards the end of Paul's life. This is why Philippians is called one of the "prison epistles." It may have been written *to* the Philippians, but it was written *from* Rome. The chain of both history for Clement and custody for his written work could not be clearer or stronger. In his letter to the Corinthians he is also reflecting on how believers of the Messiah should walk out their faith in Corinth as well as in Rome:

"These things therefore being manifest to us, and since we look into the depths of the divine knowledge, <u>it behooves us to do all things in [their proper] order, which the Lord has commanded us to perform at stated times</u>. He has enjoined offerings [to be presented] and service to be performed [to Him], and that not

thoughtlessly or irregularly, but at the appointed times and hours.

Where and by whom He desires these things to be done, He Himself has fixed by His own supreme will, in order that all things being piously done according to His good pleasure may be acceptable unto Him. <u>Those, therefore, who present their offerings at the appointed times, are accepted and blessed</u>; for inasmuch as they follow the laws of the Lord, they sin not. For his own peculiar services are assigned to the high priest, and their own proper place is prescribed to the priests, and their own special ministrations devolve on the <u>Levites</u>. The layman is bound by the laws that pertain to laymen." (Chapter 40)

"Let every one of you, my brothers, give thanks to God in his own order, living in all good conscience, with a becoming degree of seriousness, and not going beyond the rule of the ministry prescribed to him. <u>Not in every place</u>, brothers, are the daily sacrifices offered, or the peace-offerings, or the sin-offerings and the trespass-offerings, <u>but in Jerusalem only</u>. And even there they are not offered in any place, <u>but only at the altar before the temple</u>, that which is offered being first carefully examined by the high priest and the ministers already mentioned. Those, therefore, who do anything beyond that which is agreeable to His will, are punished with death. You see, my brothers, <u>that the greater the knowledge that has been confirmed to us, the greater also is the danger to which we are exposed</u>." (Chapter 41)

We need to ask ourselves why a chief bishop of the Roman Church would advocate keeping God's Laws as it is written and not being persuaded otherwise by man, preaching as a latter-day King Josiah, urging the faithful to also keep the Feasts of YHWH. If you remember, King Josiah was the king before Judah was taken into captivity by Nebuchadnezzar of Babylon. He destroyed all pagan worship after reading from the Torah scroll that was hidden in the Temple, reinstating the Passover Feast which had not been done in centuries.

Clement knew the history of the Jewish people, and recognized them as the elect of God (Chapter 29) but also that, as Gentiles, they were grafted in to the Messiah (Romans 11:17-21). He wanted his people to honor God and His commandments, as Yeshua and the Apostles did, with feasts of rejoicing *every few months* throughout the year. There are about seven times a year that the people of YHWH give thanks and praise to Him and three of these feasts last 8 days. How could that be called a burden to have such festivals about once every three months?

For this is the love of God, that we keep His commandments; and His commandments are not burdensome. (1 John 5:3 NAU)

The sacred year begins in the spring with Passover and the Feast of Unleavened Bread, honoring the deliverance of God's people from bondage in Egypt. For those of us who are believers, this 8-day feast— nowadays referred to in short as Passover—also commemorates the suffering, death and resurrection of Yeshua the Messiah. This feast was so important to Yeshua that he was determined to keep it, knowing he was about to die in a matter of hours.

Next, nearly two months later, comes the Feast of Weeks, or Pentecost, which celebrated the start of the wheat harvest and was also the occasion for the miracle of the languages in Acts 2. Pentecost then completed the spring harvests and pointed the people to the start of fall, beginning with the Feast of Trumpets (Rosh Hashanna), which was also the start of their civil year. Ten days later comes the Day of Atonement. This great all day fast with an extensive liturgy of prayer and repentance was also the time the faithful believed they could get their sins forgiven, and so they thanked God Almighty for His mercy.

A mere five days after that solemnity, the most joyous time of the year begins with the Feast of Tabernacles, also called Sukkot.

For 8 days we celebrate, at that time, the grape harvest and all the other blessings and provision that we have received from God all year. It was during this feast that Yeshua gave some of his most amazing teachings in John 7 and 8.

Thereafter, we have two optional feasts that Yeshua also kept, Hanukkah, an 8-day festival of lights (John 10) towards the end of the secular year and Purim, the story of deliverance told in the book of Esther. This feast taking place in the February to March timeframe is also mentioned in John 5. These rounded out the rest of the season as the faithful got ready to celebrate the next start of spring with Passover and start the whole process all over again.

Clement explains that God has by His own supreme will given His people the time, place and by whom these things are to be done. Today this is regarded as an appointed time to meet with our Creator even though the Temple no longer exists, and the priests are no longer able to do sacrifices. Clement clearly intends for his people to continue doing these feasts so that they may be, as he says, "accepted and blessed," and that "for as much as they follow the laws of the Lord, they sin not."

There is no doubt that when Clement mentions "appointed times and hours" he is referring to the feasts mandated in the books of Moses. The Greek word he uses, *kairois*, is in fact the same word used for those feasts in the Greek translation of the Pentateuch, such as in Leviticus 23:4.

Let us continue to look at Clement's Letter to the Corinthians on the topic of leadership with these choice statements of wisdom:

"The Apostles have preached the Gospel to us from the Lord Jesus Christ…and thus preaching through countries and cities, they appointed the first fruits [of their labors], <u>having first proved them by the Spirit</u>, to be bishops and deacons of those who should afterwards believe…for thus says the Scripture in a

certain place, 'I will appoint their bishops in righteousness and their deacons in faith.'" (Chapter 42)

It is worth noting that Clement's Greek word for "bishop" really means something closer to "overseer" or "supervisor" which also harks back to a Hebrew term for a person carrying out commandments as a servant (Isaiah 60:17). None of these terms however carry the sense of the full Catholic term for "bishop" as they promote it today. He explains the original temperament and characteristics of those who should be serving in these positions as follows:

"Our Apostles also knew, through our Lord Jesus Christ, and there would be strife on account of the office of the episcopate...they appointed those [ministers] already mentioned, and afterwards gave instructions, that when they should fall asleep, other approved men should succeed them in their ministry. We are of the opinion, therefore, that those appointed by them, or afterwards by other eminent men, <u>with the consent of the whole church, and who blamelessly served the flock of Christ in a humble, peaceable, and disinterested spirit, and have for a long time possessed the good opinion of all</u>...our sin will not be small, if we eject from the episcopate those who have blamelessly and holily fulfilled its duties." (Chapter 44)

These requirements may not be met by all our leaders today, but it is something that Church and other assemblies should strive towards going forward. Remember, that while the leaders have their roles, the Church, you, also have a role to raise up your leaders through encouragement and demands for a more excellent standard—humble, peaceable, and with a disinterested spirit, i.e., putting God and Church before themselves.

And so, we now conclude our detailed look at Clement's Letter to the Corinthians with these final insights:

"Look carefully into the Scriptures, which are the <u>true utterances</u> of the Holy Spirit. Observe that nothing of an unjust or counterfeit character in written in them." (Chapter 45)

"Let us cleave, therefore, to the innocent and righteous, since these are the elect of God. Why are there strifes, and tumults, and divisions, and schisms, and wars among you? <u>Have we not [all] one God and one Christ?</u>...Why do we divide and tear to pieces the members of Christ...Remember the words of our Lord Jesus Christ, how he said, 'Woe to that man [by whom offenses come]! It is better for him that he had never been born than that he should cast a stumbling block before one of my elect...Your schism has subverted [the faith of] many, has discouraged many, has given rise to doubt in many, and has caused grief to us all. And still your sedition continues.'" (Chapter 46)

"Take up the epistle of the blessed Apostle Paul. What did he write to you at the time when the Gospel first began to be preached? <u>But now reflect who those are that have perverted you.</u>" (Chapter 47)

"Let us therefore, with all haste, put an end to this [state of things]; and let us fall down before the Lord, and beseech Him with tears, that He would mercifully be reconciled to us, <u>and restore us</u> to our former seemly and holy practice of brotherly love...Let a man be faithful; let him be powerful in the utterance of knowledge; let him be wise in judging of words; let him be pure in all his deeds; yet the more he seems to be superior to others [in these respects], the more humble minded ought he to be, and to seek the common good of all and not merely his own advantage." (Chapter 48)

"Let him who has loved in Christ <u>keep the commandments of Christ</u>." (Chapter 49)

"Blessed are we, beloved, <u>if we keep the commandments of God</u> in the harmony of love; that so through love our sins may be

forgiven us…This blessedness comes upon those who have been chosen by God through Jesus Christ our Lord." (Chapter 50)

"You understand, beloved, you understand well the Sacred Scriptures and you have looked very earnestly into the oracles of God. Call then these things to your remembrance." (Chapter 53)

"You see, beloved, that protection is afforded to those that are chastened of the Lord; for since God is good, He corrects us, that we may be admonished by His holy chastisement." (Chapter 56)

"For it is better for you that you should occupy a humble but honorable place in the flock of Christ, than that, being highly exalted, you should be cast out from the hope of His people." (Chapter 57)

Clement also tells us how to live and give thanks to God with a degree of seriousness that is manifested by being obedient to our Creator and living by the teachings of Yeshua. Clement calls on his fellow believers to realize that the more they grow in knowledge and responsibility, the greater is the danger which they are exposed to should they fail to live up to their obligations.

Ignatius of Antioch

However, less than twenty years later, there is a shift away from all things "Jewish." After Clement died, another powerful teacher arose named Ignatius, bishop of Syrian Antioch. Dated from just before his martyrdom in 108 CE, Ignatius was allowed by his Roman captors to send his letters out to various leaders and friends before being headed off to his own execution.

Ignatius was also among the first in what will become a series of increasingly strident and powerful voices that will begin to view the Torah as something incompatible with belief in "the Christ." In his zeal to evangelize Christianity and to proclaim in his epistles love for our Savior, he writes things that perhaps, had he been more of a student of human behavior and history, he might have restated differently to avoid misinterpretation. While his letters show his reverence for the Most-High God, one can see a bias towards Jesus Christ whom he also calls "God," thus blurring the lines or distinctions between Savior-Messiah and God Almighty

Neither Clement nor Polycarp refer to Jesus Christ as "God" in their epistles, but as our Savior, Lord or the Son of God, maintaining the distinction between God and His Son. The impact of this title to Yeshua (Jesus) is only seen much later either when churches refer to YHWH as the God of the Old Testament and Jesus as the God of the New Testament or they start talking of the Father, the Son, and the Holy Spirit as three persons or a tri-unity. Today, most of their prayers are focused on Jesus rather than his Heavenly Father. Correct terminology matters.

Furthermore, the Greek word *pneuma* means "spirit" or "wind," but when it was mistranslated into English, the Holy Spirit was wrongly referred to as the *Holy Ghost*. A ghost is a spirit of a deceased person and our God is very much alive!

If this seems of little consequence, remember that decisions made, even seemingly minor ones, can have ripple effects with huge consequences. It took the Church away from our God, YHWH, and the keeping of His Laws, commandments and statutes. The lessons of the Hebrew people, that disobedience brings calamity, which Clement also warned about, were ignored. This was because the Church saw themselves as separate from their Jewish brothers and sisters who also believed in the Messiah.

I am quoting exclusively from Ignatius' "short version letters" as they are considered the most reliable and accurate. By contrast, the "long version letters" contain the words of a later redactor centuries after Ignatius died. That being said, let's begin by looking at the newer negative take on the Torah that was begun in the early years of the 2nd century through Ignatius, in his Letter to the Magnesians, Chapters 8 and 10:

Be not deceived with strange doctrines, or with old fables, <u>which are unprofitable</u>. For if we still live according to the Jewish law, <u>we acknowledge that we have not received grace</u>. - Early Church Fathers, p. 62.

It is absurd to profess Jesus Christ and to Judaize. <u>For Christianity did not embrace Judaism, but Judaism Christianity</u>, so that every tongue which believes might be gathered to God. - Early Church Fathers, p. 63.

Let us not, therefore, be insensible to His kindness. For were He to reward us according to our works, we should cease to be. Therefore, having become His disciples, <u>let us learn to live according to the principles of Christianity. For whosoever is called by any other name besides this, is not of God</u>. – Early Church Fathers, p. 63.

These are strong words coming from a man who never met the Messiah but is claiming to know the Apostle John while still introducing division between Judaism and Christianity. His writings, whether he intended to do so or not, opened the door to anti-Semitism in the Roman Catholic Church. This is evident from how an unknown Catholic redactor from the 4th century understood, expanded and reinterpreted Ignatius' original words which are appended to his letter:

It is absurd to speak of Jesus Christ with the tongue, and to cherish in the mind a Judaism which has now come to an end. <u>For where there is Christianity there cannot be Judaism</u>.

Let's pause for a moment and ask ourselves, "How could Ignatius and the Church accept the Apostle Paul as one their founding fathers and deny Judaism?" Luke is recounting what Paul says about himself below:

But perceiving that one group were Sadducees and the other Pharisees, Paul began crying out in the Council, "Brethren, I am a Pharisee, a son of Pharisees; I am on trial for the hope and resurrection of the dead!" (Acts 23:6 NAU)

Therefore, to reject Paul and Judaism is to deny the very foundations on which the Church rests. So how could a beloved early church father like Ignatius have written such a thing? We believe after reading all his epistles carefully, that this view is more complicated than it appears on the surface. He was under arrest and in a hurry, with limited time to write to his church in Antioch and others. So, before he was executed, he draws on what he has, perhaps, seen in Antioch and wants to excite the believers about our Savior and the Good News, to encourage them to be strong in their belief and do good works.

However, unintended consequences can have as much effect as those we intend. We see this when Ignatius goes even further in attempting to institute the substitution of the original Saturday Sabbath in favor of the *Lord's Day* on Sunday:

If, therefore, those who were brought up in the ancient order of things have come to the possession of a new hope, no longer observing the Sabbath, but living in the observance of the Lord's Day. – Early Church Fathers, p. 62.

The same Catholic redactor expands on the above in an even stronger language:

Let us therefore no longer keep the Sabbath after the Jewish manner and rejoice in days of idleness; for "he that does not work, let him not eat." For say the [holy] oracles, "In the sweat

117

of thy face shalt thou eat thy bread." But let every one of you keep the Sabbath after a spiritual manner, rejoicing in meditation on the law, not in relaxation of the body...And after the observance of the Sabbath, let every friend of Christ keep the Lord's Day as a festival, the resurrection-day, the queen and chief of all the days [of the week]. — Early Church Fathers, p. 62.

This statement is however in clear violation of what Yeshua teaches, when he said in Matthew 5:17 "Do not think that I have come to loosen Torah or the Prophets" and goes on to explain that he came to fill them full with proper understanding. Also, in Luke 16:17 he says, "But it is easier for heaven and earth to pass away than for one stroke of a letter of the Law (Torah) to fail." That being said, contrary to Ignatius, this is what we are commanded by our Heavenly Father to do and Clement agreed:

*Remember the sabbath day, to keep it holy. Six days you shall labor and do all your work, but the seventh day is a sabbath of the LORD your God; in it you shall not do any work, you or your son or your daughter, your male or your female servant...
(Exodus 20:8-10 NAU)*

*For six days work may be done, but on the seventh day there is a sabbath of complete rest, holy to the LORD; whoever does any work on the sabbath day shall surely be put to death.......
(Exodus 31:15 NAU)*

Which is why Yeshua also says this about the day of rest:

But pray that your flight will not be in the winter, or on a Sabbath. (Matthew 24:20 NAU)

Yeshua and his disciples, all born into Judaism, kept the Sabbath. In Matthew 12:2-12 and in many of his conversations with the Pharisees, Yeshua was removing the "fences" they had made regarding the keeping of the Sabbath. He was not talking about not observing the Sabbath but was explaining to them, the

Pharisees, and teaching or re-training his disciples on what is permissible during the Sabbath.

So, as believers, should we or should we not keep this Set-Apart day? Did the Apostles as they preached the Gospel ever separate themselves from their Jewish faith? The Twelve knew very well the full history of the Hebrew Bible (Luke 24:44). They therefore never separated themselves from their covenant with God, but instead looked at Yeshua as the ultimate and best expression of that faith.

Hence, we can conclude, Ignatius got it wrong, for the original "Christianity," which was an extension of *The Way* (Acts 24:14), did most certainly embrace Judaism, the faith of their Savior.

Clement also knew that the price for abandoning the Divine Laws YHWH God Almighty gave was banishment, death or extinction. Our Heavenly Father is a loving God. He is patient and forgiving but, at the same time, when repentance is not forthcoming, He must bring about judgment on His children. Does not a parent punish a child because he loves the child?

We saw this play out repeatedly in history, with Adam and Eve being banished from Eden, everyone except Noah and his family being destroyed in the Flood, the destruction of Sodom and Gomorrah, the exile of the northern tribes of Israel into Assyria and the southern tribes into Babylon and finally the Romans destroying the Temple and the exile of the Jews from their land for more than 1,800 years until the establishment of the state of Israel in 1948. I think for the people who went through all these hardships, they would beg to differ with Ignatius when he calls the obedience to Torah "unprofitable!"

Take a good look around you and all the problems in the world that are affecting you and consider who speaks truth. Could following the Word of God from Genesis to Revelation have a

119

positive effect on your family, your health, the food we all eat, your finances and even the governmental leadership we live under? As you may recall, Israel and then Judah both fell after a time of prosperity along with every empire or great nation since then.

Another important thing that Ignatius began to do was to suggest a lesser reliance on the Hebrew Bible in establishing faith-based positions. Whereas Paul in Acts 17 was determined to prove to the Jews in Berea that all his beliefs about the Messiah conformed to Scripture, Ignatius suggests another path in some rather nuanced language:

> *When I heard some saying, If I do not find it in the ancient Scriptures, I will not believe the Gospel; on my saying to them, It is written, they answered me, That remains to be proved. But to me Jesus Christ is in the place of all that is ancient: His cross, and death, and resurrection, and the faith, which is by Him, are undefiled monuments of antiquity; by which I desire, through your prayers, to be justified. - Letter to the Philadelphians, Chapter 8, Phillip Schaff, Early Church Fathers, p. 84.*

Let us think about what he said in view of the following:

> *But the Gospel possesses something transcendent [above the former dispensation], viz., the appearance of our Lord Jesus Christ, His passion and resurrection. For the beloved prophets announced Him, but the Gospel is the perfection of immortality. – Letter to the Philadelphians, Chapter 9, Early Church Fathers, p. 84.*

By putting the Messiah in opposition to "all that is ancient," Ignatius is paving the way for the Scriptures to be divided into what we call today the Old Testament and the New Testament. Whether by accident or design, these ideas made room for teachings of Replacement Theology and New Testament supercessionism, as opposed to all Scripture informing or building up your faith.

Also, by Ignatius elevating human beings to near-divine status, the checks and balances that could have prevailed in the Church were under attack:

I exhort you to study to do all things with a divine harmony, <u>while your bishop presides in the place of God</u>, and your presbyters in the place of the assembly of the apostles. – Letter to the Magnesians, Chapter 6, Early Church Fathers, p. 61.

For it is written, "God resists the proud." Let us be careful, then, not to set ourselves <u>in opposition to the bishop</u>, in order that we may be subject to God. - Letter to the Ephesians, Chapter 5, Early Church Fathers, p. 51.

But the Spirit proclaimed these words: <u>Do nothing without the bishop</u>. – Letter to the Philadelphians, Chapter 7, Early Church Fathers, pp. 83-84.

I don't think he foresaw the time when Church leadership could be anything less than perfect. However, for the Church and other religious organizations connected with Judaism and Christianity, there still is a safeguard in the Word, just as there is for our country through the rule of law, but neither of these safeguards should be ignored or misused.

A point of interest here is that Yeshua rebuked the Pharisees and Sadducees who comprised the Sanhedrin for the extra rules and traditions they imposed and yet, when some of the early church leaders put man-made traditions above Scripture, they too were creating oral law, just like the Pharisees. Ironically, they also ignored Messiah's advice not to let traditions nullify Scripture (Matthew 15:2-3).

Once the die was cast that put church rulings or decisions in a superior position to Scripture, a wholesale movement away from the unity of Torah and Gospel preached by Clement of Rome took root, in what eventually became the Roman Catholic Church.

Papias, Polycarp and Anicetus

Despite these trends set by Ignatius, others like Papias and Polycarp protested this alteration, urging their followers to go back to the ancient paths of the Messiah and his Apostles. Papias was the third chief bishop of Hierapolis in Phrygia, in modern-day Turkey, from 100-163 CE. He flourished as an influential writer and teacher from about 95-120 CE and died at the ripe old age of 103.

Papias was a student and friend of Polycarp, a disciple of John and the quotes we have from Papias are either fragments that came from his pen or were excerpted by later Church Fathers in the 3rd and 4th centuries, most notably by Eusebius, who was Constantine's biographer. Eusebius speaks of Papias as a man most learned in all things, and well acquainted with the Scriptures.

While Papias does not write, as far as we can tell, on the issue of Torah observance for Christians, he does seem to reference a deep skepticism for the way the earliest beliefs he knew in the Church were now changing in the middle of the 2nd century. Put simply, the written tradition he is reading is not lining up with what he knew from those who had direct and personal encounters with the actual Apostles, as he indicates here:

For I did not, like the multitude, take pleasure in those who spoke much, but in those who taught the truth; nor in those who related strange commandments, but in those who rehearsed the commandments given by the Lord to faith, and proceeding from truth itself.

If, then, anyone who had attended on the elders came, I asked minutely after their sayings, what Andrew or Peter said, or what

was said by Philip, or by Thomas, or by James, or by John, or by
Matthew, or by any other of the Lord's disciples: which things
Aristion and the presbyter John, the disciples of the Lord, say.
For I imagined that what was to be got from books was not so
profitable to me as what came from the living and abiding voice.
- Papias (130 CE), Exposition #1, Phillip Schaff, Early Church
Fathers, p. 153.

Again, Papias may be very clever in the way he doesn't quite spell things out, but, nevertheless, there is a distinction he says, being made between "commandments given by the Lord to faith" and "strange commandments," just as there is a distinction between the "teachings of the disciples" and "what I got from books." It would then seem likely that the former definitions are viewed more favorably than the latter ones, because the former ones were the originals.

In his letters, referred to as the *Fragments of Papias,* he tells us he is not prone to exaggeration, that he takes care to only write down the truth of what he hears from those who have had direct contact with the Apostles. One such thing that he hears, which gave me great pleasure to share with you, is this:

As the presbyters say, then those who are deemed worthy of an
abode in heaven shall go there, others shall enjoy the delights of
Paradise, and others shall possess the splendor of the city; for
everywhere the Savior will be seen, according as they shall be
worthy who see Him. But that there is this distinction between the
habitation of those who produce a hundred-fold, and that of those
who produce sixty-fold, and that of those who produce thirty-
fold; for the first will be taken up into the heavens, the second
class will dwell in Paradise, and the last will inhabit the city; and
that on this account the Lord said, "In my Father's house are
many mansions:" for all things belong to God, who supplies all
with a suitable dwelling-place, even as His word says, that a
share is given to all by the Father, according as each one is or

123

*shall be worthy. And this is the couch in which they shall recline
who feast, being invited to the wedding. The presbyters, the
disciples of the apostles, say that this is the gradation and
arrangement of those who are saved, and that they advance
through steps of this nature; and that, moreover, they ascend
through the Spirit to the Son, and through the Son to the Father;
and that in due time the Son will yield up His work to the Father,
even as it is said by the apostle. – Chapter 5, p. 154*

I hope and pray that you do not take your salvation casually.
Whatever your situation at present is, there is an eternity of
wonderful things to look forward to if we walk in the ways of our
Heavenly Father and His Son. As the road ahead is a bumpy one
to come, stay strong and you will discover how you have been
kidnapped from God Almighty and sold a *false bill of goods*.

For now, however, we have an extremely interesting situation
with our next apostolic witness, another student of the Apostle
John known as Polycarp. He became the second chief bishop of
Smyrna from 69-155 CE. Like Papias, Polycarp also lived a very
long and productive life well into the second half of the 2nd century.
The manner of his arrest and the miracle that preceded his death is
a good read for anyone interested. Polycarp is also referred to, not
only as an illustrious teacher, but also as a preeminent martyr.

Ancient records speak of Polycarp as a humble yet tenacious
servant who submitted himself completely to Messiah for eighty-
six years. The way he did this he clearly states in his own letter to
the Philippian assembly:

*But He who raised Him up from the dead will raise up us also, if
we do His will, and walk in His commandments, and love what
He loved, keeping ourselves from all unrighteousness,
covetousness, love of money, evil speaking, false witness; not
rendering evil for evil, or railing for railing, or blow for blow, or*

*cursing for cursing. - Polycarp, Epistle to the Philippians, Phillip
Schaff, Early Church Fathers, p. 33.*

While he does not mention YHWH by Name, Polycarp is
acknowledging His power to raise Yeshua from the dead (Acts
13:30) and us if we live by God's will and commandments and
keep away from sin. But Polycarp did far more than just teach the
"moral code" of the Ten Commandments. He also walked his faith
out in action, as a Torah-observant Feast-keeper.

One of the Feasts that Polycarp insisted he and his fellow
believers keep was Passover, so much so that when he got to Rome
he drew the ire of Anicetus, the chief bishop there. Anicetus was
the 11th chief bishop of Rome from about 153-168 CE, a few
generations removed from Clement. Polycarp's assistant, Irenaeus,
recounts this series of events a mere two to three decades after they
happened:

*Notwithstanding this, those who did not keep [the feast in this
way] were peacefully disposed towards those who came to them
from other dioceses...And when the blessed Polycarp was
sojourning in Rome in the time of Anicetus, although a slight
controversy had arisen among them as to certain other points,
they were at once well inclined towards each other [with regard
to the matter in hand], not willing that any quarrel should arise
between them upon this head.*

*Neither could Anicetus persuade Polycarp <u>not to observe what he
had always observed with John the disciple of our Lord, and the
other apostles</u> with whom he had associated; neither could
Polycarp persuade Anicetus to observe it, <u>as he said that he
ought to follow the customs of the presbyters that had preceded
him</u>. - Irenaeus, Fragment #3, from Phillip Schaff, Early Church
Fathers, p. 569.*

Polycarp is another early church father observing the Feasts of
YHWH practiced by Yeshua and the apostles and as such Anicetus

recognizes he has no power over Polycarp, to force him to tow the corporate line of Rome. As there was no "Pope" serving a "mother church" at this time, the chief bishop of one important assembly was, for the most part, just as powerful as the chief bishop of another.

As such, Polycarp, because he was on Anicetus' "home turf," could not force his Roman counterpart's compliance to keep Passover either, leaving "toleration" as the only path forward for both men.

However, the most important fact is what Irenaeus says at the end. Anicetus comments to Polycarp that he needs to in effect ignore the way of the Apostles who were taught by Yeshua and instead follow the customs that prevailed in Rome. Remember those letters of Ignatius that talked of being in unity with the bishop? Well, this is what we teach when asked about the need to stay unified: Unity without purity is a dangerous road to travel on.

Another important early witness to these events who knew Polycarp personally was Polycrates, bishop of Ephesus. He confirms this debate is about keeping Passover, which was a widely accepted practice amongst the Christians he knew:

I speak of Philip, one of the twelve apostles, who is laid to rest at Hierapolis; and his two daughters, who arrived at old age unmarried; his other daughter also, who passed her life under the influence of the Holy Spirit, and reposes at Ephesus; John, moreover, who reclined on the Lord's bosom, and who became a priest wearing the mitre and a witness and a teacher—he rests at Ephesus. Then there is Polycarp, both bishop and martyr at Smyrna...These all kept the passover on the fourteenth day of the month, in accordance with the Gospel, without ever deviating from it, but keeping to the rule of faith.

Moreover I also, Polycrates, who am the least of you all, in accordance with the tradition of my relatives, some of whom I *have succeeded—<u>seven of my relatives were bishops, and I am the eighth, and my relatives always observed the day when the people put away the leaven</u>—I myself, brethren, I say, who am sixty-five years old in the Lord, and have fallen in with the brethren in all parts of the world, and have read through all Holy Scripture, <u>am not frightened at the things which are said to terrify us</u>. For those who are greater than I have said, <u>"We ought to obey God rather than men."</u> – Polycrates, Bishop of Ephesus (ca. 180 CE), Epistle to Victor of Rome, from Phillip Schaff, Early Church Fathers, pp. 773-774. Also see Eusebius, Ecclesiastical History, 5:24*

Passover is a time when the leaven is removed from our homes, according to Exodus 12:15. Contrary to what Ignatius was saying about absolute obedience to their bishops, Polycrates has a different opinion. He is instead pointing out the fallibility of men who, while having good intentions and doing good works, may not have proper understanding, which can sometimes lead the faithful away from the truth of God. Notice also he has observed that when persuasion fails, intimidation follows, because he says that he is, "not frightened at the things which are said to terrify us" and that "we ought to obey God rather than men."

And finally, Eusebius, having access to all these original documents, puts his historical perspective down, writing about these events nearly two centuries later:

For as the bishops of the West did not deem it necessary to dishonor the tradition handed down to them by Peter and by Paul, and as, on the other hand, the Asiatic bishops persisted in following the rules laid down by John the evangelist, <u>they unanimously agreed to continue in the observance of the festival according to their respective customs</u>, without separation from communion with each other. - Eusebius (325 CE), Ecclesiastical History, Book 7, Chapter 19, Phillip Schaff, Early Church Fathers, p. 390.

The unity shown in their decision is in opposition to the teachings of Messiah Yeshua and his disciples. Ask yourself, "Is it better for me to have unity with man and not with God—to go against His commandments?" or "How can I say that I love my Savior when I don't obey him?" The answers to these questions lie with Yeshua, "And you should love Master YHWH with all your heart and with all your soul and with all your mind, and with all of your strength. This is the first commandment" (Mark 12:30). Let us pray for wisdom and discernment as we move forward.

Was what our Savior said meant for Israel only and not for those grafted in? Torah observance was initially taught and observed in the Gentile churches by the Apostles and their disciples. But the true position later became called a "tradition" that was to be respected, but not followed. Such were the teachings by Rome and sadly, sometime after Clement, Polycarp and others like them, these ideas by the Church became permanent until today.

Justin Martyr

Around this same time, we had a very influential teacher and writer Justin Martyr, who was assassinated around the year 165 CE. Justin was born a pagan but converted to Christianity in his early thirties and has left behind a very sizable body of work considering he lived in such an early period of Christian history.

In the *Introductory Note to the Writings of Justin Martyr* (Early Church Fathers, p. 160), we are told Justin was born in Flavia Neapolis, a city of Samaria and also given some other surprising facts about this early leader who, after prolonged stints in Greek philosophy, subsequently helped set the foundations of the Catholic Church, and the churches that followed. They write:

After trying all other systems, his elevated tastes and refined perceptions made him a disciple of Socrates and Plato.

The conversion of such a man marks a new era in the gospel history. The sub-apostolic age begins with the first Christian author, the founder of theological literature. It introduced to mankind, as the mother of true philosophy, the despised teaching of those Galileans to whom their Master had said, "Ye are the light of the world."

It is the mission of Justin to be a star in the West, leading its Wise Men to the cradle of Bethlehem.

He wore his philosopher's gown after his conversion, as a token that he had attained the only true philosophy.

So, what impact did Socrates and the study of Greek philosophy from a pagan culture have on Justin's way of thinking? When Socrates was at his trial for impiety and corrupting the youth, he is famously recorded as having said: "The unexamined life is not worth living," and chose death rather than exile. Justin embraced Socrates' philosophy, and was also more confident in the work he embarked upon, after knowing that Alexander the Great had Aristotle, a student of Socrates, as his teacher.

One of these seminal apologetical works Justin did was called *The Dialogue with Trypho the Jew*. While some Catholic theologians believe this debate really happened and identify the famous 2nd century Rabbi Tarphon as Justin's "Trypho," most non-Catholic scholars have viewed the entire event as fictitious. Further, the idea that a young and relatively inexperienced leader like Justin engaged a rabbi of Tarphon's extremely high status, seems very unlikely. Not surprisingly, virtually all Orthodox Jewish authorities view this entire story from Justin as a myth, since it seemingly took place either during or immediately after the Bar Kochba revolt.

Having said that, *The Dialogue with Trypho the Jew* is a very important historical document because of what Justin *himself* says about his belief, whether or not the debate really happened.

According to Justin, he was passing through Ephesus where he encountered Trypho. After exchanging some friendly greetings, the two soon enter a debate about Messiah. In that debate, Trypho becomes the foil of all the "bad Torah" that Justin clearly despises, and Justin's complete refutation of Trypho's positions is meant to send the message that, forty years after Clement of Rome, no "legalism" will be tolerated in what is rapidly becoming the Roman Catholic Church.

So where does Justin even get the idea that a faith based on Torah is conforming to legalism? The answer seems to be with Ignatius who, after influencing the believers was embraced by Rome as one of their own after his martyrdom. Justin observes that barely two decades passed after the assemblies, founded by the disciples, shifted away from Clement and Polycarp's pro-Torah view being the cornerstone of every church, to following Ignatius in a different direction.

Going back to 108 CE, Ignatius had his original manuscript letters prepared before he was led off to die. His couriers faithfully sent these to his friends and colleagues leading powerful assemblies in Ephesus, Rome, Smyrna, Philadelphia and other important places. These letters were not just widely copied in the original places they were sent to, but also widely circulated amongst these early churches and reviewed by their chief bishops.

And so, we have, not even three decades later, Justin Martyr through his writing about Trypho the Jew turning Ignatius' suggestions into an integral expression of Christianity:

"Is there any other matter, my friends, in which we are blamed, than this, that we live not after the law, and are not circumcised

in the flesh as your forefathers were, and do not observe sabbaths as you do?"

Said Trypho, "Moreover, I am aware that your precepts in the so-called Gospel are so wonderful and so great, that I suspect no one can keep them; for I have carefully read them. But this is what we are most at a loss about: that you, professing to be pious, and supposing yourselves better than others, are not in any particular separated from them, and do not alter your mode of living from the nations, in that you <u>observe no festivals or sabbaths</u>, and do not have the <u>rite of circumcision</u>; and further, resting your hopes on a man that was crucified, you yet expect to obtain some good thing from God, while you do not obey His commandments...But you, despising this covenant rashly, reject the consequent duties, and attempt to persuade yourselves that you know God, when, however, you perform none of those things which they do who fear God." (Chapter 10, p. 199)

Let us look again at a few things Trypho said, which may express the sentiments of many Jews, even though the conversation may not in fact have taken place. The Scripture-based festivals that are being referred to above are to honor God, to give Him thanks, and are also a time to gather for fellowship. Christmas was not even a church celebration in the early years. If you are curious, you can go to the following website to get the history of how and when Christmas came about (https://www.history.com/topics/christmas/history-of-christmas), and also this one about the Christmas tree (https://www.history.com/topics/christmas/history-of-christmas-trees).

Additionally, the Sabbath, while commanded, helps to rejuvenate oneself, something that not many people realize today. As for the "rite of circumcision," it is a sign of covenant with YHWH, God Almighty. Some of you may not have realized that it took Abraham 24 years after walking with God before he circumcised himself at age 99. God Almighty did not impose it on him before he had understanding, but neither did Abraham walk around trying to avoid it. As for Easter, we will be discussing that soon.

Before we go on to Justin's response, let us explain something about "the law." By Yeshua's time, oral traditions had been added to the "Law of Moses," or Torah, as it was given by God.

The Greek word *nomos*, also in Aramaic as *namusa*, can mean either "law" or "customs of men." When Paul is saying "But if you are led by the Spirit, you are not under the law," he is talking about the traditions of the Pharisees that are masquerading as Torah. Paul uses shortcuts when he is talking to folks around him because he believes they understand the context of what he is saying. Remember what we discussed earlier: The Holy Spirit never contradicts the Word of God.

Most translations, unfortunately, do not distinguish between the two when they use the word *law*. In our next translation, we hope to make this distinction clearer so that the reader will be able to discern the "Law" (Torah) that needs to be kept and the "law" which includes traditions of the rabbis. The following translations below make that distinction for Paul's comments:

- *I am a Jew, born in Tarsus of Cilicia, but brought up in this city, educated under Gamaliel, strictly according to the Law of our fathers, being zealous for God just as you all are today (Acts 22:3)*
- *To the Jews I became as a Jew, so that I might win Jews; to those who are under the law, as under the law though not being myself under the law, so that I might win those who are under the law. (1 Corinthians 9:20)*
- *Tell me, you who want to be under law, do you not listen to the Law? (Galatians 4:21)*

- *And I testify again to every man who receives circumcision, that he is under obligation to keep the whole Law. (Galatians 5:3)*
- *But before faith came, we were kept in custody under the law, being shut up to the faith which was later to be revealed. (Galatians 3:23)*

In the first verse, he is a Jew according to the "Law" given by God to his fathers, but in the second verse, he is saying he is not under the "law," created by man including traditions disguising itself as God's Law (Torah). This should also explain clearly to you the next two Scripture quotes as referring to the "Law of Moses." In the last example, the Jews he is speaking to know their history and understand it as *fences*—traditions and customs— which were necessary. The prevailing rabbinic theory was that these "fences" were useful in keeping Jews safe from committing transgressions. Paul, however, is saying that the "law" was only useful until such a time as this, when the Messiah once again taught or "revealed" the truth of their faith which he says was "shut up" or hidden from them.

Justin, much like Ignatius before him, goes on to describe to the rabbi how the new way of Christianity replaced what came before:

But now for I have read that there shall be a final law, and a covenant, the chiefest of all, which it is now incumbent on all men to observe, as many as are seeking after the inheritance of God...<u>For the law promulgated on Horeb (Mt. Sinai) is now old</u> and belongs to yourselves alone; but this is for all universally. Now, law placed against law has abrogated that which is before it, and a covenant which comes after in like manner has put an end to the previous one; and an eternal and final law--namely, Christ --has been given to us, and the covenant is trustworthy, after which there shall be no law, no commandment, no ordinance... And by Jeremiah, concerning this same <u>new</u> covenant, He thus speaks: 'Behold, the days come, saith the Lord, *that I will make a <u>new</u> covenant with the house of Israel and with the house of Judah; not according to the covenant which I made with their fathers, in the day that I took them by the hand, to bring them out of the land of Egypt'. (Chapter 11, pp 199-200)*

This, dear reader, is what we call Replacement Theology and New Testament supercessionism. In Hebrew, the word *chadash* can mean either "new" or "renewed." Although, both Yeshua and Paul (Romans 3:29-31, 7:12) state that the First Covenant is not disappearing but is eternal, the latter meaning of "renewed" is more likely. Moreover, since the First Covenant was broken by Israel and Judah due to disobedience, not because it was destroyed, Yeshua came to renew the covenant. He did not come with a new covenant, disregarding the old (Matthew 5:17-20).

Yeshua also came to give us proper understanding which we did not possess. As John, a beloved disciple of his, and the author of the Book of Revelation, further explains:

By this we know that we love the children of God, when we love God and observe His commandments. (1 John 5:2 NAU)

If we say that we have fellowship with Him and yet walk in the darkness, we lie and do not practice the truth. (1 John 1:6 NAU)

Our Messiah came to give us salvation and to teach us how to live and walk according to the Ways of his Father, so that we too may be pleasing to Him. But man, in his less than infinite wisdom, is slowing chipping away at our salvation.

Let us now look at some of the other things Justin gives his opinion on in *The Dialogue with Trypho the Jew*, contrary to the words of Yeshua Messiah and John:

The <u>new</u> law requires you <u>to keep perpetual sabbath</u>, and you, because you are idle for one day, suppose you are pious, not discerning why this has been commanded you: and <u>if you eat</u>

<u>unleavened bread</u>, you say the will of God has been fulfilled. The Lord our God does not take pleasure in such observances.
(Chapter 12, p. 200)

For we too would observe the fleshly circumcision, and the Sabbaths, and in short all the feasts, if we did not know for what reason they were enjoined you, namely, on account of your transgressions and the hardness of your hearts… how is it, Trypho, that we would not observe those rites which do not harm us—I speak of fleshly circumcision, and Sabbaths, and feasts?
(Chapter 18, p. 203)

Ignatius' emphasis on keeping the "Lord's Day"—Sunday—rather than the seventh day Sabbath that the Apostles and other Early Church leaders kept, began gently with the suggestion of equivalence, that either day was fine or it was also okay to keep both, as he said in his Letter to the Magnesians Chapter 9: "*And after the observance of the Sabbath, let every friend of Messiah keep the Lord's Day as a festival, the resurrection-day, the queen and chief of all the days [of the week].*"

Since Ignatius was the first leader to offer such sentiments in chapter 8 of his Letter to the Magnesians that "for if we still live according to the Jewish law, we acknowledge that we have not received grace," whether he intended to make a total break away from the Commandments or not, his words appear to have been very quickly adopted to mean such by later leaders like Justin. Then, with Rome's view now altered in favor of Ignatius' view, Justin becomes in effect their teacher and joins the growing body of Gentile assemblies in this anti-Torah viewpoint.

So, what is the Sabbath and was it to be done away with by those who proclaimed to be followers of Yeshua? Did Messiah and his Apostles preach that?

You shall work six days, but on the seventh day you shall rest;
even during plowing time and harvest you shall rest. (Exodus
34:21 NAU)

Jesus said to them, "The Sabbath was made for man, and not man
for the Sabbath. So the Son of Man is Lord even of the Sabbath."
(Mark 2:27-28 NAU)

From what Justin said, if the Sabbath is no longer to be observed, what is the Son of Man (Jesus) the Lord of? Are we going to be selective in what part of the "New" Testament we accept and what we discard? Did we not read many times that Yeshua and his Apostles were at the Temple or synagogues on sabbaths?

I hope you are strapped in for this roller coaster ride, for Justin inspired more people in his wake, for good and bad, than many other leaders who evangelized during these early years. He was educated in philosophy, had a certain level of practical wisdom and he knew how to use the rhetoric of his time to promote Christianity, Christians, and himself.

Nobody keeps a "perpetual sabbath" because then you are doing nothing every day of the week. All these regulations of circumcision, keeping Sabbath and the Feasts were given before Israel sinned. In fact, they were given as a joyful thing on the occasion of their freedom from bondage. Since many believers do not rest from their normal activities on the Sabbath, they are tired, exhausted and have little or no time for things that are important: God, marriage, children, family and fulfilling their calling. So, let us see what else Justin prescribes for the people of God in his conversation with Trypho:

This circumcision is not, however, necessary for all men, but for
you alone, in order that, as I have already said, you may suffer
these things which you now justly suffer (Using Adam, Abel,

136

Enoch, Lot, Noah who were all righteous and uncircumcised)...Moreover, all those righteous men already mentioned, though they kept no Sabbaths, were pleasing to God; and after them Abraham with all his descendants until Moses, under whom your nation appeared unrighteous and ungrateful to God, making a calf in the wilderness. (Chapter 19, pp. 203-204)

Moreover, you were commanded to abstain from certain kinds of food, in order that you might keep God before your eyes while you ate and drank, seeing that you were prone and very ready to depart from His knowledge, as Moses also affirms: 'The people ate and drank, and rose up to play.' (Chapter 20, p. 204)

Moreover, that God enjoined you to keep the Sabbath, and impose on you other precepts for a sign, as I have already said, on account of your unrighteousness, and that of your fathers—as He declares that for the sake of the nations, lest His name be profaned among them, therefore He permitted some of you to remain alive.

Did Yeshua's mother circumcise him because of his sins or the sins of his fathers? Was not God Almighty his Father?

And when eight days had passed, before His circumcision, His name was then called Yeshua, the name given by the angel before He was conceived in the womb. (Luke 2:21)

Circumcision is nothing, and uncircumcision is nothing, but what matters is the keeping of the commandments of God. (1 Corinthians 7:19 NAU)

What Paul is saying here is that ritual alone is not important. It is instead obedience to all the commandments of God Almighty, including circumcision, that matters. That is also why Paul keeps reminding Gentiles of Abraham who, though born a Gentile, on hearing God, did as he was told before he got circumcised at the age of 99 (Genesis 17:24). As for the keeping of the Feasts, we read the following:

And they observed the Feast of Unleavened Bread seven days with joy, for the LORD had caused them to rejoice, and had turned the heart of the king of Assyria toward them to encourage them in the work of the house of God, the God of Israel. (Ezra 6:22 NAU)

And from Yeshua and his disciples who also kept the Feasts we have this:

Now before the Feast of the Passover, Jesus knowing that His hour had come that He would depart out of this world to the Father, having loved His own who were in the world, He loved them to the end. (John 13:1 NAU)

For some were supposing, because Judas had the money box, that Jesus was saying to him, "Buy the things we have need of for the feast"; or else, that he should give something to the poor. (John 13:29 NAU)

If you keep My commandments, you will abide in My love; just as I have kept My Father's commandments and abide in His love. (John 15:10 NAU)

Regarding the keeping of the Feast of Tabernacles, also called Sukkot or the Feast of Booths, we read in John 7:2 that when "the feast of the Jews, the Feast of Booths, was near" Yeshua said to his brothers:

"Go up to the feast yourselves; I do not go up to this feast because My time has not yet fully come." Having said these things to them, He stayed in Galilee. But when His brothers had gone up to the feast, then He Himself also went up, not publicly, but as if, in secret. (John 7:8-10 NAU)

Clearly then Tabernacles was an especially important feast for all of them to honor, so much so that Messiah went up secretly even at risk to his own life. As for the keeping of Hanukkah, the

Festival of Lights or Dedication, we see Yeshua honors even this optional feast:

At that time the Feast of the Dedication took place at Jerusalem; it was winter, and Jesus was walking in the temple in the portico of Solomon. (John 10:22-23 NAU)

These are only a few examples of how the commandments of God were still in observance during the time of Yeshua, as we see him and his Apostles later teaching at the Temple and synagogues during all these feasts.

Consider this: If you knew you were going to die within a few hours, would you make it a point to spend those precious few hours preparing for and observing the Passover? Well, your Savior did. Also, in John chapters 7 and 8, we see Yeshua and the disciples, participating in the Feast of Tabernacles (Sukkot). When you read and study the Scripture, please be mindful that God's Word is always right; it is our interpretation of it is that is fallible. History has proven the Scripture, like God Himself, to be both infallible and trustworthy.

In the example below, you will see how God saved His people because they obeyed His commandments. We thought you might like a different perspective on what Ignatius has referred to as "unprofitable," i.e., the keeping of the old Law, which also gives instructions on the touching and burial of the dead. Do you recall that in preparation for Passover, the people removed from their home all old wheat and leavening?

Well, in 1349, a horrific plague known as the "Black Death" swept through western Europe. By the time it concluded four years later, more than half of the continent's population had perished. However, for the Jews, they had a vastly different outcome.

The Black Death, or "Bubonic Plague" as it has since become known, was spread through infected rats and the insects that carried it. It was also spread through infected water mixed with human feces. For the Christians, it was their own lack of hygiene that doomed them to die in massive numbers, in a culture that believed it was best to only bathe twice a year.

But for the Jews, their Torah-based lifestyle reduced their deaths from the plague by more than 90%. This was because of two commandments: First, the fact that they had to get rid of their old grain at the start of spring before Passover greatly minimized the spread of the disease through their food supply. And second, the requirements in Leviticus that the dead and human waste be buried outside their camp cut the spread of plague from coming to them from dirty water.

When the Black Death ended in 1353, Christian leaders across the continent, rather than seeing how the Jews avoided death by following the commandments of God, accused them of working with Satan to poison the Christian's wells. Thus, a new and violent false justification for anti-Semitism was born out of that disaster.

Science today has also proven that certain foods are not healthy. In Deuteronomy chapter 14, you will find an "approved list" of foods that will be good for you and a list of those which are not good for you. There are animals that since the time of Noah are called "clean" and "unclean." We have plenty of "clean" food to eat and farmers can change over to raising these clean animals for our consumption, but we need to be calling for such a change through what we consume. There is a law of supply and demand and, like we said earlier, the enemy has sold you a *false bill of goods* that is to your detriment.

So why was Justin so against the Jews and their keeping of the old Law? In his work called *The First Apology* we get a hint of this reason. Justin wrote this letter to the Emperor Antoninus Pius and others as a petition saying, "on behalf of those of all nations who are unjustly hated and wantonly abused, myself being one of them." Referencing the Greek Torah that Ptolemy had translated from Hebrew by the 70 scribes for his library in Alexandria, Egypt, Justin writes:

They (the Greek Torah readings) are also in the possession of all Jews throughout the world; but they, though they read, do not understand what is said, but count us foes and enemies; and, like yourselves, they kill and punish us whenever they have the power, as you can well believe. For in the Jewish War which lately raged, Barchochebas, the leader of the revolt of the Jews, gave orders that Christians alone should be led to cruel punishments, unless they would deny Jesus Christ and utter blasphemy. (Chapter 31 p. 173)

But Jesus Christ stretched forth His hands, being crucified by the Jews speaking against Him, and denying that He was the Christ... And after He was crucified they cast lots upon His vesture. (Chapter 35 p. 174)

First, perhaps the reason the Jews did not understand the Torah was because it was in Greek, not Hebrew, and there may have been mistranslations. Or perhaps it is Justin that did not understand what it said by taking verses out of context. As for his second allegation, that the Christians were persecuted by the Jews during this "Jewish War," this is not accurate. Bar Kochba did not give such instructions and neither was he in a position to do so. Rabbinic Jews, Messianic Jews (believers of Yeshua), along with the Gentiles that were following Yeshua and the Apostles, were all being persecuted by the Romans who were pagan worshipers. Any Torah observant believer was being persecuted.

The Romans wanted their emperor to be regarded as King and god. By contrast, all the early disciples and believers of the

Messiah were Jews and subject to the Torah command that they should not worship any other god except for the Most-High, YHWH. As Gentiles then started to come into the movement and followed their teachings, they too refused to participate in pagan worship and accept the emperor as a god. Therefore, contrary to what Justin said, both Jews and Gentiles were being persecuted. The Rabbinic Jews may not have liked their people following Yeshua, but that does not mean that they used this "Jewish War" against the Gentile believers as Justin alleges.

Unfortunately, today, the sacrifice of these early believers, Jews and Christians, is not even considered when many go into religious places and bow down to statues, worship other gods or eat food sacrificed to idols.

Also, as most of you know, it was the Romans that crucified Yeshua and the Roman soldiers that cast lots for his clothes. Because of the discourse that had arisen with Yeshua's presence in Jerusalem, and those who now followed him, some in Jewish leadership who did not believe that he was indeed the Messiah feared for the safety of their people, and so they handed him over to the Romans.

"If we let Him go on like this, all men will believe in Him, and the Romans will come and take away both our place and our nation." But one of them, Caiaphas, who was high priest that year, said to them, "You know nothing at all, nor do you take into account that it is expedient for you that one man die for the people, and that the whole nation not perish." Now he did not say this on his own initiative, but being high priest that year, he prophesied that Jesus was going to die for the nation, and not for the nation only, but in order that He might also gather together into one the children of God who are scattered abroad. (John 11:48-52 NAU)

As high priest, Caiaphas was well versed in the Torah and the prophets, as most of the learned Jews were, and therefore was bringing to mind the prophesy in Isaiah 53, that the Messiah will die for his people (see especially verses 5-7). Their knowledge of Scripture also informed them through Exodus 20:5-6 that their sin will be visited on their children to the third and fourth generation, and this was a small price they felt they would have to pay to save the nation.

It is easy for us to say, sitting here today, that by handing Yeshua over to the Roman authorities, the Jews showed a lack of faith and knowledge. However, because it was prophesied, who are we to judge them if this was what God had always intended for His Son and the salvation of His people? Did not God harden Pharaoh's heart so that His people – the Hebrews and the foreigners that went with Moses – could be saved? Would Christianity, based on the crucifixion, death and resurrection, have spread so widely and with such fervor if their Savior died a natural death or of old age?

Simply put, in his letter, Justin quotes, out of context in many cases, from many of the prophets like Isaiah, Jeremiah and Zechariah to back up his theology and emphasize that God is no longer with the people of the Old Covenant. He also alleges that the Jews who rejected the Messiah are not a part of this New Covenant either. They have sinned and therefore may be punished. But this standard does not apply to them, the Christians, who have accepted the New Covenant and believe they are walking in righteousness.

And that it was foreknown that these infamous things should be uttered against those who confessed Christ, and that those who slandered Him, and said that it was well to preserve the ancient customs, should be miserable, hear what was briefly said by Isaiah; it is this: "Woe unto them that call sweet bitter, and bitter sweet." (Chapter 49, p. 179)

143

Isaiah is talking about judgement coming down upon his people for not keeping the Torah (5:20). It is hard to ascertain whether the issue is with Justin's lack of knowledge of Semitic languages like Hebrew, or because he was reading from the Septuagint, the Greek translation of the Scripture from which he also takes things out of context, like the following:

And in what kind of sensation and punishment the wicked are to be, hear from what was said in like manner with reference to this; it is as follows…Tribe by tribe they shall mourn, and then they shall look on Him whom they have pierced; and they shall say, Why, O Lord, hast Thou made us to err from Thy way? The glory which our fathers blessed, has for us been turned into shame." (Chapter 42, p. 180)

He is using Isaiah 63:17 and Zechariah 12:3-14, again to emphasize that the ancient customs should no longer be followed, ignoring that God Almighty has commanded these to be observed.

I have included the Scripture verses to make it easier for you to look them up for yourself along with the context to see if they were applied correctly. This is just another example of where he goes to Scripture to make his point, that the Gentile Christians are blessed compared to the unbelieving Jewish people. If you read just two verses past 63:17, you will see that Isaiah is referring prophetically to the Temple in Judah which will be burnt down by Nebuchadnezzar and, as we mentioned earlier, happened during the reign of King Zedekiah.

Why, O LORD, do You cause us to stray from Your ways and harden our heart from fearing You? Return for the sake of Your servants, the tribes of Your heritage. Your holy people possessed Your sanctuary for a little while, Our adversaries have trodden it down. We have become like those over whom You have never ruled, like those who were not called by Your name. (Isaiah 63:17-19 NAU)

144

Zechariah 12:9-14 is about the destruction of the Second Temple of YHWH that will happen after Yeshua is crucified and the judgment against the Romans who destroyed it. While the Jews lamented the loss of their Temple, so did the early believers of Yeshua, especially those who were in Jerusalem.

While abandoning Greek philosophy for Christianity, Justin may have inevitably fused Greek pagan theology with biblical theology in a process known as *syncretism*. In his *The First Apology* we see, in the footnotes, how he is quoting Plato and Socrates and how he uses that in context to his bible discussion

Justin, in his zeal and undeniable passion for his Savior, nevertheless tends to skip over parts of Scripture that do not lend to the theology he is trying to promote, that is to say he "cherry picks" and uses them as "sound bites," outside of the context for which they were intended. By doing this repeatedly, he is on a slippery slope. It is what we call false compression of Scripture, creative editing, or creative interpretation, and this is going on even today in our assemblies.

We do not know where he may have acquired his misconceptions about Jews, whether they were while he studied with the Greeks, or elsewhere. However, when we study Scripture, especially the Prophets, we must be aware of history, context, language and culture, along with the expressions and abbreviations used.

So, what about this so-called Jewish War in which its leaders gave orders that Christians alone should be led to cruel punishments, "unless they would deny Jesus Christ and utter blasphemy?" Let's see if that's true in the next topic.

The Jewish Wars

Where is this city that was believed to have God himself inhabiting therein? It is now demolished to the very foundations...some unfortunate old men also lie upon the ashes of the temple, and a few women are there preserved alive by the enemy for our bitter shame and reproach...And I cannot but wish that we had all died before we had seen that holy city demolished by the hands of our enemies, or the foundations of our holy temple dug up after so profane a manner. (Josephus, The Jewish War, 7:376-379, ca. 90 CE)

The historian Josephus was an eyewitness and active participant in all the tumultuous events that led up to the destruction of the Second Temple in 70 CE. The rebellion, which began over one very small regrettable incident, would soon engulf the entire Jewish nation and put all of her people at risk of genocide. Josephus tells us that more than a million Jewish victims lay dead in the streets of Jerusalem and elsewhere.

For the purposes of telling the story of this book, there are a few events which occurred just after the Messiah came that shed greater light on the frailties of the human condition, and show the massive ramifications caused by those frailties, than the two Jewish Revolts against Rome.

In order to understand these events and their consequences, we need to go back in time and ask two critical questions. First, what were the circumstances that led to the First Revolt and second, given the devastating and cataclysmic disaster that followed, how could the sons or grandsons of the architects of that first debacle even consider revolting again?

In the spring of 66 CE, the trouble began in Caesarea, about 30 miles north of Jerusalem. A pagan man sacrificed a bird on the grounds of a synagogue, which ritually defiled the area right near its entrance (The Jewish War, 2:289). Outraged, the Jews began beating the offender while others in the city came to defend him. The Roman garrison intervened to try to restore order, but this attempt only got more crowds of people fighting each other. They killed many of the Roman soldiers and fled to a nearby city.

Later, the Jewish rebels petitioned the Roman governor Florus, who was stationed in Caesarea, for help, but although they paid him a huge bribe of eight talents, he went to Jerusalem and raided the Temple treasury—claiming it was for payment of back taxes but stealing it for himself. The Jews in Jerusalem, many of whom were not inclined to rebel against Rome for the previous provocation in Caesarea, were now fully mobilized against Florus and his troops. As a result, the First Jewish Revolt was now in full swing.

However, the revolt and its ultimate consequences would have been far more devastating if not for the Jews who, with some of the believers, ran to the mountains, because Yeshua had warned his people to leave Jerusalem when she was surrounded by armies (see also Luke 21:20-26). Early Church records confirm that many of them did indeed run for the mountains. Two 4th century historians, Eusebius (Church History, Book 3, Chapter 5) and Epiphanius (Panarion, Chapters 29-30), tell us that believers in Messiah took shelter in Pella—modern-day Jordan—just before the outbreak of hostilities.

They would stay there for the duration of the war and only a few would hazard a return to Jerusalem after it ended. As for the rest, the vast majority of Nazarenes (Jewish believers) migrated to the rival Parthian Empire where some became part of the Assyrian Church of the East. Included among them were leaders who were from Yeshua's own extended family.

Other Jewish leaders were compelled to stay and fight. One such leader, Yosef bar Matitiyahu, later to be known as the Jewish historian Josephus, became the leader of the rebels in Galilee. For more than a year, he proved brutally effective in slowing the Roman advance, inflicting some of the heaviest casualties of the entire war upon them.

Then in the summer of 67 CE, he and his commanders became trapped at Yotapata, a series of caves in Galilee, while the Romans were laying siege to a nearby city. As that siege turned into several weeks, Yosef and his men began to starve and so, rather than surrender to the Romans, they decided to commit suicide.

But Yosef, who was now the last survivor, found he could not honor the pact. Instead, he surrendered to general Vespasian and his son Titus, who was second in command. He told Vespasian that while he was hiding out in the caves, he had had a divine vision of the general soon becoming emperor. Vespasian, for his part, took an immediate liking to Yosef and, though he considered him a slave, found him to be a very useful translator as groups of Jewish rebels began to surrender.

By the year 69 CE, Yosef's vision had proved completely accurate. After Emperor Nero died by suicide, Vespasian became emperor as predicted. His son, Titus, was left to continue to prosecute the war while his father returned to Rome.

Yosef, who had now been given his freedom, prospered in the service of the Romans but earned the fierce hatred of his people as a traitor because of it. And yet, were it not for Yosef pleading for his people with his friend the Emperor, it is likely hundreds of thousands of additional Jews would have perished by the time the revolt ended.

Another act that further alienated him from his people happened when Yosef took on a Roman name—Flavius— the family name of Vespasian and Titus—and turned his Hebrew name into its Latin equivalent, Josephus. He will spend the next three decades writing his historical account of both the Jewish War and all the biblical events that preceded it. He also remarried and lived to see three sons from his new wife grow to adulthood while he remained a privileged member of the Roman Emperor's household.

Truly, while Josephus' outcome is exceptional, the rest of his people did not fare nearly so well during this first revolt. Many of the Jews who escaped into the Parthian Empire, a fierce rival to the Roman Empire, were forever exiled from their Jerusalem kin, while others were made slaves and shipped back to Rome to build the Coliseum.

This famous Roman Coliseum that so many tourists flock to see these days was a temple of death, where the Jews and tens of thousands of early Christians, gathered from the provinces Rome conquered, suffered horrific torture by burning and being torn apart by wild beasts that were all a part of the Roman games.

Further, while the precise numbers are not known, the well-established Jewish communities that we spoke of earlier, throughout ancient Persia, India, Babylon and even parts of Africa, each received a huge influx of refugees seeking to escape Roman wrath. While Jerusalem had been a magnet, drawing exiles to the joy of Temple worship at feast time, an Exodus in reverse was now happening, as Judea emptied herself out and her people scattered to other nations once more. Messianic Jews and Gentile believers now carried their faith outside of Jerusalem—probably the only silver lining of this war.

But there was another Jew who helped the Romans during the First Revolt, Yochanan ben Zakkai, who was, in return, given permission to establish rabbinic academies in Galilee. These learning academies, for all intents and purposes, gave birth to Rabbinic Judaism and prevented Judaism itself from going extinct.

In some other cases, Jews, who simply waited out the conflict and quietly returned to Jerusalem years later, were pretty much ignored by Roman authorities, so long as they did not cause trouble. Even though the Temple was gone, survivors of the priesthood were allowed to do sacrifices in other parts of the country. There was hope among the people of God in Israel, that if they could just hang on a few years, maybe they could get Roman permission to rebuild the Temple and restore the city again, just as in the days of Ezra and Nehemiah under Persian rule.

According to the famous scholar Lawrence Schiffman (Revolt and Restoration, pp. 161-162), even though Roman regulations for living in Jerusalem made life very hard, many Jews managed to thrive in that limited system, while others suffered greatly through famine and abject poverty, with their rights severely curtailed under Roman law.

Slowly, though, the rabbis were becoming restless under Roman rule. They issued a number of rulings that stressed the critical necessity of getting the Temple back with all due speed. Six decades later, with memories of the overt brutality of the Romans in the First Revolt rapidly fading, pressure was building to force the issue once again.

However, unlike the First Revolt, there was no authoritative and continuous account from someone of the caliber of Josephus to chronicle this war. Instead, what we know about this rebellion comes down from a variety of sources, including Roman, Rabbinic and Early Church tradition. In the Talmud for example, the story is told that the Emperor Hadrian visited Jerusalem in 130 CE and promised the Jews he would allow them to rebuild the city and Temple. The Jews naturally rejoiced, until one of Hadrian's counselors, whom some sources say was a Samaritan, persuaded the emperor to build a temple to Zeus overlooking the Temple ruins.

While Eusebius and other sources don't mention Hadrian's initial promise, there can be no doubt that the emperor's decision to turn Jerusalem into a pagan city was the spark that lit this second tragic rebellion. Hadrian even named the new pagan city after his own family, Aelia. He then added to that name the term *capitolina*, to refer to the new shrine, basically renaming the entire city after him and the pagan temple he built.

This decision sparked the second war with Rome. The rebellion began with a group of rabbis, led by the famous Akiva, who believed that God was once more about to deliver the Jewish people from pagan hands. Recalling Numbers 24:17 and the prophecy that a star would come out of Jacob, Akiva found a charismatic leader named Shimon and dubbed him *Bar Kochba*, or "son of the star."

For three years, Shimon Bar Kochba's rebels were remarkably successful against Roman troops, but the Roman commanders figured out their enemies' tactics and adjusted their plans accordingly. Soon Bar Kochba was fighting on defense, but the irony was that tens of thousands of Jews who didn't really believe he was the Messiah, felt they had to join his ranks because it was their best chance of gaining emancipation from Rome. Even the followers of Yeshua joined the fight for a time, until they soured on the prospect of calling Bar Kochba the Messiah, because Yeshua their true Messiah had died and resurrected a century earlier.

In rabbinic sources and according to the opinions of modern historians, many who have studied this war have called it attempted genocide, because the Jewish people were trying to hold on to their faith and the land given to them by God Almighty. If it were not for them, the birthplace of our Messiah and Christianity, Jerusalem and Israel, might have been permanently and completely taken away from us today.

However, it was certainly the start of a long and painful exile of the Jewish people from their land. The emperors after Hadrian only allowed the Jews entry back to Jerusalem on their fast day that commemorated the destruction of both of their Temples. Otherwise both they and their Messianic cousins were banned from entering the holy city again under penalty of death.

Even in Roman records, the level of slaughter beyond the normal conventions of war is acknowledged. The historian Cassius Dio, for example, said nearly 600,000 Jews in 50 fortified towns and nearly a thousand villages all perished. Dio's figures are considered accurate in part because his accounts are based on Roman census figures conducted before and after the war. To put that number in perspective, about as many people would die in the American Civil War, which lasted more than a year longer in duration (1861-1865).

In the wake of this disastrous Second Revolt, Rome imposed even more punishments on the Jews. It was the beginning of their exile from Judea. When they did so, Jerusalem, now a thoroughly pagan city, was overrun by pigs defecating in the streets of the once sacred city, near where the Temple used to stand. Jerusalem also lost her status as an important city in the Empire, both to the Roman pagans who destroyed her and to the Gentile Christians who now completely replaced the Jewish hierarchy that used to rule there.

In his writings Constantine's biographer Eusebius tells us of another true cost of this conflict, which was the end of the Hebrew bishops ruling in Jerusalem:

The chronology of the bishops of Jerusalem I have nowhere found preserved in writing; for tradition says that they were all short lived. But I have learned this much from writings, <u>that until the siege of the Jews, which took place under Hadrian, there were fifteen bishops in succession there, all of whom are said to have been of Hebrew descent</u>, and to have received the knowledge of Christ in purity, so that they were approved by those who were able to judge of such matters, <u>and were deemed worthy of the episcopate</u>.

For their whole church consisted then of believing Hebrews who continued from the days of the apostles until the siege which took place at this time; in which siege the Jews, having again rebelled against the Romans, were conquered after severe battles. But since the bishops of the circumcision ceased at this time, it is proper to give here a list of their names from the beginning.

The first, then, was James, the so-called brother of the Lord; the second, Symeon the third, Justus; the fourth, Zacchaeus; the fifth, Tobias; the sixth, Benjamin; the seventh, John; the eighth, Matthias; the ninth, Philip; the tenth, Seneca; the eleventh, Justus; the twelfth, Levi; the thirteenth, Ephres; the fourteenth, Joseph; and finally, the fifteenth, Judas. These are the bishops of Jerusalem that lived between the age of the apostles and the time referred to, all of them belonging to the circumcision. – Eusebius, Church History, Book 4, Chapter 5, Early Church Fathers, p.176.

After the Jews were expelled from their home for good, the 16th bishop of Jerusalem, a Roman named Marcus, will soon purge all Jewish influence from the faith as Jerusalem becomes a thoroughly Gentile and pagan city. Even Jerusalem's prestige as a major church hub is stripped from her. The Gentile believers who remained were now reporting to Caesarea instead of Jerusalem.

And so, the stage was set for the vast majority of Yeshua's followers to embrace a thoroughly Gentile and anti-Torah version of the faith. Parts of the *True Way* were now hidden from the people. The bias against the Jews seemed to extend to the Jewish believers as well, and what was put forth by Ignatius turned much darker in the next generation of leaders, beginning with Justin Martyr.

While much can be said about Ignatius and Justin who have added value to the Church and the evangelism of Christianity, no man should be put on a pedestal and venerated because of his martyrdom and have a theology built around what he said. We are all human and have our blind spots but, as leaders, we must be careful what we choose to confirm or deny, especially when it comes to all things related to our Heavenly Father, His Word and His Son.

You, as a believer, now need to decide whether God's Law given to the Jewish people that formed the foundations of your faith, which the Church decided to disregard or nullify in their teachings, should be a part of mainstream Christianity going forward. Consider starting with observing the Sabbath (a day of rest) and the Feasts (usually a time of fellowship), followed by the kosher guidelines (for your health). Do this as a church and we are certain you will receive unexpected favor and joy. Assemblies in alignment with Him will be blessed.

The evolution away from the original Messianic vision of the faith is startling and all happening within a mere hundred years or so after the resurrection. We went from Clement of Rome saying *"Those, therefore, who present their offerings at the appointed times, are accepted and blessed; for inasmuch as they follow the laws of the Lord (YHWH) they sin not,"* to Polycarp's "tradition" of keeping Passover that he received from the apostles being tolerated but not binding, to now Justin and the Church completely divorcing Torah observance, the keeping of God's commandments from present-day Christianity.

154

The Heresies of Marcion and Valentinus

MARCION

The noble Polycarp, who we talked about already, was said to be so humble that he offered to teach the Gospel to the people who were trying to torture and murder him. When it comes then to the archetype of the self-sacrificing and selfless hero, there is no one who fits that mode better than Polycarp.

However, at the other end of the spectrum to oppose him, is the greatest heretic and threat to the true faith, a man named Marcion of Sinope, who lived from about 85-160 CE.

So, what happened when these two opposing forces met in Rome? For one thing, we find out the gentle and humble Polycarp has a backbone and is more than able to face the heretic down in public. On one occasion when they met, Marcion asked Polycarp, *do you know me?* and Polycarp's answer was simple and direct:

"I do know you, the first-born of Satan."

Such was the horror which the apostles and their disciples had against holding even verbal communication with any corrupters of the truth. - Irenaeus, Against Heresies, Book 3, Chapter 3, paragraph 4, Early Church Fathers, p. 416.

What made Marcion so evil and dangerous? For one thing, he used his great wealth to give a massive bribe to the Roman Catholic Church, hoping to persuade it to his point of view. When this did not work and Marcion was excommunicated in 144 CE, he left Rome and set up his own rival churches in Asia Minor (Turkey) where he taught his own doctrines.

Marcion's wicked tenure is also especially punctuated by two ironic facts. First, it was Marcion who coined the terms "Old Testament" and "New Testament." More than that, in a time when western Christianity was moving at a glacial pace in trying to figure out what Renewed Covenant books should make it into their canon, Marcion inadvertently spurred them into passionate action by offering only a highly redacted Gospel of Luke and ten letters of Paul for his "Bible;" while simultaneously throwing out the entirety of the Hebrew Bible and the remainder of the sixteen Renewed Covenant books because he did not like them.

And yet, if not for Marcion, the western church would not have had the impetus to seek broad agreement from their ranks on what their own canon should be; they only found that consensus when they had a common enemy to refute. Basically, the Gospels, Acts and Paul's letters found early acceptance, while the rest would not get certified in the west until the end of the 4th century.

The second irony is that even though we don't have his teachings recorded in his own hand today, what we know of his heresy comes from those who hated his teachings and put down their opinions about what they heard and read. Marcion's influence may have been forever checked by the end of the 2nd century if not for this "venting" process, that kept those same bad ideas circulated through the pens of his enemies.

In the first place, how arrogantly do the Marcionites build up their stupid system, bringing forward a new god, as if we were ashamed of the old one…what new god is there, except for a false one? - Tertullian, Against Marcion, Book I, Early Church Fathers, Chapter 8, p. 276.

Replacement Theology and New Testament supercessionism received much greater emphasis by Marcion, who dismissed the Old Testament altogether. However, Marcion was so extreme in his methods, that some 2nd century leaders, like Irenaeus the bishop of Lyon, in France, clearly recognized the danger and warned the flock accordingly:

The rule of truth which we hold, is, that there is one God Almighty, who made all things by His Word, and fashioned and formed, out of that which had no existence, all things which exist. Thus says the Scripture, to that effect "By the Word of the Lord were the heavens established, and all the might of them, by the spirit of His mouth."

And again, "All things were made by Him, and without Him was nothing made." There is no exception or deduction stated; but the Father made all things by Him, whether visible or invisible, objects of sense or of intelligence, temporal, on account of a certain character given them, or eternal; and these eternal things He did not make by angels, or by any powers separated from His Ennoea (divine intent).

For God needs none of all these things, but is He who, by His Word and Spirit, makes, and disposes, and governs all things, and commands all things into existence,--He who formed the world (for the world is of all),--He who fashioned man,--He [who] is the God of Abraham, and the God of Isaac, and the God of Jacob, above whom there is no other God, nor initial principle, nor power, nor pleroma,--He is the Father of our Lord Jesus Christ, as we shall prove.

Holding, therefore, this rule, we shall easily show, notwithstanding the great variety and multitude of their opinions, that these men have deviated from the truth; for almost all the different sects of heretics admit that there is one God; but then, by their pernicious doctrines, they change [this truth into error], even as the Gentiles do through idolatry, thus proving themselves ungrateful to Him that created them. – Against Heresies, Book 1, Chapter 22, Early Church Fathers, p. 249.

The reality is that Irenaeus may in fact be a bit too charitable here, for Marcion did not cloak his idolatrous ideas in monotheistic garb but rather proclaimed his brand of dualism boldly and without artifice, as Tertullian explains here:

The heretic of Pontus introduces two Gods, like the twin Symplegades [clashing rocks] of his own shipwreck: One whom it was impossible to deny, i.e. our Creator; and one whom he will never be able to prove, i.e. his own god. The unhappy man gained the first idea of his conceit from the simple passage of our Lord's saying, which has reference to human beings and not divine ones, wherein He disposes of those examples of a good tree and a corrupt one; how that "the good tree bringeth not forth corrupt fruit, neither the corrupt tree good fruit." Which means, that an honest mind and good faith cannot produce evil deeds, any more than an evil disposition can produce good deeds.

Now (like many other persons nowadays, especially those who have a heretical proclivity), while morbidly brooding over the question of the origin of evil, his perception became blunted by the very irregularity of his researches; and when he found the Creator declaring, "I am He that createth evil," inasmuch as he had already concluded from other arguments, which are satisfactory to every perverted mind, that God is the author of evil, so he now applied to the Creator the figure of the corrupt tree bringing forth evil fruit, that is, moral evil, and then presumed that there ought to be another god, after the analogy of the good tree producing its good fruit. Accordingly, finding in Christ a different disposition, as it were—one of a simple and pure benevolence —differing from the Creator, he readily argued that in his Christ had been revealed a new and strange divinity; and then with a little leaven he leavened the whole lump of the faith, flavoring it with the acidity of his own heresy. -Tertullian, The Five Books Against Marcion, Book 1, Chapter 2, Early Church Fathers, p. 272.

The evil genius of Marcion in the end rests on two things. First, his great wealth and tremendous skills promoting his beliefs in the public arena make his ideas particularly hard to ignore, forcing them to have to be actively countered with great effort. Second, Marcion knows how to take what people know and expect from Scripture and gradually lead them down his own twisted path of interpretation that operates on its own seemingly logical premises.

Once these premises are accepted, the very idea of refuting Marcionite doctrine through Scripture becomes impossible because, like any cult leader proclaims, anyone who says anything contrary simply has not been initiated into the "higher truth." There are many mainstream religious and spiritual leaders who have also recognized this and used it to their advantage. As even Adolph Hitler once pointed out, a lie repeated often enough eventually is believed as the truth.

VALENTINUS

A contemporary of Marcion, and one just as popular and dangerous as he was, is Valentinus. Like Marcion, Valentinus positioned himself at first as a very wealthy patron of the Roman Catholic Church. According to Tertullian, Valentinus used his wealth and influence in an attempt to become the chief bishop of Rome, but this plot ultimately failed, so Valentinus sought another road for the power he craved.

He built and headed "learning academies" throughout Rome where students could go to study the Scriptures. His desire was to do through stealth what he could not do by bribery. He attempted to train up the next generation of church leaders to wield influence long after he was gone from the world. One of the ways he did this was to look at what beliefs created the most problems, and then work a solution that kept his theology intact. His "solution" would then make it seem he was more conventional than he actually was.

For example, Valentinus took the strict dualism of Marcion, i.e. that the God of the Old Testament was different from that of the New Testament and said instead that such terminology was just a metaphor for the One God.

However, unlike Marcion, Valentinus sought to hide who he really was and actually pretended to be a conventional Catholic teacher and theologian. Valentinus did not attempt to either throw out or suppress Scripture books directly; instead, he sought to persuade his students that the Bible had a special secret meaning and application that was diametrically opposed to what it literally said.

Valentinus, like all Gnostics, did not believe Messiah was human, but rather a divine being who put on the appearance of flesh. As a result, Yeshua's death did not atone for our sins because he did not and could not really die in the first place. The Gnostics further postulated that Deity could not truly unite with flesh, which, in turn, led them to believe Messiah's flesh was an illusion.

Nevertheless, he took pains to hide his anti-Scripture views within his esoteric and creative theology and claimed they came from Scripture. He knew that if his students threw out Scripture, they could never be accepted as Catholic leaders, so he simply showed them a different way to think about it. That way, if some did ascend the conventional Catholic hierarchy later to the status of archbishop or even higher, Valentinus' views would continue to prevail within the mainline faith.

The effect of Valentinus' teachings was profound. One of his most successful and powerful students, a man named Heracleon, was praised for his great learning even by those who thought he was a heretic. Other more conventional church leaders, such as Origen and Clement of Alexandria, praised and accepted much of what Heracleon had to say, giving some parts of it a passport into the wider church. Valentinus had many schools and tons of students and would keep sending student after student into the Catholic Church, in the hopes that more of his teachings would be absorbed by the Church.

In other words, rather than paint himself as a heretic, Valentinus sold his beliefs through his schools as if they were a franchise opportunity within the wider Catholic Church. While appearing righteous, the students of Valentinus were in effect "sleeper cells" waiting for a time when Valentinus or his later chiefs would wake them up to their true spirituality and mission against Rome. In fact, the damage wrought by Valentinus is still being felt today, just in a different form.

We see many people either trying to deny the plain Word or to filter it through other sources, whether that is extra-biblical works like 1 Enoch, Jewish mysticism through Kabbalah or a variety of "new age" theories.

In essence, the template for how all these splinter groups operate as they pretend to support Scripture, yet simultaneously go far away from it, was pretty much developed by Valentinus, whose methods remain popular even if the man himself is largely unknown today.

It was therefore inevitable that when belief in the Messiah took Rome by storm at the end of the 1st and beginning of the 2nd centuries CE, some of this cultural corruption imagery would transfer to their beliefs about the early Christians as well. That is exactly what happened when a minor 2nd century CE leader in the Roman Church was made famous by some graffiti in the underground tombs of the city. The leader, Alexamenos, was shown venerating a crucifixion victim with the body of a man and the head of a donkey. The crude Latin inscription on it translated out to, *Alexamenos worships his god.*

Going a bit deeper, Valentinus, perhaps even to a greater degree than Marcion, was able to put forth his heresies as if they were the intent of the original Scripture. He used it to his advantage and combined it with other sources, as Irenaeus explains:

Such, then, is their system, which neither the prophets announced, nor the Lord taught, nor the apostles delivered, but of which they boast that beyond all others they have a perfect knowledge. They gather their views from other sources than the Scriptures and, to use a common proverb, they strive to weave ropes of sand, while they endeavor to adapt with an air of probability to their own peculiar assertions the parables of the Lord, the sayings of the prophets, and the words of the apostles, in order that their scheme may not seem altogether without support.

In doing so, however, they disregard the order and the connection of the Scriptures, and so far as in them lies, dismember and destroy the truth. By transferring passages, and dressing them up anew, and making one thing out of another, they succeed in deluding many through their wicked art in adapting the oracles of the Lord to their opinions.

Then, again, as to those things outside of their Pleroma, the following are some specimens of what they attempt to accommodate out of the Scriptures to their opinions. – Irenaeus, Against Heresies, Book 1, Chapter 8, Early Church Fathers, p.326.

In a sense then, the Valentinian model is more dangerous, because even those who avoid the traps of inventing "new scripture" or omitting Holy Writ, may nevertheless fall into the trap of using Scripture wrongly and/or combining it with outside sources in an attempt to find the "true" interpretation. Not only do these same habits carry on today in a variety of different trendy forms, we also see Peter warning that such was happening in his own day:

Therefore, beloved, since you look for these things, be diligent to be found by Him in peace, spotless and blameless, and regard the patience of our Lord as salvation; just as also our beloved brother Paul, according to the wisdom given him, wrote to you, as also in all his letters, speaking in them of these things, in which are some things hard to understand, <u>which the untaught and unstable distort, as they do also the rest of the Scriptures, to their own destruction</u>. (2 Peter 3:14-16 NAU)

In other words, the Valentinian definition of success is simply that no one recognizes them and what they are doing as something outside of mainstream Christianity, so that their opponents will passively absorb their ideas and believe what was presented to them to be the way things were always intended to be.

When considering Marcion and Valentinus, the bottom line is that both attempted to destroy the core salvation model that the Messiah literally died to bring to the world. For the former this was done by taking out every Scriptural witness that explained who the Messiah was and when and how he would come. Since Yeshua himself said that his teaching was not his own but was that of his Father who sent him (John 7:16), by disregarding the Old Testament, little to no trace of the true "Good News" by the prophets carried into Marcionite thinking, leaving Marcion to put into that vacuum whatever ideas he liked.

As for Valentinus, his threats to the truth were two-fold. First, the general heresy of the Gnostics which totally denied core tenets like the virgin birth and Yeshua's atonement sacrifice. And second, the entire misinformation campaign Valentinus used to totally cloak his true beliefs and position his ideas as one possible interpretation of Scripture, rather than the repudiation of Scripture. Again, however, nothing either of these men did is surprising in the sense that Yeshua saw the danger in advance:

At that time many will fall away and will betray one another and hate one another. <u>Many false prophets will arise and will mislead many. Because lawlessness is increased, most people's love will grow cold.</u> But the one who endures to the end, he will be saved. <u>This gospel of the kingdom shall be preached in the whole world as a testimony to all the nations, and then the end will come.</u>
(Matthew 24:10-14 NAU)

Irenaeus

Our next important Early Church leader, Irenaeus, was faced with a series of extremely daunting challenges. He himself tells us that he was, in his early youth, acquainted with Polycarp and needs all the wisdom and experience he can get when he is elevated for leadership:

Irenaeus became the bishop of Lyons, in France, during the latter quarter of the second century. Eusebius states (Hist. Eccl., v. 4) that he was, while yet a presbyter, sent with a letter, from certain members of the Church of Lyons awaiting martyrdom, to Eleutherus, bishop of Rome; and that (v. 5) he succeeded Pothinus as bishop of Lyons, probably about A.D. 177. - Introductory Note to Irenaeus Against Heresies, Early Church Fathers, p. 313.

Irenaeus was uniquely positioned and qualified to begin the first extensive categorization and systematic refutation of the heresies in his midst. While some work along these lines was first initiated by Justin, Irenaeus is not doing refutation as a side note as Justin often did, but rather addressing the heresies head-on in his writings. The editors of Early Church Fathers, put the matter well this way:

The work of Irenaeus Against Heresies is one of the most precious remains of early Christian antiquity. It is devoted, on the one hand, to an account and refutation of those multiform Gnostic heresies which prevailed in the latter half of the second century; and, on the other hand, to an exposition <u>and defense of the Catholic faith.</u> - Ibid p. 311

In the prosecution of this plan, the author divides his work into five books. The first of these contains a minute description of the tenets of the <u>various heretical sects, with occasional brief remarks in illustration of their absurdity, and in confirmation of the truth to which they were opposed</u>. - <u>Ibid</u> p. 311

However, this massive endeavor was not a purely academic exercise for Irenaeus, since matters of heresy were about to hit him far too close to his spiritual home for comfort. Regarding his trip to Rome to meet Eleutherus, this is what is recorded:

But he had the mortification of finding the Montanist heresy patronized by Eleutherus the Bishop of Rome; and there he met an old friend from the school of Polycarp, who had embraced the Valentinian heresy. <u>That the intolerable absurdities of Gnosticism should have gained so many disciples</u> and proved itself an adversary to be grappled with and not despised, <u>throws light on the condition of the human mind under heathenism, even when it professed "knowledge" and "philosophy."</u> The task of Irenaeus was twofold: (1) to render it impossible for anyone to confound Gnosticism with Christianity, and (2) to make it impossible for such a monstrous system to survive, or ever to rise again...Irenaeus demonstrated its essential unity with the old mythology, and with heathen systems of philosophy. – Introductory Note to Irenaeus Against Heresies, Early Church Fathers, p. 309.

Furthermore, the very idea that he would find another student of his master corrupted by Gnosticism, may have also been a powerful personal motive to "call out" or expose the bishop of Rome for who he was.

Our purpose in telling you about Marcion and Valentinus is to illustrate how quickly and deeply such heresy penetrated the Roman Catholic Church going all the way to the top and how that affected the unsuspecting believers in the years to come. Scripture warns us against such heresies:

But false prophets also arose among the people, just as there will also be false teachers among you, who will secretly introduce destructive heresies, even denying the Master who bought them, bringing swift destruction upon themselves. (2 Peter 2:1 NAU)

This prophecy however is not confined to only heretics. Yeshua knew what the future would bring—that false teachers, prophets and leaders will come to lead us astray, and so he warned us against those people with hidden agendas coming "in sheep's clothing."

Such was also the case when Irenaeus watched and recorded the struggles of his former master. Polycarp had stood his ground against Anicetus the chief bishop of Rome about the observance of Passover because Anicetus preferred to honor the resurrection day with an emphasis on the eucharist.

Nevertheless, just a few decades later, new Roman leadership threatened to undo that peace. In 189 CE, Victor became the bishop of Rome and we are told:

The beautiful concordat between East and West, in which Polycarp and Anicetus had left the question, was now disturbed by Victor, Bishop of Rome, whose turbulent spirit would not accept the compromise of his predecessor. Irenaeus remonstrates with him in a Catholic spirit and overrules his impetuous temper. At the Council of Nicea, the rule for the observance of Easter was finally settled by the whole Church; and the forbearing example of Irenaeus, no doubt contributed greatly to this happy result. - Ibid, p. 310.

This new bishop of Rome took very harsh measures for enforcing uniformity throughout the Church as to the observance of the paschal solemnities. On account of the severity thus evinced, Irenaeus addressed to him a letter (only a fragment of which remains), warning him that if he persisted in the course on which he had entered, the effect would be to rend the Catholic Church in pieces. This letter had the desired result; and the question was more temperately debated, until finally settled by the Council of Nicea. – Ibid, p. 313.

The "happy result" was simply a later viewpoint prevailing over an earlier one, but that did not mean the issue was settled either by Irenaeus or the Council of Nicea in 325 CE. Instead, there is a bit of re-branding going on. The original issue was whether a Christian should calculate the timing of "Easter"—more properly— "Resurrection Day," based on the timing of Passover or by another method. Constantine, however, said directly that he wanted "nothing to do with that Jewish crowd" when rendering his decision.

The truth is, there would have been no impetus from Polycarp or others like him to time "Easter" by Passover if they were not celebrating the resurrection as part of the wider Passover Feast. Even the Catholic term *eucharist* is tied to Passover, as it simply refers to the unleavened bread that Yeshua gave thanks for at his own Passover meal (Luke 22:19). Paul uses this occasion also to teach the Corinthians to remember Messiah whenever they gathered (1 Corinthians 11:23-27). But just because Paul wanted that more frequent commemoration certainly does not mean he wanted the Corinthians to forego observing Passover. It was not his intent to substitute one for the other.

Your boasting is not good. Do you not know that a little leaven leavens the whole lump of dough? Clean out the old leaven so that you may be a new lump, just as you are in fact unleavened. For Christ our Passover also has been sacrificed. Therefore let us celebrate the feast, not with old leaven, nor with the leaven of malice and wickedness, but with the unleavened bread of sincerity and truth. (1 Corinthians 5:6-8 NAU)

It is also important to note that the term *eucharistos* was also applied to the Passover wine as well as the unleavened bread (Matthew 26:27, Mark 14:23), which basically enshrined the entire Passover feast as the original communion.

These details matter for a simple reason. Reading the Church sources suggest that one group in the "Easter Controversy" kept the "Eucharist" while the other did not, but this is misleading. The reality is both Polycarp and Anicetus took the "Eucharist" in terms of a *kind of communion*, so there was never any question about that.

Instead, the controversy was over whether to do so in its original construct of the Passover Seder meal or to divorce themselves completely from that original inspiration. Fast forward a few decades after Polycarp's time and it becomes clear that the spiritual politics between Rome and other assemblies had changed—away from God's ordained feast.

Many centuries later, the *pascha*, instead of being celebrated as Passover, became known as Easter. The first translation of the Bible into English was done by John Wycliffe in 1382 and he refers to *pesach* as *pask*, even in Acts 12:4. The term *passover*, which is now used by both Jews and Christians, was first coined by William Tyndale in his bible published in 1536, though strangely enough, in Acts 12:4 he uses the term *easter* instead.

However, it was only after the King James Bible in 1611 that the branding as "easter" in English gets popularized, but the NAU, NIV and even the New King James have gone back to using *passover*, the original English meaning for *pesach*.

So why was the issue not truly settled in Nicea? Well, the Council of Nicea left out of their ranks those who, by definition, had a different viewpoint. Constantine could not compel bishops outside his jurisdiction to attend, let alone sign on, to his imperial branding of the faith. In Syria, bishops with a pro-Catholic view were invited while dissenters that had a more "Jewish" influence were left behind by design. The Assyrian Church of the East, which was comprised of Aramaic speaking Christians, did not show up, but only issued partial agreements back to Constantine after the fact. As for the Jewish followers of Messiah known as the Nazarenes (Acts 24:5, 14), even though they lived side by side with their Gentile counterparts, not even one from their number was invited or attempted to attend.

History also tells us that many issues Constantine thought were "decided" at Nicea—everything from what books the Bible should have in it to formulations on Godhead and the human/divine nature or natures of Messiah—were merely papered over for later councils of Carthage, Ephesus, Chalcedon and others to deal with over the next century and a half.

However, what Irenaeus did most certainly do is give the earliest effective defense for the version of the faith that would be later embraced by Constantine:

Irenaeus had manifestly taken great pains to make himself acquainted with the various heretical systems which he describes. His mode of exposing and refuting these is generally very effective. It is plain that he possessed a good share of learning, and that he had a firm grasp of the doctrines of Scripture. –

Introductory Note to Irenaeus Against Heresies, Early Church Fathers, p. 312.

Eusebius, Constantine's biographer, relies heavily on Irenaeus' level of effectiveness, quoting long portions of his writings verbatim and applying the same arguments, approaches and techniques to the heretics of his own time. Eusebius, in other words, was trying to do his part to make Irenaeus' own goals a reality for himself and his emperor.

And yet, as compelling an advocate for the Roman Catholic faith as Irenaeus was, this chief literary opponent of heresy was not totally immune from heretical ideas himself:

But at times he gives expression to very strange opinions. He is, for example, quite peculiar in imagining that our Lord lived to be an old man, and that His public ministry embraced at least ten years. But though, on these and some other points, the judgment of Irenaeus is clearly at fault, his work contains a vast deal of sound and valuable exposition of Scripture, in opposition to the fanciful systems of interpretation which prevailed in his day. - Ibid, p. 312.

Unlike many others in his position, Irenaeus must be credited also for never losing sight of his overall vision, which he passionately believed—that the Catholic Church possesses one and the same faith throughout the whole world. How that sense of unity will hold up in the centuries to come is, of course, another story.

Eusebius, Constantine and others out of that tradition

In the three centuries following the resurrection of the Messiah, both Judaism and Christianity underwent massive transformations through a variety of wars and hardships. In the midst of both groups, there was no greater agent of change than Emperor Constantine I. And yet, of all the amazing things Constantine did, perhaps the most remarkable of them all was him becoming emperor in the first place, and this is the key to understanding everything that happened afterwards.

Constantine had no Roman royal blood. His father, Flavius Constantius, was a commoner who rose to leadership in the Roman army of the Emperor Diocletian. Then Flavius began a relationship with Helena, who was also of low birth, and the result of their union was Constantine, born in 272 CE.

But, in the year 285, Diocletian made a fateful decision to divide his empire into an eastern half and a western half. The emperor focused on directly ruling the eastern half, which was headquartered in Turkey, while he gave the western half headquartered at Milan Italy to a man named Maximian. This was done for political reasons, and each emperor had his own administrative court and standing army that made each one independent from the other.

It was at that point that Constantine's father saw an opportunity for advancement. The new co-emperor Maximian wanted to find a suitable husband for his stepdaughter, Theodora. Flavius, who may or may not have officially married Constantine's mother Helena, actively courted Theodora and married her a few years later.

171

As for Constantine, although he cared for his mother, she gave him permission to live with his father and seek out his political fortune. Constantine then went on to a distinguished military career while his father rose to greater and greater prominence in Maximian's court over the next decade and a half.

Eventually, Flavius won, lost, and then won back again, the right to be emperor in the west. He died in battle in the year 306. On his deathbed, he commanded his troops to make his son Constantine his successor. Those troops in turn gave Constantine all the power he needed to subdue his many enemies, and he became emperor of the west by year's end.

Throughout his younger years, Constantine spent a great deal of time in the court of both the eastern and the western emperors. Much of his education and training, especially in his formative years, was with Diocletian. Constantine was also an eyewitness to a particular series of dark events that would seal the fate of thousands of innocent Christians.

In 302 CE, when Constantine was in the royal court, Diocletian asked that a prophetic ruling be given him from the oracle of Apollo, the prophet to the Greek god of wisdom, on what to do about the Christians. Constantine was also there when the answer came back early the following year: Persecute all of them and kill any of them who get in your way.

Diocletian then unleashed a wave of terror unlike anything the Christians had seen before, even far worse than that of Emperor Nero back in the 1st century. Christians, especially leaders who opposed oppressive rules forcing them to do pagan sacrifices, were routinely tortured and then burned alive, or torn apart by wild beasts. Such violent spectacles filled Roman amphitheaters and gladiator games held throughout every major city in the Empire.

The horrific details from these executions also hark back to how the noble bishop Polycarp was executed in his hometown of Smyrna, hundreds of miles away from Rome. Constantine saw many of these horrors but did not participate in carrying them out.

As alluded to earlier, it is important to understand these biographical highlights before we get into Constantine's actions, because this was a person who was in near constant warfare with one rival or another for most of his adult life. He was someone who longed for unity and stability, in his royal house and family as well as throughout his Empire. The fact that he had to fight and contend for every scrap of power he got steeled in him a resolve that he could somehow unite the entire Roman Empire under his will, but this turned out to be far more difficult than he thought.

The eastern co-emperor Maximian made being a Christian a capital offense in the year 304. At this time, all parts of the Roman Empire embraced the "religious ruling" of the oracle of Apollo. Nevertheless, while Constantine was fending off rivals to his own growing power, he seems to have also marveled at the resistance and resilience of the Christians that his contemporaries were persecuting.

Although Constantine will eventually become the great protector of western Christianity, the true extent of his personal Christian faith remains a mystery. Even the most generous assessment in that area still has him as a pagan for most of his life. He is someone who comes to see Christianity more as a tool for political unification rather than as a way of life and faith.

One of the numerous rivals for his throne was Maxentius, who mounted a fearsome rebellion that lasted four years. Maxentius in fact became so brutal that even his father, who was co-emperor, turned against him. By that time however, Maxentius was too strong to be overthrown, so Constantine was left to deal with him another time.

That fateful moment came, according to Eusebius, at the Battle of Milvian Bridge. On the eve before the battle, October 27th of 312, Constantine was said to have a vision of a "cross" in the sky and hear a divine voice proclaim in Latin *in hoc signo vinces* or "by this sign, conquer."

Instead, the cross that Constantine purportedly saw was actually the merging of the two Greek letters that, when combined had an overall cross shape. It is this symbol, called the Chi-Rho after the names of the Greek letters, that Constantine had painted on the shields of his army. By the end of the next day, the enemy army had been routed and Maxentius died by drowning in the Tiber River. He had attempted to retreat across the Milvian Bridge, which promptly collapsed as he went across it.

But Maxentius was not the only opponent Constantine had to contend with. The eastern co-emperor Galerius, who had long opposed Constantine and also vigorously persecuted Christians, reversed course just before he died. He issued the Edict of Toleration and granted legal protection to Christians in the east. Constantine knew now was the time to act, so he began work on a similar royal declaration known as the Edict of Milan.

Like Galerius' declaration, the Edict of Milan gave Christians protected legal status and lifted the death penalty off of them. Constantine, though, went further and made it Roman law for all lands and possessions which had been stolen from Christian communities to be returned to them immediately, though the claims of individual Christians who had lost private property were not considered at this time.

Their newly given protected status meant it was illegal for anyone in the Roman Empire to persecute Christians solely on the basis of their faith. There is even a provision for those who illegally owned Christian property to apply for compensation from the empire after returning it to their rightful owners. Eusebius also comments on this important moment as a turning point in the history of the Early Church:

Moreover, the emperor's edicts, permeated with his humane spirit, were published among us also, as they had been among the inhabitants of the other division of the empire; and his laws, which breathed a spirit of piety toward God, gave promise of manifold blessings, since they secured many advantages to his provincial subjects in every nation, and at the same time prescribed measures suited to the exigencies of the churches of God.

For first of all they recalled those who, in consequence of their refusal to join in idol worship, had been driven to exile, or ejected from their homes by the governors of their respective provinces...Such were the benefits secured by the emperor's written mandates to the persons of those who had thus suffered for the faith, and his laws made ample provision for their property also. – Life of Constantine Book 2, Chapters 20-21, Early Church Fathers, p. 505.

While this edict then is the true emergence of western Christianity from the shadow of Roman persecution, the Christian faith would not become the official religion of Rome until 380 CE. Meanwhile, in the years immediately following the Edict of Milan, Jews in Constantine's empire began to lose rights even though previously Judaism was considered a protected faith under Roman law.

Would the decisions of the early church fathers to go along with Constantine have been different if not for these fortunes showered upon them, almost like a bride? Sadly, we may never know.

175

As Constantine began to embrace Christianity, he sought the counsel of powerful bishops to hammer out a unified Christian theology. Nearly everyone he talked to imparted anti-Semitic ideas to the emperor.

Constantine already knew well the histories of Jewish rebellions against Rome and to these were added other accounts citing places and dates where different groups of Jews created problems for Christians. Sometimes these Jewish incursions were massive, while at other times it was only one small group which got greatly exaggerated into being all the Jews throughout the empire. Either way, there can be no doubt that Constantine found opposition to the Jews a point on which nearly all *his bishops* agreed, and so he became open to suggestions about what to do with them. He would then act on those suggestions about a decade later.

Also, what is most remarkable is that, in a very odd turn of events, Constantine's efforts to give protection and rights to Christians, also paved the way for him becoming emperor over the entire Roman Empire. When he began work on the Edict of Milan, Constantine co-labored with Licinius, his co-emperor for the eastern half of the empire. Both men agreed to publicly proclaim and act on every provision of the Edict and, for a while, both did just that.

But, by 324, it was clear that Licinius had gone back on his word, and the persecutions he renewed against the Christians had the potential to force hundreds of thousands of refugees into Constantine's jurisdiction. This gave Constantine the pretext he needed to invade the east and dethrone his rival, and in very short order, there was no one left to challenge his supremacy, either in the east or west.

It was at that moment, the last few months of the year 324, that Constantine made another fateful decision: He would now move the capital of his empire from Rome to Turkey, at a place known as Byzantium. This Greek city was recently rebuilt by previous emperors, based on Roman urban principles. It was also one of the best fortified cities in the world, well-placed along strategic and military routes that dominated the region. Later Constantine would rededicate his new capital by naming it after himself, Constantinople, and it would continue as a Christian power base for another thousand years, more than nine centuries after the Roman Empire fell in the west.

In the following year, Constantine turned his attention to unifying the Christian faith at the Council of Nicea. This was a massive meeting of hundreds of western bishops under Constantine's command. While there, he affirmed proper status for Christianity, addressed some heretical movements in their midst and enacted several anti-Jewish laws. Sunday, thereafter, became the official rest day of the Roman Empire, and anyone found celebrating the original Saturday Sabbath, Jew or Gentile, was severely punished.

Similar bans were made on circumcision and other Jewish practices, up to and including making it illegal for a Christian to keep the Torah under penalty of death. It was also decided that Easter, instead of Passover, would be celebrated in the churches from that point.

The Council of Nicea in 325 also made progress in coming to a broad agreement as to what books would comprise the Bible, both Old and New Testaments. Other matters though, such as finding proper formulations for Trinity or Godhead and developing a framework for a common theology, would take a lot more time to reach final agreement. It is fair to say that a comprehensive, though not complete, vision of what western Christianity would

177

eventually look like came out of this Christian council and away from the original teachings of the apostles.

Beloved, if our heart does not condemn us, we have confidence before God; and whatever we ask we receive from Him, <u>because we keep His commandments and do the things that are pleasing in His sight</u>. (1 John 3:21-22 NAU)

As for Constantine, the remaining fourteen years of his life were spent creating churches for the newly emancipated and protected Christians to worship in. Constantine provided financial resources to individuals and the church, land and buildings to be used for meetings. Every need was provided for. As the bishops of the churches now received an infusion of wealth from the emperor, their goals became that of the Church as opposed to that of God's Law for all mankind and all generations. In their eyes, they had a "new" covenant to justify their actions.

But was this covenant new or was it misrepresented by a select few in the early church years? Perhaps while those few did not want to be bothered by commandments of God, they saw an opportunity for power and status through this new way.

To achieve his goal of creating more churches, Constantine traveled to Jerusalem with Eusebius, who was born in Caesarea, to find the places where the Messiah actually walked.

After his advisors informed the emperor that the burial place of Yeshua was located underneath the shrine to Jupiter built by Hadrian two centuries earlier, Constantine promptly ordered the Roman temple destroyed. The remains of a cave were found under it, which the emperor's mother Helena and others identified as the exact burial place Yeshua was laid before his resurrection. From this very same spot would eventually arise the Church of the Holy Sepulcher, which tradition claimed to encompass both the tomb and the very place of the crucifixion.

178

Although archaeology has confirmed it is not the spot the tourists go to, they do say his tomb is somewhere in that area, perhaps within a half-mile radius. Other important churches, such as the Church of the Nativity in Bethlehem, were also built at this time, around the year 326.

After Constantine returned home, he began turning his city of Constantinople into a showplace. Christian relics and ancient artifacts were brought in from all over the empire to adorn this city. Some of these were said to be the rod of Moses or fragments of the True Cross, but the extent of these and others' authenticity have yet to be confirmed.

The attachment to physical objects, such as having statues and relics, are there even in our Catholic churches today. As one former Hindu said to us at a world-famous Roman Catholic Church in Canada, "It is like going into a Hindu temple where one has many statues to worship"—Oy vey!

Scripture is very clear on the subject of praying before such objects:

You shall not make for yourself an image in the form of anything in heaven above or on the earth beneath or in the waters below. You shall not bow down to them or worship them. (Exodus 20:4-5 NIV)

For all the gods of the nations are idols, but the LORD made the heavens. (1 Chronicles 16:26 NIV)

Dear children, keep yourselves from idols. (1 John 5:21 NIV)

Even so, Constantine's overall impact on Christianity and the wider world cannot be overstated. His innovations and achievements have truly stood the test of time and propelled the Roman Catholic Church to what it is today. It is therefore certain that the legacy of the world's one billion Roman Catholics would not be nearly so important but for his efforts.

According to Eusebius, he finally sought to be educated on the Christian faith after he fell ill and was baptized just before he died, in 337 CE. Thus, ended the life of one of history's most important yet enigmatic of figures.

As for Constantine's biographer Eusebius, he also had a major voice that shapes the wider Christian world. In many ways Eusebius rendered an extremely important service in the cause of world history; he had imperial backing and resources to write the first official biography of the Catholic Church.

It is almost impossible to fathom in our modern times what an enormous undertaking this was for him. Eusebius was the bishop of Caesarea which boasted a very impressive collection of ancient manuscripts about the Bible and the Church. In addition to that, the full resources of the Vatican libraries in Rome were also made available to him, though the Vatican as we know it today did not exist back then. From these archives, and Eusebius mentions having several others, he must sift through tens of thousands of documents and put together a coherent narrative that does justice to all its individual and discrete pieces of history.

That some form of bias might arise from such a colossal and painstaking work is probably inevitable, but there are unfortunately places where Eusebius' judgment can be seriously called into question.

Nevertheless, on the positive side, we can track his overall accuracy, because earlier fragments of what he quotes from are available to cross-reference. In the case of Josephus for example, there is little doubt that Eusebius is properly excerpting passages from Josephus' Greek text. However, there are times when

Eusebius either jumps to incorrect conclusions from that text, or shows his bias in his evaluation of those events:

> *And in the sixth book he writes as follows: "Of those that perished by famine in the city (during the Jewish wars) the number was countless, and the miseries they underwent unspeakable. For if so much as the shadow of food appeared in any house, there was war, and the dearest friends engaged in hand-to-hand conflict with one another and snatched from each other the most wretched supports of life." <u>Such was the reward which the Jews received for their wickedness and impiety, against the Christ of God</u>. – Church History, Book 3, Chapter 20, 32, Early Church Fathers, pp. 140-141.*

As a result, some scholars choose to put little stock in his overall work, but others thought using that kind of broad brush is ultimately unwarranted. In the interest of fairness, Eusebius also believes the Catholic Church's tendency to excess is at least partially to blame for the hardships of his times which, unfortunately, seems prevalent even in the modern churches and assemblies of believers:

> *<u>But when on account of the abundant freedom, we fell into laxity and sloth, and envied and reviled each other</u>, and were almost, as it were, taking up arms against one another, rulers assailing rulers with words like spears, and people forming parties against people, <u>and monstrous hypocrisy and dissimulation rising to the greatest height of wickedness, the divine judgment with forbearance</u>, as is its pleasure, while the multitudes yet continued to assemble, gently and moderately harassed the episcopacy. – Church History, Book 8, Chapter 1, Early Church Fathers, p. 323.*

Eusebius is at least honest about when he is inserting his opinions between the sources he uses. From there, a careful reader can still gain great value from what he quotes and set aside the historian's suspicious feelings and tendencies. What remains from that process is, therefore, still a work of great importance for the study of the western church. We are, overall, in a far better position to have it with its flaws, than to not have it at all.

John Chrysostom (344-407 CE)

Following the Council of Nicea, a western early church leader named John Chrysostom stepped up his attacks against Jews. Is it any wonder that the Jews then became wary of the Christians? It seemed they never knew which way the wind would blow:

The synagogue is worse than a brothel...it is the den of scoundrels and the repair of wild beasts...the temple of demons devoted to idolatrous cults...the refuge of brigands and debauchers, and the cavern of devils. It is a criminal assembly of Jews...a place of meeting for the assassins of Messiah... a house worse than a drinking shop...a den of thieves, a house of ill fame, a dwelling of iniquity, the refuge of devils, a gulf and an abyss of perdition."..."I would say the same things about their souls... As for me, I hate the synagogue...I hate the Jews for the same reason. - Homilies against the Jews (387 CE)

St. Augustine (354-430 CE)

Our next church leader on the other hand is St. Augustine, who has also often been accused of anti-Semitism in his writings, but for a variety of reasons his situation is less clear. Let us begin with this famous excerpt from "Confessions":

How hateful to me are the enemies of your Scripture! How I wish that you would slay them (the Jews) with your two-edged sword,

182

so that there should be none to oppose your word! Gladly would I have them die to themselves and live to you! - Confessions, 12:14

Many references to this line of Augustine insert the phrase "the Jews," where Augustine just says "them." There have been those over the centuries who interpreted Augustine as condoning Jewish persecution, but it may be things are not quite that simple or cut and dried.

For one thing, while it seems probable his "them" *includes* Jews whom he thinks are the enemies of Scripture, there is no evidence of his writings being exclusively targeted only against Jews. In reading carefully, we see that Augustine is not prescribing murder but that his "enemies" die to themselves, i.e. become humble and stop sinning.

Augustine nonetheless was also a product of his time, so it is important to remember the main motivation behind his passionate writings. In 410 CE, Rome was viciously sacked by Visigoth armies led by a man named Alaric. The Visigoths, who were from Germany, were begging for Roman help with their famine and asked to be made citizens of the Empire to have greater protections. When these requests were refused, and Alaric saw his people die by the thousands, he resolved to take by force what his people needed.

However, the citizens of Rome who witnessed Alaric's wrath were instead quick to blame it on the Roman people embracing Christianity and abandoning the traditional gods. It is easy to forget that Rome and much of that region was still pagan. Augustine then sought to prove this was not true and in the process he calls out nearly everybody in the Empire to show that their sin, remaining as pagans, was the cause of the disaster.

Therefore, the possibility that Augustine was misinterpreted, and hate being preached against the Jews had little to do with him, seems a lot more probable, but one can also see how Jews learning of Augustine's message might have thought he was advocating violence against them.

And finally, when one reads Augustine's masterpiece *City of God* it is clear he attacks pagans, Jews and Christians he disagrees with in fairly equal measure, along with a hopeful note for all concerned to come to repentance as well:

It is true that wicked men do many things contrary to God's will; but so great is His wisdom and power, that all things which seem adverse to His purpose do still tend towards those just and good ends and issues which He Himself has foreknown. And consequently, when God is said to change His will, as when, e.g., He becomes angry with those to whom He was gentle, it is rather they than He who are changed, and they find Him changed in so far as their experience of suffering at His hand is new, as the sun is changed to injured eyes, and becomes as it were fierce from being mild, and hurtful from being delightful, though in itself it remains the same as it was. That also is called the will of God which He does in the hearts of those who obey His commandments. – City of God, Book 22, Chapter 2, Early Church Fathers, p. 480.

In the wake of Augustine's ministry though Christological controversies on how to discuss Godhead (Trinity) and the quantity and character of the nature or natures of Messiah would continue to divide the church, resulting in the Christian councils at Ephesus (431 CE) and Chalcedon (451 CE). One of the issues was whether Mary was to be regarded as "the Mother of God."

On Nestorius and His Controversy

In the spring of 428 CE, a man named Nestorius became the chief bishop of Constantinople. At that time, the Roman Church was heavily promoting the idea of the Virgin Mary as a kind of co-redeemer and elevated her even further with the title of *theotokos*, "God bearer." When Nestorius heard this idea, he vigorously opposed it. Since God was an uncreated Being, he argued, God could not have a mother.

Nestorius' opponents took his simple view and expanded it into a much wider debate on whether Messiah had one or two natures. The reality though is far more nuanced concerning what Nestorius actually believed. He once stated, for example, that "the two-fold nature is one," which was actually similar to the way his opponents described it, but they did not take it that way. In other words, from Nestorius' viewpoint, singularity or plurality was a matter of spiritual perspective, but to his opponents this "perspective" was tantamount to stripping the Messiah of his divinity, which Nestorius never intended or did.

He was later "invited" to defend himself at the Council of Ephesus in 431 CE, only to find out that even before he arrived, he was judged and condemned as a heretic. Led by Bishop Cyril of Alexandria, they removed Nestorius from his position and excommunicated him from the faith. Despite this, even church leaders who agreed with the Council's decision thought Nestorius was denied the due process of a fair hearing.

However, this harsh punishment was not sufficient for St. Cyril. His group, backed with the sanction of Pope Celestine I, contacted the Aramaic Church of the East. They asked their patriarch to also condemn and excommunicate Nestorius. But when the Church of East wrote back and said Nestorius was right and they were wrong, the Roman Church labelled them *Nestorians* to suggest they were a new assembly, rather than one founded by the Apostles.

This unfair insult and denial of the Church of the East's heritage lasted well into the 20th century. It was only finally repudiated and removed by Rome when Patriarch Mar Dinkha IV complained and Pope John Paul II apologized. By the end of the 1990's, Rome and the Church of the East reconciled as each one recognized the separate independent liturgy and leadership of the other.

Nevertheless, the controversy created by what Nestorius said, as well as what others falsely claimed he said, still haunts both the eastern and western churches to this day. Even the eastern church, who made him a saint, doesn't agree with everything that was attributed to him. Meanwhile, when more extensive writings of Nestorius were discovered in 1895, the general opinion of him in the west improved, but objections to the way he expressed his beliefs still remained.

In the end, the saga of Nestorius demonstrates how well-meaning believers can sometimes isolate their own people over what may have largely been a matter of semantics.

When the Roman Catholic Church issued revised Godhead terminology from Chalcedon, many churches who agreed with the previous definitions from Nicea in 325 objected to the new formula which included direct worship of the Virgin Mary. Eventually this would cause the eastern and western churches to split in 1054. Other issues that divided Christians from the Catholic West included the Roman emphasis on venerating statues in their churches.

St. Thomas Aquinas (1271 CE)

For these next two church leaders, St. Thomas Aquinas and Martin Luther, the law of unintended consequences is once again on full display. For Aquinas, he makes the point that while the Jews deserve persecution for their perceived misdeeds, the Christian should practice restraint in that persecution. In making this plea however, Aquinas comes up with a series of instructions that foreshadow the actions of the Nazis by more than six centuries, particularly with regard to making them wear distinctive clothing to identify themselves:

To which question (proposed in this unqualified way) it can be answered that although, as the laws say, the Jews by reason of their fault are sentenced to perpetual servitude and thus the lords of the lands in which they dwell may take things from them as though they were their own—with, nonetheless, this restraint observed that the necessary subsidies of life in no way be taken from them, because it still is necessary that we "walk honestly even in the presence of those who are outsiders (I Thess. 4:11)," "lest the name of the Lord be blasphemed (I Tim. 6:1)," and the Apostle admonishes the faithful by his example that (I Cor. 10:32-33), "they be without offense in the presence of the Jews and the Gentiles and in the Church of God"—this seems to be what should be observed, that, as the laws have determined, the services coerced from them do not demand things that they had not been accustomed to do in times gone by, because those things that are unexpected more often rattle souls…

Finally, you ask whether it is good that Jews throughout your province are compelled to wear a sign distinguishing them from Christians. The reply to this is plain: <u>that, according to a statute of the general Council, Jews of each sex in all Christian</u>

provinces, and all the time, should be distinguished from other people by some clothing. - *St. Thomas Aquinas (1271 CE), Letter on the Treatment of the Jews*

Ironically of course Jews were already wearing distinctive clothing that clearly identified who they were, such as tzit-tzit tassels on the corners of the men's clothing, beards and woolen clothes of a particular distinctive variety and so on. Jews were in fact proud to dress in a Set-Apart way, both men and women, because it came from a need to observe Torah that they dressed modestly. But that was not enough for Aquinas and others of his ilk.

Instead, they wanted to shame Jews by making them wear degrading outfits of Gentile design rather than modest attire commanded by Scripture. From here, one can draw a straight line directly from this suggestion of Aquinas to the ghettos established by the Nazis and the eventual setting up of the death camps.

In fact, the only other writer who had even greater influence on Nazi policy towards the Jews is our next example.

Martin Luther (1483-1546 CE)

Martin Luther was a passionate man who often resorted to graphic terminology to make his points. Such was true whether his target consisted of Jews or his own Catholic Church that he was seeking to reform. Also, Luther's kind of fiery rhetoric has roots that go back centuries in Christian discourse, and this form and style was sometimes meant to be taken as more hyperbolic than literal.

For example, consider the famous *Inferno* poem by Dante Alighieri, written around the year 1300. Dante's vivid descriptions of the nine levels of hell would shape Catholic thought in a huge way for centuries. And yet, modern scholars have long recognized that the poet's impetus was not exclusively theological or altruistic. It turned out that some of the people he described in the worst tortures of hell bore a striking resemblance to his political enemies who had him exiled from his native city of Florence. In much the same way as Dante, Luther's polemics are often expressed in extraordinarily strong and even violent images. Even though some took it with a proverbial grain of salt, not all did.

While Luther's true intentions are a subject of debate and interpretation, there can be no doubt that those who followed him took him at face value and used Luther's words as a justification for Jewish persecution. Adolph Hitler had Luther's book *On the Jews and their Lies* on his bookshelf, and it seems he took a lot of inspiration from it, passing into German law what Luther only suggested:

What shall we Christians do with this rejected and condemned people, the Jews: First, to set fire to their synagogues or schools. This is to be done in honor of our Lord and of Christendom, so that God might see that we are Christians.

Second, I advise that their houses also be razed and destroyed.

Third, I advise that all their prayer books and Talmudic writings, in which such idolatry, lies, cursing, and blasphemy are taught, be taken from them.

Fourth, I advise that their rabbis be forbidden to teach henceforth on pain of loss of life and limb.

Fifth, I advise that safe-conduct on the highways be abolished completely for the Jews. For they have no business in the countryside.

Sixth, I advise that usury be prohibited to them, and that all cash and treasure of silver and gold be taken from them.

Seventh, I recommend putting a flail, an ax, a hoe, a spade, a distaff, or a spindle into the hands of young, strong Jews and Jewesses and letting them earn their bread in the sweat of their brow. But if we are afraid that they might harm us or our wives, children, servants, cattle, etc., then let us emulate the common sense of other nations such as France, Spain, Bohemia and then eject them forever from the country. - On the Jews and Their Lies (1543)

Although we still see such violence and hatred against Jews in isolated communities, it must also be pointed out that the vast majority of Lutherans today took Luther at his word, and subsequently passed resolutions repudiating his anti-Semitism, no longer quoting from those controversial writings. Nevertheless, the question remains: Did Luther really mean it?

My personal take is that while Luther was clearly "venting" at Jews for their perceived intransigence, he was only dealing in the present moment of his current frustration. After about twenty years of overtures to the Jews to get them to accept Christ and Christianity failed, he took the rejection personally.

Many of us would like to believe that had Luther truly known the full and horrific extent to which his words would have been taken in the Holocaust, he might have expressed his religious zeal in a different way to curtail anti-Semitism.

Also, the totality and scope of Luther's writings is so massive that it could fill the space of several sets of encyclopedias, and these voluminous teachings must be used in context with the smaller batches of quotes to see his full message, which is often focused on the grace of God.

And finally, in the spirit of fairness and giving him the benefit of the doubt, Luther did not always feel great hatred towards the Jewish people. Quite different from his later writings in 1543 are his earlier statements in this excerpt from 1523:

If I had been a Jew and had seen such dolts and blockheads govern and teach the Christian faith, I would sooner have become a hog than a Christian. They have dealt with the Jews as if they were dogs rather than human beings; they have done little else than deride them and seize their property. When they baptize them they show them nothing of Christian doctrine or life, but only subject them to popishness and mockery...If the apostles, who also were Jews, had dealt with us Gentiles as we Gentiles deal with the Jews, there would never have been a Christian among the Gentiles...

When we are inclined to boast of our position [as Christians] we should remember that we are but Gentiles, while the Jews are of the lineage of Christ. <u>We are aliens and in-laws; they are blood relatives</u>, cousins, and brothers of our Lord. Therefore, if one is to boast of flesh and blood the Jews are actually nearer to Christ than we are...If we really want to help them, we must be guided in our dealings with them not <u>by papal law</u> but by the law of Christian love. We must receive them cordially, and permit them to trade and work with us, that they may have occasion and opportunity to associate with us, hear our Christian teaching, and witness our Christian life. If some of them should prove stiff-necked, what of it? After all, we ourselves are not all good Christians either. - That Jesus Christ was born a Jew (1523)

From an unbiased perspective though, the problem is that the positive views of the Jews were from Luther's youth, while the negative views were those he preached literally to his death. Which viewpoint should you actually believe was from this son of the church?

If we wish to find a scapegoat on whose shoulders we may lay the miseries which Germany has brought upon the world, I am more and more convinced that the worst evil genius of that country is not Hitler or Bismarck or Frederick the Great, but Martin Luther.

- Reverend William Ralph Inge, Anglican Prelate and Professor of Divinity of Cambridge University, 1944.

Two Jewish children from the Warsaw Ghetto (1940) wearing degrading images of the Star of David sewn into their clothing as commanded by the Nazis.

The Legacy of Hitler, Protestantism and the Roman Catholic Church

I do insist on the certainty that sooner or later, once we hold power...Luther, if he could be with us, would give us his blessing.
– Adolph Hitler

While Europe continued to vigorously contend whether Catholicism or Protestantism was the better faith, the sobering reality was that for either one, long legacies of anti-Jewish sentiments were well-represented both in churches and in their leadership. The Spanish Inquisition's brutal torture of Jews, Muslims and others they deemed less than worthy was only disbanded in 1834. Further, between 1478 and 1834 there was a movement of the Catholic Church in Spain where anyone who was not towing the line of the Church was under suspicion. Some were put in the dungeons on torture racks until they either converted or died.

However, even in places that did not physically torture or murder Jews, the pattern for viewing Jews as either racially or morally inferior was deeply ingrained in the cultural values of both western and eastern Europe. In Russia, the Czars actively allowed and encouraged people to harass Jews wherever and whenever they could, with legal officials happily looking the other way.

Out of this environment eventually grew a cottage industry of anti-Semitic books and pamphlets in both old Russia and the Soviet Union which replaced her. The bestseller of them all was the *Protocols of the Elders of Zion*, a vicious book which made the case for wholesale murder of Jews to prevent them from taking over the world. Everyone from Adolph Hitler to Henry Ford to the aviator and celebrity Charles Lindbergh promoted these ideas, not just in Germany and Russia, but in the United States as well.

These same people also regularly consulted Luther's *On the Jews and their Lies* along with the writings of Aquinas, Chrysostom and others. Anti-Semitism did not just become a hateful doctrine tolerated in society. It grew slowly at first, but later a blueprint of genocidal and specific steps emerged. In the 1800's, they first segregated the Jews into ghettos (with their special markings on their clothes) followed by denying them basic rights of owning land and working in certain occupations.

Eventually it progressed to sending soldiers to isolated villages to wipe Jewish enclaves out wherever possible, before being fully realized in the death camps of places like Auschwitz, Poland, which murdered more than six million innocent victims. Hitler also timed his first nationwide public persecution of the Jews in 1938, the famous "Night of Broken Glass" or Kristallnacht, to coincide with Luther's birthday of November 10th that year.

However, the relationship between Hitler and Roman Catholic anti-Semitism is a completely different matter. Luther may have escalated the discrimination of Jews, but Pope Pius 12th, who was in charge at the Vatican when the Holocaust was going on, took a much more active role in helping the Nazis escape justice after the fact.

Remarkably, such assistance was also despite how the Nazis persecuted tens of thousands of Catholic priests and bishops. Basically, any Christian or church leader who protested the Nazi agenda against Jews, Communists, Gypsies or anyone else who disagreed with them, faced destruction of their churches and the murder of their priests, along with the elderly and the sick. These accounted for another five million victims at the hands of Hitler, totaling eleven million lives. Many Catholics too were sent to the death camps in Auschwitz, Bergen-Belsen, and other places, where they died alongside the Jews in their midst.

Meanwhile, as these faithful Catholics were suffering, their Vatican leaders were pressured to agree and implement the Anti-Jewish policies of Pope Pius 12th, because canon law from 1870 declared that the Pope, meaning *papa or father* was infallible. So where did this idea of Vatican leaders conforming come from?

If you remember, we had previously mentioned that there was a time when there was no "mother church," but it was the chief bishops who oversaw their respective areas. When one such chief bishop, Ignatius, introduced the idea "your bishop presides in the place of God," and you do not set yourself "in opposition to the bishop," he set the stage before his death in 108 CE for how canon law will later view its Pope—as someone who is infallible.

As a result, in the 1940's, even Vatican and church leaders who had a crisis of conscience and knew that the pope and the Nazis were wrong, felt unable to speak up. They would not break ranks. It is because of situations like this that Yeshua said:

Do not call anyone on earth your father; for One is your Father, He who is in heaven. (Matthew 23:9 NAU)

However, there was at least one notable exception to that rule of silence. A Polish bishop named Karol Woltiya actively defied Catholic hierarchy and sheltered Jews from the Nazis. Woltiya would eventually rise to the rank of Archbishop of Krakow and in 1967, he removed the Catholic Church's curse against the Jewish people through the council known as Vatican II. By 1981 Woltiya became better known to the world as Pope John Paul II, and he did much to undo the damage of his predecessors against Jews and others.

Then, in 2015, classified documents about the Nazis, not just from Germany but through intelligence agencies across Europe and the United States, were released. Bob Baer, who was a CIA analyst for more than 20 years, digitized these documents and conducted a three-year investigation that ultimately aired on the History Channel as "Hunting Hitler." With the release of literally millions of previously classified documents, the full extent of Nazi preparations, even in America, before, during and after the war was revealed for the first time, along with confirming other details that had come to light since the end of World War II.

Hitler and his commanders had made plans to escape Germany and find safe haven in various Nazi hotspots around the world. These included places like Spain, where the dictator Francisco Franco made sure that Hitler and his senior staff had places to hide out and plan a Fourth Reich. Other places that had facilities built for the Nazis—whether or not the Nazis themselves were able to take advantage of them—included Norway and Argentina, the latter being where we know Hitler's second in command, Adolph Eichmann, got sanctuary.

However, the role of the Roman Catholic Church is something that surprised even seasoned Nazi hunters. Baer and his team found proof that the Pope with the vast resources of the Vatican, had issued new passports with brand-new identities, under an assumed name, for these architects of the Holocaust to start their lives over. The passports from Vatican City would then be used to generate new passports in other countries that would further hide their identities.

As a result, the people under Hitler who were most responsible for killing innocent millions were given papal sanction to live the rest of their long lives in peace and comfort, never being forced to account for what they did. In most cases they died with their vast fortunes intact, which they plundered from the European Jews they murdered.

This sent an extremely clear message to the Jews: Allowing others to control their fate, subject to the whims of racist dictators or religious leaders, was no longer an option. The *Christian* countries they had been living in for centuries abandoned them to near extinction, so now they could wait no longer. The pressure was on for an independent state. For the sake of their own preservation, world leaders finally changed their policies so as not to have blood on their hands and granted Jews the right to return and establish the modern state of Israel.

Nowadays, although in some places persecuting Jews is becoming more popular after long being dormant, most Christians seem to have really taken the warnings and lessons of the Holocaust to heart. They have, to a tremendous degree, embraced the Jewish people as their brethren, while agreeing to disagree on their differences.

Roman Catholic overtures of apology to Jews also began to receive wider acceptance, because of the efforts of Pope John Paul II. We pray and hope the current pontiff, Pope Francis (Jorge Mario Bergoglio), will endeavor to enlighten Christians more on their Jewish roots and, on a personal note, give us access to the earliest Renewed Covenant manuscript that is in the custody of the Vatican.

The effect of these cultural paradigm shifts is also being felt in the ongoing dialogue that has emerged in recent decades between believers in Yeshua who keep the Torah and feasts and those who do not, which ironically has also put all of us back into the original debates that surrounded the separation of Judaism from Christianity.

In fact, had the division between Jews and Christians not been so wide, each of them may have helped the other to discover the truth and the salvation brought by Messiah. Instead, through lies and deception born from the enemy's destructive and evil plans, both sides experienced centuries of exile, isolation and war as a consequence of being *kidnapped from God*.

However, our Creator in His infinite mercy, has provided a way for all of us to return home to Him. As prophesied in Daniel 12:4, the words that were concealed until the end of time are being revealed with many of God's people coming together, during this Information Age, when knowledge travels back and forth and greatly increases.

Let us therefore be wise. Choose righteousness over self-righteousness and learn from the mistakes of our ancestors.

Destructive forces are at work in the city; threats and lies never leave its streets.

If an enemy were insulting me, I could endure it; if a foe were rising against me, I could hide. But it is you, a man like myself, my companion, my close friend, with whom I once enjoyed sweet fellowship at the house of God, as we walked about among the worshipers. Let death take my enemies by surprise; let them go down alive to the realm of the dead, for evil finds lodging among them.

As for me, I call to God, and the LORD saves me. Evening, morning and noon I cry out in distress, and he hears my voice.

He rescues me unharmed from the battle waged against me, even though many oppose me…

Cast your cares on the LORD and he will sustain you; he will never let the righteous be shaken.

But you, God, will bring down the wicked into the pit of decay; the bloodthirsty and deceitful will not live out half their days. But as for me, I trust in you.

(Psalm 55:11-18, 22-23 NIV)

SECTION FIVE

The Scattering of God's People from the Beginning

*And someone said to Him, "Lord, are there just a few who are
being saved?" And He said to them, "Strive to enter through the
narrow door; for many, I tell you, will seek to enter and will not
be able. "Once the head of the house gets up and shuts the door,
and you begin to stand outside and knock on the door, saying,
'Lord, open up to us!' then He will answer and say to you, 'I do
not know where you are from.' (Luke 13:23-25 NAU)*

In the previous sections we learnt how God's people were
scattered from Noah's time onwards. Throughout this book, we
have seen one overarching pattern for the human extended family:
Some of them become united in our Creator's purpose while others
are, for a time at least, cut off because of disobedience or bad
circumstances caused by wars, politics and personal agendas of
those with influence.

We are attempting to share with you also why we need to
desperately return to our Heavenly Father so that His kingdom will
reign here on earth. It is up to us, the normally quiet ones who love

our God, to rise up and say *no* to all the evil and injustice in this world.

And so, the first step is to be equipped, to know your own ancestral and faith history, the history of the world, along with prayer and study of the Word.

The second step is to go into spiritual battle, armed with the Word of God, against those who are ruled by power and greed on one extreme and fear on the other. That is why Yeshua said:

Do not think that I came to bring peace on the earth; I did not come to bring peace, but a sword. (Matthew 10:34 NAU)

He also said in Matthew 8:26:

"Why are you afraid, you men of little faith?" (Matthew 8:26)

If we can't stand up against unrighteousness or evil, how are we going to build up our faith, like David, to have the *knowing* that God is with us? We collectively, as believers, need to once again take control of the future of our children and the generations to follow.

Just as it would not be prudent for the commander of an army to send his soldiers into battle without knowing who the enemy is, how strong they are, the terrain, etc., it would not be wise for us to go against our opponents without our armor, which is why Yeshua said:

Behold, I send you out as sheep in the midst of wolves; so be shrewd as serpents and innocent as doves. (Matthew 10:16 NAU)

We have to make our assemblies, churches and government strong, and that my friends is only possible if God Almighty is with us. We can quibble about this and that and stay divided, which is the tactic of the enemy along with keeping us ignorant of the truth, or we can become united for the greater good. Let us look at Zechariah 8:11-15 and Revelation 7:4, 9-10:

'But now I will not treat the remnant of this people as in the former days,' declares the LORD of hosts. 'For there will be peace for the seed: the vine will yield its fruit, the land will yield its produce and the heavens will give their dew; and I will cause the remnant of this people to inherit all these things. 'It will come about that just as you were a curse among the nations, O house of Judah and house of Israel, so I will save you that you may become a blessing. Do not fear; let your hands be strong.' "For thus says the LORD of hosts, 'Just as I purposed to do harm to you when your fathers provoked Me to wrath,' says the LORD of hosts, 'and I have not relented, so I have again purposed in these days to do good to Jerusalem and to the house of Judah. Do not fear! (Zechariah 8:11-15 NAU)

And I heard the number of those who were sealed, one hundred and forty-four thousand sealed from every tribe of the sons of Israel...After these things I looked, and behold, a great multitude which no one could count, from every nation and all tribes and peoples and tongues, standing before the throne and before the Lamb, clothed in white robes, and palm branches were in their hands; and they cry out with a loud voice, saying, "Salvation to our God who sits on the throne, and to the Lamb." (Revelation 7:4, 9-10 NAU)

Beginning with Adam, who had three sons that were named and many other children who were not, only Seth produced seed that was worthy of remembrance and continuing forward. The same is true of the next eight generations—many unnamed sons and daughters come about, but only one special heir from that line is identified and continues forwards until we get to Noah.

Then, after the Flood, only eight people survive with three sons producing seed for the world. While these lines are named and remembered, the Bible tends to focus on the lineage of just one son, Shem, the father of the Hebrew people. The descendants of the other two sons, Ham and Japheth, however, are not forgotten. They will fill most of the world for their special purposes under God Almighty while they are scattered and will receive their kingdom opportunity to return home to Him.

From Shem's line will eventually come Abraham, who is himself one of three sons, to receive a special blessing. His progeny will bless the entire world and be as numerous as the stars of the heavens.

Nevertheless, here too God is making further refinements to which parts of Abraham's family get which blessing. Ishmael gets lands that are comprised of many Arab nations today, as do the sons of Abraham by his third wife, Keturah, but Isaac and his sons get Canaan, a Promised Land much bigger than the modern state of Israel. Later, from Abraham's grandson Jacob will come the twelve tribes that are today collectively known as Israel, while Jacob's elder brother Esau, like Ishmael, receives a separate inheritance and purpose as well—as more are scattered.

After centuries of struggle, one lineage of the people of God are brought together into a unified earthly kingdom led by Saul, David and Solomon. However, even during this period of the united monarchy, certain divisions would manifest as one royal house gives way to another. The first separation happens with Saul and his descendants being rejected from establishing a dynasty. So royal rule, which began from the tribe of Benjamin under Saul, switched to Judah under King David.

Naturally, some of Saul's sons did not take kindly to this change, so there was civil war for the first few years of David's reign. Eventually, however, David prevailed and completely consolidated his power, while Saul's family was almost completely wiped out in the end.

In total, the golden age of the united monarchy of Saul, David and Solomon only lasted 120 years from 1051 to 931 BCE. After them, Solomon's son Rehoboam promptly brought all their efforts to naught. Within 5 years of his taking power, the kingdom split with his own at Jerusalem and the northern breakaway kingdom at Samaria under Jeroboam. God's people will go to other places because of their sin until they find their way home.

The Twelve Tribes were now two different nations. Judah, Benjamin and Levi, including the priests, made up the kingdom of Judah, while the rest were called the kingdom of Israel. There would be tension and occasional war between these two kingdoms for the next two centuries.

As we have seen, many remarkable righteous kings in Judah cried out to YHWH for help and were blessed with miracles. Jehoshaphat is generally regarded as one of these righteous kings, but he makes one critical mistake in allowing his son to marry the daughter of Ahab and Jezebel, pagan worshipers, who rule the northern kingdom.

Jehoshaphat's reforms will however set the standard against which later kings like Hezekiah and Josiah will measure their attempts to return to covenant.

One of the most mysterious incidents where God's people were scattered is only mentioned by the prophet Obadiah, the chief steward of King Ahab, in around 860 BCE. Obadiah's details are sketchy but what we do know is that a group of Edomites, descendants of Esau, attacked Judeans living in Jerusalem. Apparently, some in the northern tribes were joined with Esau's folks against Judah and the battle was so fierce that many from Judah got on ships and left Jerusalem for "Sepharad," which is Spain.

Others from the northern tribes also left, for reasons not clear, and eventually settled in "Zarephath" which is now part of France. Some rabbis believe Obadiah is describing an event he witnessed in his own day because the prophet appears to relate it in flashback. Others believe this to be a prophecy that happened about a century or so later, as part of the wider Assyrian invasion.

While the former scenario appears more plausible, what we know is that there are still Jewish communities in Spain and France that trace their lineage back to this time. There have even been cases where people, who thought their families were Christian going back many generations, found out they had Jewish blood; their ancestors having suppressed their lineage due to persecution.

One such person who is a friend of ours discovered his Jewish roots went back so far that the family name was even recognized by some rabbis in Israel. When our Creator calls, no matter what our circumstance in life may be, we are drawn to His call like bees to honey. We have this burning desire for the truth and that takes us on an intense study of the Scripture, looking deeper into what is only touched on from the pulpits.

Those who are called have and will put aside our biases because now we have a common desire: we cannot live without our Heavenly Father. It is what we choose to do after that which determines what happens to us. That is why Yeshua said, "For many are called, but few *are* chosen." (Matthew 22:14 NAU)

Northern Kingdom and the First Samaritans

With no such righteous kings in Israel's future, the entire line of Ahab and that of the northern kingdom was ultimately doomed to be destroyed. In 722 BCE, the Assyrians invaded the kingdom of Israel and took the ten tribes into captivity, away from the land they lived in.

From there we track the Assyrian advance to the kingdom of Judah. Assyria invaded Jerusalem in 700 BCE during the reign of the righteous king Hezekiah, but our God, YHWH, wiped out the entire Assyrian army overnight, all 185,000 of them. While Assyria never sent back the Hebrew people who they took from Samaria two decades earlier, they were no longer harassing the kingdom of Judah in the south. Josephus tells us that, by his day eight centuries later, those 10 tribes were still in Assyria or lost as no one was sure where they went or what happened to them.

However, one of the most important developments in the wake of the 722 BCE Assyrian invasion of the northern kingdom of Israel, was the ongoing development and possible re-invention of the Samaritan people. The Samaritan story is an important one which needs to be dealt with here almost as a separate unit from the rest of our topics, being told from beginning to end.

The Samaritans began as a separate pagan enclave living near the city of Samaria for some time prior to the Assyrian invasion. We don't know much about them except what Scripture informs us.

In any case, the Samaritans who were about to be confronted by Assyria are described this way in 2 Kings 17:29: *Every nation still made gods of its own and put them in the houses of the high places which the people of Samaria had made, every nation in their cities in which they lived.*

After the invasion, however, most of these earlier "Samaritans" were killed. The few who remained, along with remnants of the northern tribes not exiled, eventually interbred with their Assyrian occupiers. As a result, most the Samaritans we know of today are from this reconstituted amalgamation.

It is also certain that this latest version of the Samaritans abandoned the paganism of their ancestors. Instead, they embraced their partial Israelite roots, believing again in YHWH, preserving His Torah and keeping His Feasts, while at the same time putting their own individual spin on how they chose to worship Him.

Unlike other groups who crossed borders, the Samaritans remained in the same region as their brother Jews but were cut off from the main group based on religion. Because they were often barred from the Temple, they set up their own rival shrine on Mount Gerizim, along with their own separate priesthood and cultic traditions, including having strategically altered the Torah text to suit their sectarian needs.

So why are the Samaritans so important for Christians to understand? Most of you know of the Samaritan woman at the well who is surprised that Yeshua, a man from Judah, would speak to her because of her ethnicity. But Yeshua treats her and the others with her with respect in John 4, while also acknowledging their deficiencies when compared with the rest of Judah: "You worship what you do not know while we worship what we know because salvation is from the Jews" (John 4:22). We have to come back to the true teachings of Yeshua and the apostles, back to *the Way*

It is also incredibly significant that Yeshua did not deny their heritage outright. When they referred to themselves as direct descendants of the patriarch Jacob, who is later called Israel (John 4:12-21), Yeshua neither contradicted them, nor did that necessarily mean he accepted their claim completely. Instead, it may be that his main focus was bringing salvation to all peoples (John 4:13, 23-24), not certifying individual and narrowing ancestral claims. Such is the great reach and influence of the Samaritan people, from ancient days to that of the Gospels themselves.

Having said that, Yeshua combats the prevailing prejudices associated with the Samaritan people (Luke 10:25-37). What is exceedingly ironic, though, is that the Pharisees accused Messiah of being a Samaritan himself to delegitimize his message against them (John 8:48), but now we need to return to looking at other events after the Assyrian invasion.

Judah, Her Exile and the Aftermath

As we keep on this journey of how God's people dispersed, try to understand how we are all connected in spite of the division and re-unification of the Jewish people. Sub-cultures came about every time they travelled across borders, accounting for why so many are discovering their Jewish roots through DNA testing. But what is also important is to understand how many got *grafted in*.

In about 650 BCE King Manasseh decided to put an idol in the Holy of Holies (2 Kings 21:4). However, if such a perversion ever happened with the Ark present, Scripture strongly suggests the entire city would have been in danger of complete destruction (1 Samuel 5:1-12), so it may be the Ark was taken out of Jerusalem before that time for safe-keeping.

However, Manasseh's overall program of oppression and murder was more than sufficient justification for a major contingent with their priests and other leaders to leave the country. Archaeology tells us where many of these refugees eventually ended up. Betzalel Porten, who was once Professor Emeritus of Jewish history at Hebrew University in Jerusalem, explains what likely happened next:

To summarize, Manasseh's revolt against his Assyrian overlords may have led him to an alliance with Egypt. In that connection,

207

he most likely dispatched a contingency of Jewish soldiers to Egypt. At the same time, his profanation of the Jerusalem Temple and his harsh repressive policies may well have resulted in the flight into Egypt of disaffected Jerusalem priests. Both the soldiers and the priests eventually found their way up the Nile to Elephantine. There, under Egyptian tutelage, they built a temple to YHWH. - Porten, Bezalel. "Did the Ark Stop at Elephantine?" Biblical Archaeology Review 21.3 (1995): 76–77.

One of the historical sources which Dr. Porten bases his opinion on is the Letter of Aristeas, which was written in the 1st century BCE, and which states that as many as 100,000 Jews relocated to Egypt in about 650 BCE. Later waves of these Jewish exiles to Egypt were partly documented by Jeremiah (43:5-6, 44:1-14) and Ezekiel (29:9-21). The beginnings of these Jewish communities were also predicted nearly a century in advance by Isaiah (19:17-20), who spoke of five cities in Egypt where Jews and Egyptians would worship YHWH, setting up their temples with a pillar and altar, and doing sacrifices dedicated to Him. One of these places where that happened is Elephantine island.

Pharaoh Psamtik I, who was king from 664 to 610 BCE, had just removed Ethiopian usurpers who had been ruling in Egypt. In the aftermath of that struggle, the Pharaoh needed help to guard his southern border to prevent these Ethiopians from returning. To accomplish this, he stationed a large Jewish garrison on Elephantine island (Letter of Aristeas, 1:12-13), which is also referenced by the Greek historian Herodotus. In order to stay there long term, the Jewish soldiers and their families needed, at a minimum, a priesthood and an altar-shrine.

After the Jews on that island had expanded their shrine into a full-fledged temple to YHWH, records from that temple revealed they worshipped Him and a goddess together as a power couple. This pagan syncretism on the part of Egyptian Jews appears to explain the angry biblical rebukes and frequent predictions of their destruction by Isaiah, Jeremiah and Ezekiel.

Jeremiah predicted that very few of them would survive to return to Jerusalem and history shows that this group of Judean worshippers in Egypt were either mostly killed or had scattered.

In 586 BCE, it was the kingdom of Judah's turn to go into exile in Babylon. During this same time, some Jews rebelled and went to Egypt after assassinating the Jewish governor Gedaliah, who reported to Nebuchadnezzar. Jeremiah was one such prophet forced to go to Egypt with these rebels, dying a short time later.

Unlike Israel, Judah kept herself ethnically intact to some degree and was able to return to her ancestral land after 70 years, in effect putting the Davidic line back in Jerusalem. But many remained in Babylon, which they now considered their home.

When, in 536 BCE, Cyrus of Persia allowed the Jews who were at Babylon to go back home, not all did so. Some went back to Jerusalem to help rebuild the city and Temple to be ready for when the 70-year penalty ended. Others went to Persia to join brethren who had been there since the last century or two. It would be these Jews in Susa that would be the central focus of the Book of Esther.

The Esther story unfolds through a series of events dated from 499-473 BCE. One of the enduring questions regarding this account has been why a tolerant king like Xerxes I (a.k.a. "Ahasuerus"), would agree to the genocide of the Jewish people. The short answer is that he suffered several humiliating defeats at the hands of the Greeks living in his provinces before the biblical story happens. Xerxes despised the Greeks for their rebellious attitude, and Haman who hates the Jews, takes advantage of this to motivate the king to crush what he feels is just another rebellious group within the kingdom (Esther 3:7-11).

So why did Haman want to kill all Jews when he was only "offended" by one of them, Mordechai? That is because, as it turns out, Haman is a descendant of Esau. We know this because Haman is called an "Agagite" (Esther 3:1), named after King Agag who is descended from Amalek, the grandson of Esau (Genesis 36:12).

In 1 Samuel 15:3, Saul is instructed to kill the Amalekites— every man, woman and infant. We can only deduce that between the birthright that Jacob "stole" from Esau and having his people persecuted by King Saul, Haman's family has been nursing a grudge against the descendants of Jacob for an exceedingly long time. When Mordechai then refuses to honor Haman, who is Mordechai's superior by order of the king (Esther 3:1-2), it is the last straw for Haman.

Fortunately for the rest of the world, though, the plot to kill all the Jews is foiled and the feast of Purim is instituted to remember their deliverance, on February 29th, 473 BCE. Haman's attempt to wipe out the Jews in all 127 provinces of the Persian Empire is the closest ancient parallel we have to Hitler and the Holocaust.

As you may have realized by now, the Jewish people along with their culture and traditions have spread to many places around the world: Spain, France and other places in Europe, Egypt and the Middle East, to name a few. India, which was the easternmost outpost of Persian territory, also received a great many Jews from this same period of time. Persia's acceptance of Jews also made it possible for them to reside in communities literally from Ethiopia to India (Esther 1:1).

Wherever they went, some probably intermarried with the locals and therefore the seed of Abraham, Isaac and Jacob was allowed to be multiplied "as the stars of heaven" (Exodus 32:13-14).

Half a millennia later it would be these same groups of Jews throughout the Persian Empire that would also provide fertile ground for the growth of Christianity, which had greater popularity east of Jerusalem than west of her. From these 127 countries of Persia and later Parthia, Jews and early Christians could and did migrate to the rest of the known world, including China, Japan, Korea and the rest of the Orient.

As a result, with few exceptions, there is no place on earth that did not receive a massive cultural injection of the shared biblical heritage of either Judaism or Christianity or both. In Africa, Islamic opinions of biblical history joined with that of their older Jewish and Christian cousins who continued spreading that legacy throughout that continent and beyond.

It should also be pointed out that the seventy nations mentioned in Genesis 10 are all represented with current peoples and nations on the earth today. No one is left out, so no matter where you live, God Almighty has a spiritual plan for your development. The question is, are you living a righteous life in obedience to Him, or a life according to man's laws?

To bring God's people back to Him, Yeshua tells his disciples in Matthew 15:24 that he was sent "to the *sheep* which went astray from the House of Israel." The theme of YHWH reaching all nations with His Word and Truth began with the prophet Jonah journeying to Nineveh in ancient Iraq.

However, there were also earlier hints about how righteous non-Hebrews, such as Malki-Tzedek who was with Abraham in Genesis 14 and Jethro, the father-in-law of Moses, were sent to these nations. Both men were called priests of the Most-High God and these and the sons of Aaron are called by the same word in Hebrew for "priest," *kohen*.

211

The prophet Job also seems to come out of this tradition of non-Hebrew righteous men. He is from Uz, a land that was named either after the son of Aram the son of Shem, or after a descendant of Esau (Genesis 10:22-23, 36:28; 1 Chronicles 1:17).

Meanwhile, over the next century and half, many more exiles return from Babylon under Ezra. Nehemiah also returns from Persia to Jerusalem, to finish the rebuilding effort for the Temple and surrounding city. Nehemiah's elevation to becoming the Judean governor reporting to the Persian Emperor Artaxerxes I (445 BCE) was a turning point in getting everything else done, 71 years after the Temple was first rebuilt in 516 BCE. The nation of Judah once more unites under Ezra and Nehemiah, restoring the priesthood and Temple service, and setting up a religious academic infrastructure that would eventually become the envy of the world.

After Nehemiah died in 409 BCE, a man named Bagoas assumes Nehemiah's position as the new Persian governor. His appointment is confirmed in the Egyptian records known as the Elephantine papyri.

In that same year, Jews in Egypt write a protest letter to that new governor because the native Egyptians, who are now also under Persian control, damaged their temple. Having favor from earlier Persian kings, the Jews asked for funds and assistance to rebuild and repair it. Bagoas wrote back and said they had his full support to do so and, with that permission secured, the Jewish Temple was saved, at least for a generation.

But around 360 BCE, the Jews of Elephantine lost their protection. Their temple was completely destroyed and the community scattered. It is likely some of them went to Ethiopia at the other end of the Nile. Other Jews migrated to other areas of Persia and from there into India, eventually becoming a thriving community that survives even today, but we are not sure exactly when this happened or how long the migration lasted.

Alexander the Great

Meanwhile, back in Jerusalem and Judah proper, the Jews settle into a relatively quiet and uneventful part of their history, the last few decades of Persian rule. Then, in 334 BCE, a young but brilliant Macedonian general named Alexander the Great conquered the Persian Empire and assumed lordship over the entire Middle East, including Judah.

Keep in mind that during every period of war, there is movement of people in and out of regions either voluntarily or by force. The politics of the time dictate this migration as well.

After a victory next door in Gaza two years later, Alexander took the opportunity to visit Jerusalem, where a man named Yaddua was high priest. At first Yaddua was terrified but he had a vision from YHWH to open the city and receive Alexander and his army as honored guests.

Similarly, Alexander also had a dream where he was told to be friendly with the Jews, so he granted them all their requests, both in Judah and in Babylon, which he had under his control. Alexander eventually became a great friend and benefactor to them, according to Josephus (Antiquities, 11:325-337).

During this time Alexander was told that his recent military successes were most likely a fulfillment of the vision of the Prophet Daniel, who predicted a great conqueror would overwhelm the Persians and the Medes. Alexander may have also been told that Scripture places his people as descended from Javan, son of Japheth, son of Noah.

Alexander the Great's campaigns from 336-325 BCE gave him power from Greece to northwest India and across Asia and northeast Africa as he sought to export his Greek culture wherever he went. In the centuries that followed, while much the area he conquered became Christian with the migration of Jewish and Gentile believers, many of his cultural values in the arts, education, philosophy and law became embedded in the Christian Roman Empires, both east and west.

But when Alexander the Great died in June of 323 BCE, fortunes began to decline for the Jews. A series of wars broke out amongst Alexander's associates and generals. When the dust settled the two most important leaders, Seleucus Nicator and Ptolemy I, took over the regions of Syria and Egypt, respectively.

From the Maccabees to Herod the Great

A descendant of Seleucus, Antiochus IV, would become the infamous Syrian Greek king who defiled the Temple and prevented worship there for two years, mainly by slaughtering a pig on the altar and putting pig's blood on the Temple walls. The Maccabees, Jewish aristocrats, eventually drove those pagans out and rededicated the Temple, resulting in the annual commemoration known as Hanukkah, in 165 BCE.

From the Maccabees would come the Hasmoneans, a series of kings who also served as high priests. The true sons of Aaron, pure priests known as the Zadokites, were booted from power to make room for these new kings, who were neither from Judah nor were they sons of Aaron. The fugitive Zadokites eventually fled into the wilderness of Qumran to join another dissident group known as the Essenes, helping them write the Dead Sea Scrolls.

A century later, in 63 BCE, the Roman general Pompey the Great conquered Judea for Rome and made it a tax paying province, cultivating an effective partnership with the Hasmonean kings and the Jewish High Council, or Sanhedrin. Pompey would later be replaced by Julius Caesar, who continued honing these same Jewish institutional relationships. Hence, Jews would have migrated to Greece and other European places under the control of Alexander, and to Rome and other provinces under the Romans, where they had favor and prospered.

However, what no one at the time knew was that the greatest enemy to the Hasmoneans would also turn out to be the same evil king who tried to kill Messiah as an infant in the Gospel of Matthew. But, to tell Herod the Great's story effectively, we need to go back to the beginnings of his people.

As Josephus tells us, Herod, like Haman before him, was a direct descendant of Esau. For many centuries his ancestors lived a semi-nomadic and pagan existence.

Then, after the rise of the Hasmoneans, a king and High Priest known as Hyrcanus I led forces against Herod's tribe, forcing them to become Jewish through circumcision. This established a Jewish "pedigree" in theory all the way down to Herod himself, but, in actuality, his family still retained their paganism and greatly resented Hyrcanus' interference. In fact, Herod's father, Antipater, was furious about his second-class status and responded to the perceived injustice by becoming skilled in using times of chaos and war to his advantage.

In 69 BCE, a civil war broke out between two rival Hasmonean princes: Hyrcanus II and Aristobulus II. Antipater was in the inner circle of both princes because his father was a trusted advisor to their father, a king named Alexander Janneus, who died some years before the war began. Hence both warring princes looked at Antipater as a trusted family friend, a judgment they would live to regret.

Antipater's master stroke was in convincing Hyrcanus II to seek help from the Romans. He agreed and they traveled directly to Rome. Once there, Antipater promptly ingratiated himself with the Roman elite on the pretext of helping his "friend" prevail in the dispute with his brother.

When the dust finally settled, Hyrcanus II was only allowed to be high priest and his brother and opponent, Aristobulus II, was murdered. Meanwhile Antipater was made the first governor of Judea by Julius Caesar and Hyrcanus had to report to him. The Hasmoneans realized too late that they had been tricked, so they resolved to stop Antipater. In the end another rival had one of Hyrcanus' wine tasters poison and kill Antipater in 43 BCE.

But what the Hasmoneans did not know was that Antipater's son was just as clever, ruthless and determined to rule as his father. Now vowing revenge for his father's murder, Herod is determined to take the Hasmonean throne for himself.

It took six years for Herod to plan and execute his vengeance. He married Mariamne, who is of both royal and priestly stock, to strengthen his claims of being Jewish. Herod himself may not have come from David, but she did, and so his sons would likewise inherit that lineage. He had a four-year long engagement with her beginning in 41 BCE, which was enough for him to achieve his immediate political goals.

He started by gaining favor with the famous Roman general Marc Antony, who had powerful allies in the Roman Senate. Together they made the case that Herod should be declared king of the Jews and the Senate agreed, conferring that title on him in 40 BCE. Three years later, Herod convinced Marc Antony to kill the last surviving Hasmonean king Antigonus. Now there was no one to threaten Herod's final ascension to power, which he would violently protect and defend for the next 34 years.

The Spread of the Good News

As Yeshua and the Apostles come on the scene in the next century, the Good News or Gospel is announced, bringing the promise of forgiveness of sins and eternal life to all who follow them. The miracles and later resurrection of Yeshua, having been so well attested to by so many witnesses, will literally inspire millions across the Middle East and Europe to come to faith as their movement sent seismic shockwaves of change throughout the Roman world. The Renewed Covenant's emphasis on Yeshua's Great Commission to his Apostles (Matthew 28:18-20, Mark 16:15-20) emphasized the universality of his great message.

During the time of Yeshua, politics in Rome and the pagan worship of Romans, was making life for believers in Messiah very unstable and dangerous. What is remarkable is that even amongst the Pharisees and later rabbis who did not believe in him, their "spin" on Gospel events was not that these miracles did not happen—they could not deny that basic fact—but that it occurred through evil means.

However, for Yeshua's opponents, like the High Priest Caiaphas, some in the Sanhedrin and some Jews who handed him over to the Romans for punishment, they had another problem that would soon overwhelm their entire world. After the death of

Emperor Tiberius in March of 37 CE, things took a turn for the worse when his nephew Caligula ascended to the imperial throne.

Caligula, in addition to his famous homicidal and depraved madness which terrified nearly everyone, hated believers in Yeshua. He knew that both they and their Jewish counterparts would never revere him as the god he proclaimed himself to be publicly. There is no doubt that he would have gone after all of them in a horrific fashion, as he did against everyone else who defied him, had his life not been cut short.

He almost destroyed the Jerusalem Temple by insisting on putting a statue of himself as Zeus in the Holy of Holies. Were it not for the intervention of the Jewish historian Philo through his letters and the delay because of one such letter received by Petronius the governor of Syria who was given the task to erect the statue, Jerusalem would have been in ruins in 40 CE. Fortunately, in this rare instance, Caligula eventually dropped this idea.

But, when the Praetorian Guard revolted and killed, not just Caligula but his wife and child, Claudius, who was Caligula's uncle, was compelled to accept the job. It was his very lack of ambition and thoughtful temperament, along with the fact that he never plotted against anyone, that made the military coup leaders think he would make a good ruler. They were right. Claudius brought stability and calm to the empire much in the same way that Augustus and Tiberius had done before him.

While Acts 18:2 says Claudius expelled Jews from Rome for a time, his policy to Jews and Christians in his empire was generally tolerant. Claudius was also a welcome change in Judea, which had suffered greatly under the tyrant Caligula for four years before he was assassinated.

Unfortunately, Claudius' death in 54 CE was followed by his very evil successor, Nero. It would be Nero, more than any other emperor in the First Century, who would be the greatest enemy to both Jews and Christians.

To give one famous example, Nero's very name adds up to 666 in Hebrew, and he is widely believed to be the inspiration for the number of the Beast in Revelation due to his propensity to murder believers in Yeshua through a wide variety of ghastly means. However, it would be the protests from his own people about his hedonistic excesses and greed that would eventually bring him down.

Early Persecution of Christians

In July of 64 CE, Nero accidentally sets fire to Rome by burning away structures on land where he wanted to erect his pleasure palace. This project was widely condemned by the Senate and the Roman people at large as being way too expensive and dedicated to Nero's exclusive benefit and glory. Nero was only trying to burn the structures on this property, but the winds shifted in the opposite direction and nearly three quarters of Rome was destroyed. Rumors spread that Nero fiddled his violin gleefully as he watched the city burn and nearly everyone in Rome despised him, and he knew it.

So, Nero decided he needed to revamp his image, and the only way he could do that was to shift blame for the fire away from himself and onto the believers of Yeshua, perhaps the only group the people despised more than him.

Nero blamed the great fire on the Messianics and Christians, rounding up their leaders and imprisoning them. One of these, Paul, would be beheaded two years later, in the year 66, virtually the same moment the Jewish Revolt against Rome in Jerusalem was breaking out. The Temple would get destroyed four years later.

Judaism would have died out, but for the Romans allowing a few rabbinic academies in the Galilee to exist. When a second rebellion broke out and was violently put down in 136 CE, the more than 1,800 year-long exile of the Jewish people from their land began and they scattered all over the earth. As before, many Jews were made slaves of Rome. Others fled eastwards to join family in the Parthian Empire in places like Babylon and old Persia, as far as India or perhaps to north African settlements like Carthage, which is modern-day Tunisia.

One of the best documented places that the Apostles went to was India, which Thomas visited in 52 CE. The Aramaic churches he founded in Kerala and Goa are still there, as are the spiritual descendants of that original generation. Today, that group is actually named St. Thomas, but were originally called "Nazarenes," the name given to Jewish followers of Messiah (Acts 24:5-14). Ancient records tell us both large communities of Christians and Jews thrived in Syria, Turkey and India.

Also, many Indians in Trinidad and South Africa today only know of Christianity as their faith walk. In fact, in the Spring of 2020 before Covid19 hit the world, we travelled to Durban, South Africa, a hub for Indian Christians, and shared the Word with many Church leaders and other Christians, witnessing miracles on the day the Hebrew Name of God (YHWH) and Yeshua were taught.

Anyway, while the Renewed Covenant is silent on the details regarding Paul's death stating only that he was ready for it (2 Timothy 4:7), Clement of Rome, writing in the 1st century, acknowledges that Paul died "under the prefects" which refers to the Emperor and his associates there. Additionally, all sources agree this was during the time of Nero.

As for Peter, Catholic tradition says he was martyred around this same time, or perhaps a year later, but there is no evidence from Scripture or history that the fisherman ever made it to Rome at all.

Over the next seven decades, Christianity becomes progressively more Gentile. Ironically, the Christians blamed the Jewish believers who led the way to Christianity, along with the majority of tolerant rabbinic Jews, for their hardships and persecution. By aligning these Jews with those against Yeshua, the Church packaged them as one, blaming the Jews for their troubles and rejecting the Word of God given to them.

The last Jewish bishop of Jerusalem was deposed at the end of the Bar Kochba Revolt (136 CE) and a Roman named Marcus took his place (Eusebius, Church History, Book 4, Chapter 5). Jerusalem becomes a backwater, with Catholic bishops who were there, now reporting to Caesarea, which in turn was answering to Rome.

Rome will continue to persecute Jews, Messianic Jewish believers of Yeshua and Christians for the next two centuries, until Constantine grants Christians protection beginning in 313 CE. By the end of that century, Christianity is made the official religion of the Roman Empire.

The Roman Empire, though, reached its zenith during the reign of Emperor Trajan in 117 CE. After that time, however, it underwent a slow and protracted decline. In the early 300's Emperor Diocletian tried to address the growing political divisions by dividing the Empire into eastern and western halves. Constantine, however had successfully reunited the Empire prior to his death in 337 CE, except for three short years where Julian the Apostate became emperor.

Julian, who ruled from 361-363 CE, attempted to turn Rome back to her pagan roots and was an active opponent of the growing Christian Church. He became the first in a growing series of powerful voices attributing the decline of the Empire to the rise of Christianity, but most historians today attribute the fall of Rome to a much more complex series of causes.

Ironically, he gave favor to the Jews, allowing them to start rebuilding their Temple in Jerusalem. In any case, when Julian died, all the emperors after him were dedicated to Christianity.

The beginning of the end for Rome came in 410, when the Visigoth leader Alaric sacked the city. As was previously discussed, this was in response to Rome refusing to aid Alaric's people with needed food and grant them citizenship. It is estimated that seven million people perished between 395 and 455 CE, which was the peak time for the chaos this long-standing dissolution brought. Christians in these lands reverted to a more primitive and largely agrarian existence. Out of these humble beginnings would eventually arise a golden age of Catholic influence across those lands that would last until the rise of Luther.

Meanwhile, back east, the Persians also had many Messianic and Christian believers in their midst. Ever loathing Rome, when Rome became Christian, the Persians began fiercely persecuting believers around 344 CE. Many Aramaic speaking believers fled Persian territory for the more tolerant Romans, including the famous poet St. Ephrem, who spent his remaining years in Edessa, Turkey.

In 476 CE, the western Roman Empire fell and plunged Europe into the chaos we call the Dark Ages, which lasted nearly a thousand years. During this rise of feudalism, the local landlords who ruled took as taxes food the peasants produced on their lands.

The growing power of monarchies in various European countries did not however supplant the power of these local lords.

In the wake of the fall of the west, Byzantine eastern emperor Justinian the Great (ruled 527-565) sought to revive the western Empire and annex it to his own. In these efforts he was only partially successful, but he did significantly extend the eastern Empire's overall reach. Also, like Constantine before him, Justinian tried to unify the Empire under his vision of Orthodox Christianity, vigorously persecuting various heretical groups that disagreed with him.

People who held to a different vision of either Trinity or the nature of Messiah other than what the Catholic Church endorsed were harshly treated, tortured and murdered in much the same way Diocletian did. The difference now however was that it was one group of Christians trying to wipe out another group of Christians. Between these persecutions and a vast array of natural disasters such as earthquakes and tsunamis that plagued his Empire, a half a million people were killed directly while millions of others suffered as well.

Christianity grew much stronger in these places while the Jews in their midst suffered greatly at the hands of their Christian masters. During times of turmoil, we can expect Christians and Jews, at least those who are able, to have left for greener pastures, bringing with them their inter-racial culture and beliefs in its many variations.

Is it also any wonder why Jews may have started to hide their ethnicity and the practice of their faith? If not for DNA testing, many with Jewish ancestry would still be unknown to us.

However, getting back to our story, a much greater danger to both groups was coming from Saudi Arabia, where the head of a brand-new religion named Islam was born in 570 CE.

The Rise of Islam

When he turned forty years old in 610 CE, Mohammed claimed he had seen a vision of the angel Gabriel. His disciples wrote about it and the vision eventually became the Koran, the founding scriptures of the Islamic faith. Islam itself split into two factions shortly after Mohammed's death, but this was due to a dispute over who should succeed him, not what they believed doctrinally.

The Shiites thought succession of leadership from Mohammed should go to Ali, his grandson, while the Sunni majority backed a special group of spiritual and military leaders called *caliphs*. Both groups however believed that Jews and Christians were heretics to Islam (generally) and sought remedies ranging from military conquest to taxation to attempted genocide to deal with them.

From the Muslim point of view, the biggest threat to their plans of global domination was the Byzantine Empire. Founded by the Emperor Constantine, the eastern half of his Roman Empire in Turkey, later known as the Byzantine Empire, flourished in the wake of Rome falling in the 5th century.

It was the Byzantines that held absolute control over the lands in the Middle East, which the Muslims were soon to conquer. Muslim armies spread to Africa, where they took over places like Egypt and Libya.

However, Islam was not oppressive everywhere. In 640 CE, Caliph Omar allowed a small group of Jewish families to resettle in Jerusalem and granted their request to live near where the Temple used to stand. Also, in the Egyptian desert, Muslim forces granted special privileges to the Greek Orthodox convent known as St. Catherine's, which was also the traditional site of Mount Sinai.

When Muslims took over Spain and ruled it for nearly 700 years, Jews in particular did very well under their rule. The famous rabbi Rambam (Maimonides) was the court physician to the Sultan in Spain. Jews all over the Middle East also began speaking and writing in Arabic, leaving for posterity some of their most important liturgical works in that language. They would continue to prosper there until 1492, when Roman Catholic rule was finally and completely re-established under King Ferdinand and Queen Isabella, who promptly then ordered all Jews to leave Spain or die.

As parts of northern Africa received Christianity as early as 43 CE, the faithful spread throughout the rest of that continent over the next thousand years. By the early 400's Ethiopia had converted to the faith joining long standing communities in Egypt, Libya and Carthage (Tunisia) to dominate the northern half of Africa. The final push to the rest of the continent was completed by the Roman Catholic Church at the end of the 18th century.

The Muslims, who were portrayed in Christian imagination as little more than barbarians, were not supposed to defeat the Catholics who said they marched in the army of God. And yet, even major Crusader victories in places like Jerusalem and Acre were eventually turned back and the Muslims remained in essentially the same position they were before the wars started.

For example, Pope Urban II launched the First Crusade, aligned with the Byzantine Emperor in the year 1095, to expel the Muslims from the land. Called literally a "war of the cross," it was ostensibly so Christian forces could take back sacred pilgrimage sites under Islamic control. The Catholic Church proclaimed these incursions as holy wars and often granted promises of eternal life

225

in heaven and forgiveness of sins through so-called "indulgences" for those who participated.

For a brief time—from 1099 to 1187—Jerusalem remained under the protection of Christian knights known as the Templars, only to be decimated at the Battle of Hattin by the Muslim general Saladin.

Centuries later, the Muslim dominated Ottoman Empire, had control over nearly the entire Middle East, including Israel. They were generally tolerant of the Jews in their midst, but also imposed restrictions on the size of their synagogues and required them to pay a small tax to avoid conversion to Islam.

The Ottomans, though, like Saladin and others before them, also coveted Christian lands. For more than a millennium, the 20-foot-thick walls of Constantinople resisted nearly all invaders. But in 1453 the Ottoman commander known as Mehmed the Conqueror changed all that. From that time on, Constantinople was given the name it bears today: Istanbul.

In a remarkable display of tolerance, the Ottomans struck a power sharing deal with the Byzantine Orthodox Church, granting them complete autonomy to operate their churches in exchange for their accepting Ottoman rule. The arrangement, which has proven beneficial to both sides, even continues up to the present with the modern state of Turkey. However, most of the rest of Christendom fled from Muslim rule there, relocating themselves back into Catholic territory in Europe.

Early Christianity in the East

Later generations of Aramaic Christians also made it to China and left their monuments behind to prove they were there, as you will see in the following pages.

You will recall that the Western Church also underwent a series of traumatic divisions throughout the Middle Ages over questions regarding the divinity of the Virgin Mary as "mother of God" and the nature of Messiah. These clashes came to a head in 451 CE, with the Council of Chalcedon, that split the Aramaic Orthodox east from the Roman Catholic west and her new formula which included direct worship of the Virgin Mary. A much more serious east-west split happened in 1054 CE and it has been that way ever since.

This can perhaps account for one aspect of ancient Christianity that is also often ignored when discussing the spread of the faith around the world: the advance of the Aramaic Church in the first three centuries of the faith. We have already looked at how it spread to India through the efforts of St. Thomas. The fact is that Aramaic Christians were in China between 600-700 CE, centuries before the Roman Catholics. The Hsian-Fu (Xian) monument shown on the next page is in both Chinese and Aramaic, testifying to these missionaries being able "to teach the Gospel to the kings of China."

Above: Hsian-Fu (Xian) Monument commemorating the arrival of Christianity in China in 635-781 A.D. Medium: black, sub-granular limestone. Approximate Date: 781 A.D. Place of Discovery: Hsian-Fu, Shanhsi Province, China. Current Location: Pei-lin, China. It shows Aramaic and Chinese next to each other. Full monument shown here. (Photos courtesy of David Castor). Partial close-ups are shown in the next page

Above: On top of the tablet, there is a cross (the arrow points to it). Below this headpiece (second photo) is a long Chinese inscription, consisting of around 1,900 Chinese characters, sometimes glossed in Syriac (several sentences amounting to about 50 Syriac words), calling God "Veritable Majesty," the text refers to Genesis, the cross, and baptism. (Wikipedia =Xi'an Slete)

The eastern Aramaic Christians and the others who visited them later, lost track of their Asian brethren for centuries because of the nature of their persecution in China. It has only been in the last twenty years that Aramaic speaking Chinese Christians have reconnected with their brethren in the Middle East.

It is also likely that the Chinese of today are derived from Noah's son Ham and the "Sinites" who are said to be a highly productive and civilized people from the Far East (Isaiah 49:12). As such, they too are part of the final redemptive processes that brings everyone back home to our Creator.

But one of the deadliest leaders from that part of the world who came later, Genghis Khan (ca. 1162-1227), was a grave threat to both Christians and Muslims in the lands he wanted to seize. The founder of the Mongol Empire first conquered vast tracts of land in his native Mongolia, which encompasses much of both China and Russia. He then proceeded into the heart of Muslim territory and conquered Merv (part of Iran), Samarkand and several cities in Afghanistan, most with horrifically high casualties. The Muslims people were dealt a devastating blow when they lost Baghdad to one of Genghis' descendants, the general Hulagu.

Christians had much to fear from the Mongols as Genghis and his successors also attacked lands in Russia (Georgia), Turkey (Armenia) and Bulgaria, each of which boasted exceptionally large Christian congregations. It is currently estimated that tens of millions of people were killed by Genghis alone, with millions more falling to Mongol conquest over the next few centuries.

On the other hand, the Mongol conquests also had some positive aspects, such as the unification of the Silk Road, which connected trading centers across Europe and Asia, along with the spread of Christianity throughout Mongol lands, though never to the extent of having a majority. Even so, it is through missionary outreach to the Mongol and Chinese world that the faith spread to the rest of Asia, including Korea, Vietnam and Indonesia.

Meanwhile, Christian Europe also was learning to stretch her might against millions in the Far East, such as with the British domination of India. There are many examples of excessive oppression that could be offered here which were extreme even given the standards of the time, but perhaps no greater example of the extent of British depravity in India is how their policies affected and contributed to the more than 26 million Indians who perished in various famines between 1769 and 1900.

Most historians agree that uneven rainfall was only part of the overall problem, while the bulk of it was due to bad economic and administrative policies, such as overly exporting Indian produce rather than getting it to the natives who needed it first. The British cared less about feeding their colonial subjects and more about lining their pockets from sales of opium, rice and wheat. Millions of acres of arable Indian land were squandered for exportation crops rather than helping the local population which, even in the best of times, often teetered on mass starvation. What the famines did not take out, massive outbreaks of bubonic plague and influenza decimated. So, while Christianity continued to grow in India, there were obvious tradeoffs.

Christians against Christians

Another aspect of Christianity that often gets overlooked is that the Crusades were just as often about Christians fighting Christians. Constantinople, the home of Byzantine Catholics, was viciously attacked and looted by the Roman Catholic forces in 1198. Ironically, they were allies just a hundred years prior in

1095, when together they "liberated" the Holy Land. Then, from 1209-1229 there was a 20-year war against a Christian sect known as the Cathars, which many modern historians have referred to as a genocidal campaign.

In other cases, such as the Crusades at Drenthe (1228-1232), Stedinger (1233-1234) and Bosnia (1235-1241), entire major cities of controversial Christian sects were nearly completely wiped out. From 1209 to 1285, no less than five separate Crusades consisted entirely of Christian-on-Christian violence, and these attacks continued sporadically for another century and a half, only ceasing in 1485.

If the world does not look on *Crusades* held by churches as favorably as you would expect, perhaps now you know the negative connotation behind the word.

Catholic historians have sometimes suggested that the extent of some of these groups' heretical views justified the violence against them, but this becomes harder to sustain in the modern age when many criticize some quarters of Islam for doing the same thing, waging war against others solely based on religious differences.

In any case, it is estimated that three million people perished in all these conflicts by the time the Crusades ended in the 17th century, by which time the last victims consisted of those embracing the new Protestant faith. Those last Crusades, in places like Savoy (France) and Bohemia (the Czech Republic), demonstrated the desperation of the Catholic Church against a Protestant movement that now struck at their very cultural heart.

Long Standing Controversies in the Western Church

Indeed, by 1517, the Roman Catholic Church itself seemed to be doomed with the rise of Martin Luther and Protestantism. The seeds of what we now call the Protestant Reformation were planted a century and a half before Luther.

In 1382, John Wycliffe published the first English Bible, translated entirely from the Latin Vulgate, the official Bible of the Catholic Church. Wycliffe was widely condemned by Catholic authorities as a heretic, and even forty-one years after he died from a stroke, the Church exhumed his remains, tried and found him guilty of heresy, and burned his bones.

Even so, Wycliffe was a trailblazer in more than one important way. Both he and the spiritual movement he headed known as the Lollards, anticipated the major complaints of the later Protestant Reformation to an astonishing degree.

But what Luther did better than any before him was crystallize the excesses of the Catholic Church into an easy to understand format. Called the "95 Theses," he nailed a list containing 95 criticisms of the Catholic Church to the door of the Bishop of All Saints Church in Wittenberg Germany. Luther also benefitted from having access to the movable type printing press, which had been invented by Gutenberg near Luther's hometown. The massive copies of Luther's pamphlets did much to sway, at first, the lay people and then the crown heads of Europe, to his cause.

In Britain however, their Reformation began when King Henry VIII broke from the Pope who refused to annul his first marriage to Katherine of Aragon so he could legally marry Ann Boleyn. He forced bishops to sign a loyalty oath directly to his throne if they wanted his support, or face isolation and persecution by remaining

Catholic. The dispute was felt even amongst his own children, as Mary Queen of Scots remained Catholic while Elizabeth I cemented Britain as a Protestant nation.

The English Reformation also had profound impacts on both the people and the Word. Good people and families were divided over the matter. Henry VIII's most trusted advisor, Sir Thomas More, languished and died in prison rather than convert to the new Anglican faith, a hybrid of Protestantism and loyalty to the British monarchy. Not only did this create upheavals at home, but Britain's Protestantism also provoked Catholic nations to try and take her over. The Spanish sent a massive armada in 1588 to overthrow Elizabeth I and put her Catholic sister Mary on the throne. But, when the invasion failed, it strengthened the Protestant elements to keep England in that faith. In another two centuries though Catholics and Protestants would eventually learn to live peacefully with each other.

As for the Word, Henry VIII did want a Bible of his own for England that did not require papal sanction. In a very ironic twist, he had the famous Bible translator William Tyndale convicted and burned at the stake as a heretic in 1536, only to unknowingly publish Tyndale's work as his own "authorized" Scripture a year later.

This was because one of Henry VIII's advisors re-packaged Tyndale's translation as coming from "Thomas Matthews," and the king apparently loved it when he finally had a chance to read it. It would seem then that Tyndale's last wish before he burned to death came to pass: "May the King of England open his eyes!"

The legacy of Henry VIII and Tyndale would be the King James Bible. When King James I gathered together 54 scholars to do this great work in 1604, what they came up with when they finished in 1611 was 83% Tyndale's work.

However, the King James Bible as we know it today is not the same as the original. The Bible that King James "authorized" had tons of printing errors, including the famous, "thou shalt commit adultery" and many others just as serious. The original printers were heavily fined and the form of KJV that we have today came from 1769. It took more than a century and half to get the errors out, by which time King James was not in a position to authorize anything.

All modern Bibles today, Jewish and Christian, owe a huge debt to what those translators did in the early 17th century. Unfortunately, with the new revision, the last remaining acknowledgment of our Creator's Name was removed, which you saw in the 1611 photos we included. Unfortunately, as Christianity grew, the knowledge of His Name diminished.

The Stone of Destiny

One last modern example which showcases how the Bible inspires international politics and culture has to do with something called the *Stone of Destiny*. According to medieval folklore, the very stone that the patriarch Jacob is said to have slept on and turned into an anointed altar (Genesis 28:18) was brought to Scotland, some say, by Joseph of Arimathea.

It would be on that same stone that King Arthur was purportedly crowned. From that time forward, kings of Scotland would covet having that stone once used by Jacob as the proof of their authority, that is, until the King Edward I of England took it for his throne in 1296. This heinous act inspired centuries of conflict and tension between Scotland and England, leading up to the battles of William Wallace (Braveheart) and Robert the Bruce against Britain. The

Scots only ended their separatist movement after a tremendous loss of life.

The stone remained in England until it was stolen and brought back to Scotland in 1951. However, during the theft, it broke into two pieces, so it was repaired and sent back to London four months later. Along with other reasons, as the British continued to hold on to it, the Stone of Destiny added to the long simmering conflict between the two nations.

There is also a parallel history of the Irish struggling under British rule that plays into this overall story. Although firmly a part of the United Kingdom, the Scots, as well as the Irish who were Catholics, struggled for autonomy from the British who were Protestant. For the Scots, their cultural distinctiveness was recognized, but they did not have their own Parliament and they yearned for greater freedom. For the Irish, perceived discrimination in Northern Ireland kicked off a three-decades long insurrection. Thousands died in what is now broadly called "The Troubles."

And yet, the path for both groups to reconcile with Britain seems to have come through the Stone of Destiny. Queen Elizabeth II returned the stone back to Scotland in 1996 as a gesture of goodwill. The next year, 1997, Scottish Parliament was reinstated after a centuries-long absence, sending a clear message that the Queen was willing to seriously negotiate with her UK "partners." This also appears to have inspired the Irish to end their insurrection with the Good Friday Accords in 1998. Remarkably, even until now there are still modern political factors to consider with this rock that legend connects to the patriarch Jacob.

Elizabeth II was the last British monarch to be crowned with the stone under her throne and so she offered the gentle suggestion to the Scots that they may need to borrow it back when her successor replaces her in the future. The point is, even if that stone was not used by Jacob, it can certainly be said to have witnessed very biblical struggles and themes playing out in its midst for many centuries.

Scattering to the Americas and Beyond

At this point, there is one important and massive population that we have thus far left out of our discussion: the Americas. After Spain was liberated from seven centuries of Muslim rule in 1492, newly re-established monarchs such as King Ferdinand and Queen Isabella turned their attention to exploration. One of their most important explorers, Christopher Columbus, was looking for the so-called "northwest passage"—an alleged shortcut that sailors could take to China and India without having to go overland for thousands of miles.

Through the funding provided for these voyages by the king and queen, Christopher Columbus set sail for this northwest passage to India in 1492, when he stumbled upon the two continents of North and South America instead. Thinking he had arrived in India he called the First Nations people *Indians,* and that name has stuck with them until today.

Anyway, what is perhaps not well known outside the USA is that almost all of these explorations to the Americas by first the Spanish, then the Portuguese, Dutch, French and English respectively were disastrous, as they also sought territorial expansion at the expense of the indigenous people already there. A combination of constant warfare and European diseases killed tens of millions of the native populations of this "New World" they took over. Some were looking for the Fountain of Youth while others sought Eldorado, the mythical lost city of gold.

Almost all of these European explorers were seeking to spread modern Christianity, forcing conversions and murdering millions of Native Americans, Aztecs, Incas, Maya and so many others. Eventually both Protestant and Catholic forms of Christianity became prominent among the native populations, while millions from the rest of Christian Europe made their homes in what eventually becomes Canada, the United States, Mexico and Central and South America.

Also, as Britain further expanded their military and economic conquests, Christianity would be brought as far south as Australia, along with a lot of damage to the native peoples there. The former penal colony would then rise to become one of the most powerful countries in that part of the world.

Much of the dark legacy of European Colonialism, including the ideas of "taking the cross to the savages," "manifest destiny" and "white man's burden," continues to haunt the civilized world even today and will likely continue to do so for centuries in our future. Christianity too went from being persecuted to being the persecutors.

New or Renewed Covenant?

"Behold, days are coming," declares the LORD, "when I will make a new covenant with the house of Israel and with the house of Judah, <u>not like</u> the covenant which I made with their fathers in the day I took them by the hand to bring them out of the land of Egypt, My covenant which they broke, although I was a husband to them," declares the LORD.

"But this is the covenant which I will make with the house of Israel after those days," declares the LORD, "I will put My law within them and on their heart I will write it; and I will be their God, and they shall be My people. "They will not teach again, each man his neighbor and each man his brother, saying, 'Know the LORD,' for they will all know Me, from the least of them to the greatest of them," declares the LORD, "for I will forgive their iniquity, and their sin I will remember no more." (Jeremiah 31:31-34 NAU)

One of the more challenging concepts that gets debated between Messianic believers and Christians is exactly what did Jeremiah mean? The Hebrew word *chadash* can refer to either a "new" covenant or a "renewed" covenant.

Jeremiah, when read carefully, clearly reveals that the Exodus was a physical deliverance from bondage that was done, not for the sake of the Israelites, but to keep faith with the promises made to Abraham, Isaac and Jacob (Genesis 50:24, Exodus 2:24). The emancipated Hebrews, along with a mixed racial multitude that also came out with them (Exodus 12:40), were meant to go to Mount Sinai, receive the Ten Commandments and the rest of the Divine Instructions, and then take their inheritance in Canaan to be a witness to the nations (Deuteronomy 4:6).

As a result, the physical redemption was meant to be followed by a spiritual one, but that aspect failed because, as God said in the book of Jeremiah, *My covenant they broke, though I was a husband to them.* Therefore, a new way had to be found for the Almighty to reconcile with "the House of Israel."

That new way was the spiritual deliverance which would take root and flourish as it was always intended to do. The idea is simple, beautiful and profound: God will make His ways so well known to His people that it will literally be permanently memorialized on their hearts, first to the Jews and then to Gentile believers. They will look inside their hearts and find His instructions right there, so they can delight Him with obedience. Knowing that the Temple was going to be destroyed and atonement through sacrifices would no longer be possible, He sends His Only Begotten Son, Yeshua (meaning YAH saves) to show His "lost sheep" the Way.

Some Christians though believe the old covenant is no longer applicable to their faith walk, that it has been done away with, because of these lines in Hebrews and others similar to them:

But now He has obtained a more excellent ministry, by as much as He is also the mediator of a better covenant, which has been enacted on better promises. For if that first covenant had been faultless, there would have been no occasion sought for a second. (Hebrews 8:6-7 NAU)

When He said, "A new covenant," He has made the first obsolete. But whatever is becoming obsolete and growing old is ready to disappear (Hebrews 8:13 NAU)

However, what's going on here is actually a case of *conflation*, or where genuine concepts get wrongly and excessively expanded to include unintentional things. Paul's original point about covenant began at the start of chapter 7, where he began talking about high priests and the priesthood in general. He begins with the high priest Malki-Tzedek who held that office in Genesis centuries before the birth of Aaron. Then Aaron's family takes over the priesthood for many centuries until Yeshua comes in the likeness of Malki-Tzedek. What Paul is trying to teach the new believers is that even though Messiah is from Judah, and not a Levite like Aaron, he is also the new high priest of the new covenant.

When Paul is writing the Epistle to the Hebrews, the Temple is about six years away from being completely destroyed by the Romans. When that happened in 70 CE, the priesthood of Aaron was cut off so, as Paul rightly says, *where there is a change in the priesthood there is also a change in the law* (Hebrews 7:12).

The fact is, when the priesthood of Genesis (Malki-Tzedek) changed to the priesthood of Exodus (Aaron), certain rules about how sacrifices were previously done had to be radically altered. In the same way, when the high priesthood of Aaron, now without a Temple, gave way to the high priesthood of Yeshua, many things changed again, but the need for a priestly mediator between God and man remained.

What Yeshua then brought to the office of the high priesthood was, in fact, that both he and the sacrifice he made were eternal and never needed to be repeated. His sacrifice was also more effective than all the previous ones done in the Hebrew Bible combined, giving us complete forgiveness in a way that had not been possible before.

But since humans are prone to sin, repentance and getting back to righteousness was necessary. It is never rituals, Jewish or Christian, which sanctifies us. It is Master YHWH, our Creator, our Heavenly Father, who sanctifies us.

Therefore, what became obsolete was the old way of flawed *human* priests who offered largely ineffective sacrifices. That aspect and not the Covenant at Sinai, is what passed away.

At the same time, through Jeremiah, God informs us that knowledge of Him will increase among His people, *"for they will all know Me, from the least to the greatest of them."* This in turn leads to Yeshua teaching the world his Father's Law (Torah) through his words and his actions, so we may all finally get to the reward of His Father, *"I will forgive their iniquity, and their sin I will remember no more."*

A spirit glided past my face, and the hair on my body stood on end.

It stopped, but I could not tell what it was. A form stood before my eyes, and I heard a hushed voice:

'Can a mortal be more righteous than God? Can even a strong man be more pure than his Maker?

If God places no trust in his servants, if he charges his angels with error, how much more those who live in houses of clay, whose foundations are in the dust, who are crushed more readily than a moth!

Between dawn and dusk they are broken to pieces; unnoticed, they perish forever.

Are not the cords of their tent pulled up, so that they die without wisdom?'

(Job 4:15-21 NIV)

SECTION SIX

On Pandemics, Disruptions and Prophecy

All the ends of the earth will remember and turn to YHWH, and all the families of the nations will worship before You. For the kingdom is YHWH's and He rules over the nations.
(Psalm 22:27-28)

Since the focus of this book has been to show how obedience or disobedience to Divine Law affects where we are in God Almighty as a people, believers around the world understandably wonder how a once in a century pandemic like Covid-19 (Corona virus) should be viewed in connection with their faith. Is this one of the "birth pangs" that Matthew 24 warned us about, leading to Tribulation or Armageddon, or is it simply a natural, long-term consequence of living on this planet? Are some or all of us in a time of judgment, and, if so, what can we do about it?

As a first step, while the term *corona* means "crown" in Latin, we do not want to give this virus any sovereignty that belongs only to our Creator, Master YHWH, our Righteous King. Therefore, when we focus on the Almighty and His Only-begotten Son, Yeshua, we can trust that we will receive "a crown of life that God has promised to those who love him" (James 1:12) and "a crown of glory which never fades" (1 Peter 5:4).

Therefore, by all means, let us take sensible precautions against this virus, but never bow down to it in fear and hopelessness, because the True King is in control! His Crown, as well as the crowns He graciously gives to us, must supersede any crown of fear as represented by Covid-19.

And yet, the question remains: How can we view these challenging times through the lens of the massive plagues that beset the people of God throughout the Bible? Could we endure, as Moses did, losing 24,000 people to a plague in a single day (Numbers 25:1-9)?

One way to answer this question is to analyze the cycles of time in the Scripture, which reveals a kind of "sacred" math that tells a very important and special story from Genesis to Revelation. Most of us easily understand, for example, that the number seven is sacred and represents perfection, rest and peace. Similarly, the frequent use of the number forty is associated with cycles of restoration, generations, and judgment.

We see, for example, in Numbers 14:28-34, that the sons of Israel would be forced to wander in the wilderness for 40 years because they did not trust the word of their God that the land they were going to was good. This was also why, in Numbers 32:13, we are told that the 40-year punishment for Israel was chosen so that *the entire generation who had done evil was consumed.*

The other generational cycle in Scripture is that of a hundred years (e.g. Genesis 15:13-16) and within that number exists a longer framework consisting of four hundred years. Biblical time is partially reckoned in periods of 40-year generations and 400-

year long eras. However, when we multiply 40 and 100, we come to the precise length of a biblical age: 4,000 years.

I say "precise length" because, once the Scripture clearly pointed to a certain year for Adam's creation (3901 BCE), it became clear that exactly 4,000 years had passed from the creation of the first man to the death of the last Apostle, John, on the island of Patmos in 100 CE. Therefore, every moment in the Scripture, from first in Genesis to the last in Revelation, takes place within a single age. However, the math and data that shows exactly the start and end dates associated with counting the generations is a long story best told another time.

The point is that the original biblical calendar counted time, from the autumn of Adam's creation year, in increments of 40, 400 and 4,000 years. These can be tracked to a mathematical certainty so let us start with the 40-year cycle.

It is most significant that the Covid-19 virus literally emerged in the late fall because, in the fall of 2019, a generational shift occurred. An important principle to understand is that it is often the case that the sins of a previous generation must be paid off or dealt with in the opening years of the new generation. With that in mind, in September 2019 at a Sukkot or Feast of Tabernacles gathering, I taught on the generational shift that was taking place at that time and why that Sukkot was special, having no idea what was soon to happen in a matter of months. Not only the United States, but the world, was about to be plunged into a pandemic that would affect our health, economy, personal well-being, and freedom.

Now, let us go back 40 years from the generational shift of 2019 to the fall of 1979, and you will find that similar patterns were occurring. In the United States, we were dealing with double digit prime interest rates and alarming increases in inflation, tariffs and terrible gas shortages, all culminating with dozens of Americans being taken hostage in Iran by that November. During this time, there was a global economic downturn happening as well.

In fact, seemingly intractable problems continued to vex us until there was a change in leadership and the inauguration of President Ronald Reagan a year later, when he promised a return to solid biblical values. It is worth noting that, as Reagan took his presidential oath of office, the Iranian hostages were put on a plane and sent home.

The message was clear: The permissiveness and extreme liberality of the 1960's and 1970's was over, replaced by growing prosperity in the 1980's and the end of the Cold War in the early 1990's. However, when we started turning away from our Creator and His Law, the result was the growing threat of Islamic extremist terror in 1998 and 1999, the bombing of the USS Cole in October 2000 and the catastrophic September 11, 2001 attacks on New York City and Washington DC, among other places.

Forty years prior to 1979, another generational shift occurred when Hitler invaded Poland in September 1939. He met little resistance there and his campaign ushered in World War II and the Holocaust. Remarkably, though, prior to the 2001 September 11th attacks, many American historians observed that the last great transformative wake-up call was when the Japanese attacked Pearl Harbor in 1941, which was a horrific period to be sure, with more than 420,000 Americans alone losing their lives in a conflict that claimed more than seventy million deaths worldwide.

If we go back another 40 years to the fall of 1899, a similar pattern occurs at the time of that generational shift. Beginning in 1893, the United States, along with most of the western world, suffered a devastating economic depression. The issue driving the financial collapse was whether nations should only be on a gold standard or should augment their economy with a less valuable metal-based currency, such as silver. The debate fractured American and European politics, creating both social and economic instability.

Then, just as the "Panic of 1893" began to moderate slightly, a separate economic crisis hit in 1896. The "bi-metalists"—those who believed we should back our currency with both gold and silver—wanted a massive release of silver reserves to supposedly take the strain off the gold supply. But, when they eventually got that large release of silver, all investors did was redeem it for gold, which created an even worse shortage, as the overall value of the dollar degraded by 25%. Economic conditions also worsened with the United States going to war with Spain in 1898 over the mistaken belief that the Spanish deployed a mine to blow up an American ship called the Maine, docked in Havana harbor, in Cuba.

By that time, William McKinley was president, so he began efforts to deal with both crises. He negotiated an end to the Spanish American War months before the generational shift of 1899, and, by the following year in 1900, he returned the country back to the gold standard, which ended the financial crisis begun in 1893. However, in what would become a stark harbinger regarding this new generation, McKinley would die from an assassin's bullet in September of 1901.

This tragedy was next followed by the horrors of World War I, from 1914-1918. That terrible war, which killed more than 20 million people, was, in turn, followed by a vicious plague known as the Spanish Flu, which killed 100 million people and only ended in 1921. Furthermore, these events, happening in the precise middle of the generation, the 20th year, were indicative of a form of correction mentioned in the Scripture. When the spies Moses sent into Canaan came back with a false report about the land, God judged them saying:

Your corpses will drop in the wilderness, even all of your counted men, according to your complete tally from twenty years old and upwards, who have grumbled against Me (Numbers 14:29).

In 1859, another generational shift occurred when a fierce abolitionist named John Brown attempted to free slaves and begin a war to keep them free in Harper's Ferry, West Virginia. Though his rebellion only lasted three days, from October 16th to 18th, 1859, that sentiment put the North on fire for the abolitionist cause.

The anti-slavery fervor lit by John Brown's small rebellion paved the way for the anti-slavery candidate, Abraham Lincoln, to be elected president in 1860, and, before that year was out, the first states would begin seceding from the Union. The Civil War would then begin in earnest the next spring, in April of 1861. By the time it was over, President Abraham Lincoln was assassinated and 600,000 men on both sides perished in four years of bloody fighting. Then, as that generation progressed, another American president, James Garfield, would also die by assassination in 1881.

Finally, on this topic of slavery, the roots of the judgment for the Civil War generation were, in fact, laid at the start of the previous one. In April of 1820, only six months after the generational shift in the fall of 1819, President Thomas Jefferson predicted the bloody consequences of allowing slavery to continue in the United States. In a letter to his friend John Holmes, Jefferson famously compared slavery to a wild wolf, saying: "We hold the wolf by the ear, and we can neither hold him nor safely let him go."

Jefferson's prediction was remarkable when we consider that, even when the war began, most "experts" thought it would be short and painless. In fact, even as the war broke out in the spring of

1861, one congressman famously predicted he would be able to wipe up all the blood required from that conflict with a pocket handkerchief.

As already mentioned, the 40-year cycle of judgment is not the only interval of time that Scripture gives us. There have also been seismic hardships that began in connection with the start of a given 400-year period or era. For example, the fall of 499 CE began with extreme chaos associated with the dissolution of the western Roman Empire, which is widely believed to have led directly or indirectly to the death of millions. In that same year, a Persian King named Kavadh survived a coup and regained his throne, setting the stage for the prosecution of a four year-long war between him and the remnants of the Roman Empire in the year 502.

Fast forward another 400 years and, in the fall of 899 CE, the British King Alfred the Great dies, leading to great instability and war in Europe and sowing the seeds for the end of the Saxons in that country.

Next, the era shift in 1299 CE witnessed the height of the Scottish rebellions led by William Wallace, nicknamed "Braveheart," against King Edward I of England. The Roman Catholic Church also endured one of the greatest threats to its power, when a rival papacy arose in Avignon France, when the first pope to defect there was elected in 1305. Moreover, the early 1300's is also the time known as the "Little Ice Age," which began in Europe, adversely affecting crops and transforming the society of western Europe for the next five centuries.

Of course, all this analysis inevitably brings us to the start of our most recent 400-year period in the fall of 1699 CE. By the early part of the year 1700, a decades long conflict known as the *Great Northern War* erupted between Russia, Sweden, and other parts of Northern Europe. Its scope and brutality, with more than 500,000 directly killed in the conflict by 1721, was truly unprecedented for the times.

The point of all this history is not to emphasize doom and gloom. Rather, it is simply the observation that the worst of times in our civilization often bring about righteous revivals, reformations, and other key movements in the development of our Biblical faith. Society itself can also permanently change for the better in the wake of these mass disruptions.

Without the Civil War, for example, Abraham Lincoln almost certainly would not have been motivated to issue the Emancipation Proclamation which freed slaves in the states which were rebelling against the Union government. Later, that proclamation would be extended to the official ending of slavery with the 13th and 14th amendments to the Constitution.

In addition, without World War 2 and the Holocaust, the modern state of Israel might even now not be established, continuing the exile for the Jewish people that began in the 2nd century. Also, the "vengeance rockets" developed by the Nazis to terrify Europe later became the basis for the Saturn V rocket that took three American astronauts to the moon in 1969.

In other words, if you show me a war, I will show you improvements in technology that make all our lives better. Show me a terror attack, and I will show you national unity and healing in its aftermath. Show me a horrific disaster like a Katrina or massive earthquake, and I will show you how the best of us come together to love our neighbors and renew our land.

Therefore, while there may be judgment and fear all around us now, this is also the time when the promises of Psalm 91 become the most relevant for those who believe the Scripture. After all, the very advent, crucifixion and resurrection of our Lord and Savior

Yeshua the Messiah also happened during a generation of extreme hardship and persecution.

However, what really stands out for our current moment of crisis is that, while secular and religious leaders hoped Easter in 2020 could have been a great time for the United States to reopen its economy, the reality is that the lessons of Passover were far more relevant and prescient. Just as occurred at the first Passover, people stayed inside so the plague of death could literally pass over them and they would be safe and alive. This makes perfect sense when we consider that, without Passover, when Yeshua chose to make his ultimate sacrifice, we do not even get to the resurrection.

That being said, let us first look at some positive aspects stemming from this crisis. For example, as a consequence of all the "shelter in place" restrictions, families across the globe have been given the precious opportunity to spend time with each other in their homes without outside distractions, leading to a greater understanding of what is truly important. Also, the absence of our population from the public square has caused the most polluted cities on the planet, from Los Angeles to New Delhi to Beijing, to have cleaner air and water than they have had in decades, to which the new pictures of smog-free skies clearly attest. We now know that we can clean up our air, in a truly short period of time, if we have the will to do so, especially for those whose health is negatively impacted by pollution.

Moreover, as we applaud our first responders, doctors and nurses, police, and other essential workers, we have learned to appreciate their shared sacrifice and realized, more than ever, that life is precious and worth saving. For example, if God did not have a heart for Nineveh and the righteousness her citizens could and did exhibit, He would not have sent Jonah to them in the first place. In any case, the verdict of Scripture is clear: Ninevite lives matter (Jonah 4:10-11).

Perhaps, then, the most important "news" of all is a renewed appreciation for God Almighty, as we thank Him for preserving us, for keeping us alive and allowing us to reach this true season of hope.

In short, our faith, our families, and even our planet, have been given a fresh start. Out of the death and tragedy of this virus also comes renewal. We may mourn today, but we will surely rebuild tomorrow and come back stronger than we were before.

On the other hand, before we can even begin to move forwards into that future, it is also important to assess the high cost of our new enlightenment, which was paid for in the currency of human hardship, suffering and confusion stemming from our livelihoods and civil liberties being affected. We witnessed a cataclysmic crisis in our national psyche, where many facets of our shared cultural narrative, along with the common institutions that held us all together, became strained and frayed to a greater degree than any time since the Civil War. By contrast, our coming together as a nation after the September 11th attacks seem like halcyon laden nostalgia compared to how we regard some of our fellow citizens right now.

The extent of the division arising from questioning what is true and what is not is a direct and existential threat to our American ideals and the democratic norms across the world of how a free society should operate and agree to disagree. In other words, we cannot claim to be one nation under God and then ignore His own Scripture principles about loving our neighbor as ourselves and knowing how to exchange viewpoints with our brothers and sisters in a caring and compassionate manner.

And, as if all that were not troubling enough, we have seen unprecedented economic crises and deep, seemingly intractable opinions on how our government can balance our need to have an open economy with how to keep us all safe and healthy so as not to infect others with a deadly disease. But the bottom line, at least as far as Scripture is concerned, is that shared national sacrifice for the greater good and sincere collective repentance with a return to civility and respect for all brings long term blessings for the society at large.

For example, the Book of Judges is highly effective in dealing with political and theological controversies causing division amongst the nation of Israel, not so unlike our own situation. The Israelites went through much hardship. When they are not being oppressed by pagan kings of Midian or Philistines, their own divided loyalties between Father YAH and rival pagan cults are constantly tempting them to create crises, culminating with a civil war between the tribe of Benjamin and the remainder of Israel.

Other times brave leaders like Gideon are righteous for a season and answer the call to save Israel, only to lapse into paganism when victory brings them wealth and prosperity causing Israel to go into a period of apostasy. Still other times there were multiple judges ruling in different sections of the country at the same time, some better than others, but no common vision or purpose binding them together. While hesitant and sinful leaders like Samson can unite the country for a time, they ultimately cannot hold on to it for long and must sacrifice themselves for the good of the people.

The bottom line is that Judges shows that even when there is a righteous cause and a mandate from our Heavenly Father to act on it, other forces of division or competing self-interests can pull that fabric apart. The end result was, with no king in Israel, everyone did what was right in their own eyes.

So, while Paul in Romans 13:1-8 generally encourages believers to obey civilian authorities wherever possible, he also invokes doing so through the prism of keeping the

Commandments, regardless as to how the Romans felt about it (Romans 13:9-14). Such a concept is further amplified in 1 Peter 2:13-25, where we are told that even unjust rulers can be made better by seeing believers stand up for their faith in righteousness, with the burden on the believers to be both respectful to these leaders and faithful to the laws of the Messiah. However, if in spite of our best-efforts hardships still come, then 1 Peter 2:20 tells us: *When you do what is right and suffer patiently because of it, you will find favor with God.*

Messiah Yeshua also revealed this concept when he said, "Render unto Caesar the things that are Caesar's and unto God the things that are God's" (Matthew 22:17-22). This means that the Romans had certain rights, in this case to demand tax payments, but that God also required certain things from His people that could not be forbidden under Roman law. The Romans themselves well understood this, which is why they shared power with the Pharisees, Sadducees, and the Sanhedrin to balance religious sensibilities into a paradigm of Roman civil law.

However, when in other places the Romans persecuted both Jewish and Gentile believers in Messiah for not sacrificing to their Emperor, this brought them into violation with the Almighty, and it would then fall to Him to decide where, how and through whom He would administer judgment and deliverance for His people.

Finally, the lessons we are learning regarding how to live in these times are the same as those learned by our spiritual ancestors who bore up against hardships far worse than what we are now going through. Then and now, what really matters is understanding that our opponents are rarely all bad, but if we do not listen to their concerns we will be divided and without any remedy. Instead, it turns out that the arrival of such challenging times is not what is important, but rather how we face up to these challenges. With that goal in mind, let us consider what King Solomon said:

To everything there is a season, and a time to every purpose under the heaven: A time to be born, and a time to die. A time to plant, and a time to pluck up that which is planted. A time to kill, and a time to heal.

A time to break down, and a time to build up. A time to weep, and a time to laugh. A time to mourn, and a time to dance. A time to cast away stones, and a time to gather stones together. A time to embrace, and a time to refrain from embracing.

A time to get, and a time to lose. A time to keep, and a time to cast away. A time to rend, and a time to sew. A time to keep silent, and a time to speak. A time to love, and a time to hate. A time of war, and a time of peace. (Ecclesiastes 3:1-8 -KJV)

Perhaps the "new normal" that everyone is searching for is a return to God, a deeper love and commitment to our families and communities and a new global revelation for how to protect our environment and livelihoods in balanced partnership.

Have faith. We will continue to endure, for no weapon formed against us will prosper in the end (Isaiah 54:17).

Freedom is an Absolute Value

We began our time together talking about how the truth was stolen from us when we were *kidnapped from God*. Now, as we are nearing the end of our journey through the Bible and how it impacts our exile and return, it is time to take stock of what we have seen and develop some concluding principles.

One of the most important of these principles concerns our view of what freedom is because the word clearly means different things to different people, and how we define that term often says more about ourselves than the ultimate truth that Scripture provides. Indeed, the most popular version of the term is one which is self-centered and focused exclusively on the individual.

The problem, of course, is that what we desire just for ourselves can be very injurious to others. For example, Scripture commands us to love our neighbors as ourselves, but when our misplaced priorities motivate us to ignore the lessons learned from the 1918 Spanish flu epidemic and causes harm to others, will there be consequences? The One who judges is Eternal and Almighty but this much we know; this selfish form of individual-only freedom is not what Scripture enjoins.

Nor does Scripture support the total sublimation of the individual will to the state. There is, instead, in the Holy Writ a careful balancing between the rights of the individual and the mandate and mission of the government. That balancing can best be summed up in this, the first of three key statements about true freedom:

#1-Freedom is not culturally relative but is an absolute value, because man cannot substitute God's judgement regarding freedom in favor of his own.

Only Scripture's version is correct, which is why Yeshua said:

If the Son of man makes you free, then you are free indeed
(John 8:36).

A nation that has a great deal of this scriptural freedom is inherently superior to one that does not, because the freer nation is following the commandments of God. It is on this basis that the peoples of the Scripture, both then and now, are blessed by the Almighty.

For example, consider King David. As the undisputed monarch of Israel, David could be with any woman he wanted, and yet, he made the horrific choice to seduce Bathsheba, who was already married to one of his most loyal soldiers. David should have restrained his individual desire, not just for the sake of pleasing God who put him on the throne, but also for the sake of the throne itself, as the prophet Nathan boldly proclaimed to him in no uncertain terms:

> *Thus says YHWH the Mighty One of Israel, I anointed you king over Israel, and I delivered you out of the hand of Saul; and I gave you your master's house, and your master's wives into your bosom, and gave you the house of Israel and of Judah; and if that had been too little, I would have given you more of such things. Why then have you despised the commandment of YHWH, to do evil in his sight? You have killed Uriah the Hittite with the sword, and have taken his wife to be your wife, and have slain him with the sword of the children of Ammon. Now therefore the sword shall never depart from your house; because you have despised me and have taken the wife of Uriah the Hittite to be your wife. Thus says YHWH, Behold, I will raise up evil against you out of your own house, and I will take your wives before your eyes, and give them to your neighbor, and he shall lie with your wives in the sight of this sun. For you did it secretly: but I will do this thing before all Israel, and in broad daylight. (2 Samuel 12:7-12)*

David's "freedom," then, clearly was not absolute, that is, without a huge personal cost, starting with the death of his baby that Bathsheba was carrying. That tragedy was then compounded when his daughter, Tamar, was brutally raped by her half-brother, and, when David was paralyzed with inaction his rapist son was murdered by another son, Absalom. Years later, Absalom himself would rise up in rebellion, forcing David's men to kill him to save the monarchy. Another rebellious son, Adonijah, created major tumults at the very end of David's life. Following all of this was a massive plague that killed seventy thousand people in three days, all because David desired a wicked one-night stand.

The lesson is it is not enough for a man and a woman to engage in an extra-marital affair simply because they consent to be with each other. Other parties, especially spouses and children, will surely be negatively impacted. This is another example of a selfish form of individual-only freedom that Scripture forbids.

Freedom is only absolute when we walk in the ways of God Almighty. In other words, David was not able to set aside God's definitions for murder and adultery simply because he was king. Neither could his prophet, Nathan, also speaking for God, condone such sins, enable or instigate David to sin or look the other way.

Since God had also ruled out taking David's life and invalidating his royal house, the only alternative remaining was to punish him severely for the rest of his natural life. The Ten Commandments' prohibitions against adultery, committing murder and coveting the wife of your neighbor, as well as the Scriptural requirement to love one's neighbor as oneself, overrode any decision David might have made to the contrary.

Perhaps, the most interesting aspect to contemplate regarding these events is this: David received all this chastisement while clearly being deeply loved by God. He did not invalidate David's rule or his throne but kept him in power even as he was being punished. David had to learn that it was not all about his own choices in his own life. His actions affected many others.

The question is, if such is the case that a king's behavior needs to be checked, how much more must that be true for the rest of us? Scripture's version of freedom is that God empowers the king, and the king, in turn, empowers and protects his people. The rights of the individual are taken care of, but not at the expense of the good of the nation under God. At the same time, while David literally rules by divine right, his power can be taken away at any moment if he fails to live up to his obligations under covenant.

Scripture, in other words, has a preferred form of government and a sacred brand of politics that we need to understand and utilize. Fortunately, thanks to God speaking to our founding father, Moses, we know in vast detail the functions and purpose of that more perfect union. In Deuteronomy 17:14-20 for example, Moses spells out the following qualifications for a kosher Chief Executive:

> ➢ He must be someone directly chosen by God (17:15).
> ➢ He cannot be from another country (17:15).
> ➢ He will not have a great quantity of wives, or silver or gold (17:17).
> ➢ He will write a copy of Scripture's kingship laws out in the presence of the priests and keep it by his side day and night (17:18-19).
> ➢ He will learn reverential fear of his Creator and faithfully obey His laws (17:19).
> ➢ He will not be elevated above his own brothers to turn aside from the Holy Covenant (17:20).

Modern American parallels to these criteria are easy to see. We require our presidents to be born in this country and defend the Constitution, a document that commands we treat each other fairly and equally under the law. That same law also prohibits the infringement of the free exercise of faith. Further, keeping God's Word and His Law close to us is familiar to us in our legal system, as we swear to tell the truth on a Bible and put "In God we trust" on our currency, so neither we nor the president ever forget where the true power comes from. As Yeshua said to the Roman governor, Pontius Pilate: "You would have no power if it were not granted to you from above" (John 19:10-11).

On the other hand, we find all around us many politicians and some presidents who most certainly elevate themselves above their brethren, multiply excessive wealth for themselves instead of prospering the nation, take many lovers, and refuse to obey God's commandments. That being the case, is it any wonder that we have the problems we all suffer from today? We cannot reject our Heavenly Father, choose a human ruler who is in opposition to His Law and expect to have peace and prosperity. It simply does not work that way! (1 Samuel 8:7-20)

Where Deuteronomy 17:14-20 leads to, then, should not be surprising: Scripture commands a strong throne or central government, but the head of state personally is weaker than his office, being constantly checked by other branches of power. In David's case, it was the priesthood and the school of prophets.

The king of Israel was a steward, a shepherd and, occasionally, a general, yet ultimately, he merely held the throne until Yeshua the Messiah came to sit on it eternally (Daniel 7:13-14, Luke 1:31-32). Recognizing that, today's heads of state must also bow down and obey the Messiah or face the consequences (Revelation 19:15-16). As a result, no nation today, including Israel and the United States, can know peace derived from their earthly throne, if they choose a ruler that God does not endorse.

Freedom is also an absolute value in the sense that a given culture has no right to define that term for itself apart from the biblical definition. In other words, a culture has no right to assert its own traditions above the commandments in Scripture. They cannot, for example, proclaim the "freedom" to treat workers or servants as little more than animals, simply because a rich minority rules over a poor majority. They cannot say it is their culture to enslave people to whom they should be paying a just wage and providing protection. Nor can they promote a "tradition" of sexual perversion and promiscuity just because they are inclined to do so. Scripture is very clear that societies which attempt to put their own laws above the laws of God are subject to His fierce judgment and punishment (Leviticus 18:24).

#2-Biblical freedom is about family and corporate and national responsibility to guard the rights of all members of society.

As our brave men and women in the armed services know all too well, true freedom is hard to gain and easy to lose, if we fail to learn the lessons of history. The great warrior, Gideon, is an example of this pattern. After gaining an amazing victory for Israel against enemies who were far more numerous and battle tested than Israel was (Judges 6-7), Gideon retired from service and soon lapsed into paganism; the lure of idolatrous riches and fine luxury items proved too much for him. He then completed his fall from grace by returning to his other name which means *let Baal multiply* (Judges 8:27-29). In addition, we are told:

And it came to be, when Gideon was dead, that the children of Israel again went whoring after the baals and made Baal-Berith their mighty one. Thus, the children of Israel did not remember YHWH their Elohim, who had delivered them from the hands of all their enemies surrounding them. (Judges 8:33-34)

Another excellent example of this counterfeit freedom comes from Jeroboam, the first ruler of the northern kingdom, who is a perfect case study of what *not* to do. As he was fleeing to Egypt, God made it known to him, through a prophet, that ten tribes would be torn away from Solomon's line and given for him to rule.

But Jeroboam's faith in God's power was not strong enough to prevent him from seeking an illegal alliance with Egypt, who later backed his royal claim. He also had the audacity to inaugurate a new religion of his own design, complete with brand new feasts, a fabricated priesthood, and a renewed focus on golden calf worship. He, through repeated false proclamations, convinced the people to follow him. He had the bully pulpit, and he used it for his advantage, but to the detriment of his people.

The eternal truth of Sinai was traded in by Jeroboam in order to maintain power and keep the people away from the Jerusalem Temple, the true priesthood and faith. In essence, Jeroboam became Egyptian in his heart and then infected his subjects with the same kind of rebellion, all in the name of political expediency.

And yet, for all Jeroboam's many mistakes, it must be borne in the mind that his political calculations about how his people would respond were perfectly accurate. He led the ten tribes into apostasy, not in shame, but with applause and popular accolades gracing every step he took. When we look at our leaders, their politics and policies for our country, which side of the fence are we on – righteousness or self-destruction?

As we saw earlier, Jeroboam was initially successful because God sanctioned him as an instrument to punish Solomon, and Jeroboam maintained his rule for a while after losing the favor of YHWH who put him on the throne. But, in the final analysis, it was the people of the ten tribes who lost the blessings and protection of God Almighty.

We need to reclaim our rightful history as believers, going back to the original message for us, and what it really means for us today. That is why Scripture warns us in many places that bad leadership leads nations away from true freedom and into slavery, masquerading as freedom. The fact is, until our society recognizes that all people have rights and access to life, liberty, and the pursuit of happiness, we can never be absolutely free while others among us remain in bondage (Exodus 12:30-33).

#3-We either all throw off the shackles of Pharaoh and embrace freedom through servanthood to our God, or we don't get to leave Egypt.

The danger we face is going from our God-given Scriptural freedom to the enemy's counterfeit "freedom" that comforts us while enslaving us at the same time:

Notwithstanding the children rebelled against me: they walked not in my statutes, neither kept my judgments to do them, which if a man do, he shall even live in them; they polluted my sabbaths: then I said, I would pour out my fury upon them, to accomplish my anger against them in the wilderness...This is why I gave them also statutes that were not good, and judgments by which they could not live; and I polluted them in their own gifts, in that they caused to pass through the fire all that opens the womb, that I might make them desolate, to the end that they might know that I am YHWH. (Ezekiel 20:21, 25-26)

An important lesson to end this discussion is with respect to the virtues and vices of Solomon. From his humble request for a discerning heart as a little boy, to his completion of the massive Temple of God, he is rightly celebrated for his wisdom. However, such praise only applies to the first half of his forty-year long reign. Then, very subtly, the seeds of Solomon's downfall came in the form of requests from his many wives:

For it came to pass, when Solomon was old, that his wives turned away his heart after other gods: and his heart was not perfect with YHWH his Mighty One, as was the heart of David his father. For Solomon went after Ashtoreth the goddess of the Zidonians, and after Milcom the abomination of the Ammonites.

And Solomon did evil in the sight of YHWH, and did not fully follow after YHWH, as did David his father. Then Solomon built a high place for Chemosh, the abomination of Moab, in the hill that is before Jerusalem, and for Molech, the abomination of the children of Ammon, and likewise he did for all his foreign wives, who burned incense and sacrificed to their gods.

So YHWH was angry with Solomon, because his heart was turned from YHWH, the Mighty One of Israel, who had appeared to him twice, and who had commanded him concerning this thing, that he should not go after other gods: but he did not keep what YHWH commanded. So YHWH said to Solomon, Because you have done this and you have not kept my covenant and my statutes, which I have commanded you, I will surely tear the kingdom away from you, and will give it to your servant.
(1 Kings 11:4-11)

That servant, of course, was Jeroboam. So not only did Solomon's folly help weaken his own throne and be a catalyst for the fall of his people into paganism, he also enabled his dreaded enemy to take ten of the twelve tribes of Israel out of his kingdom. Indeed, the seeds of Jeroboam's success were sown in the failures of Solomon and the depravity of Solomon returning paganism to Israel, which very likely inspired Jeroboam to do the same thing for his new kingdom in the north.

At the end of the day, as the lesson was for David, so it is for the punishment and rebuke of Solomon. If even the wisest man in the world can be led astray to sin, who are we to think that our wisdom and prestige will do any better against the temptations of the world?

Solomon and Jeroboam are just two examples of leaders – affecting both the secular and religious realms – who had the support of at least some people in the nation to turn the rest of God's people away from Him and into paganism. Therefore, each one of us and collectively as a nation need to be vigilant about everything our leadership does in our name, for it is we who gave them power and authority by voting them into office.

Those who deny freedom to others deserve it not for themselves; and under the rule of a just God, cannot long retain it. –
Abraham Lincoln

SECTION SEVEN

Getting Ready to Come Home

But this is what I wrote to you, that you not keep company with anyone called a brother, if he is one who is a sexual sinner, or greedy of gain, or an idolater, or a reviler, or a drunkard or a swindler—with such a person do not even eat bread.
(1 Corinthians 5:11)

Meanwhile, as the Jews continued their exile throughout the Middle Ages, they encountered some nations who tolerated them and others who did not. In at least some of these cases the worst relations the Jews had were with those nations who were descended from peoples the prophets predicted would go to war against them. For example, the prophet Ezekiel talked about God Almighty being set against "Gog, Magog, Meshech and Tubal" who will try to destroy Israel in some future time, but Israel will ultimately prevail.

Prior to that victory, however, these nations will continue to greatly vex Israel. Gog and Magog in particular represent historic enemies of the Jews those being Germany, Austria and Russia.

This is not to say these places today, however, are evil, but rather that some from these nations have been predicted, by the prophets of old, to do evil deeds against Israel. The same is true of the Kittim, the ancient prophetic name for Rome, and what they did against the children of Abraham.

By the Middle Ages, Christians had gone from declaring Jews morally or ethnically inferior to trying to wipe them out or vastly curtail their legal rights. St. John Chrysostom once famously remarked that a synagogue was no better than a brothel while St. Thomas Aquinas and Martin Luther's suggestions on how to "manage" the Jews became part of Hitler's plans as well.

During this same period, after Chrysostom but before Hitler, oppressive rules and harsh treatment of the Jews in Europe caused many of them to go into hiding or pass themselves off as Catholics with non-Jewish names, so as not to be persecuted. As a result, many Christians today around the world are realizing that they have Jewish ancestry, or at the very least have a component of their DNA tracing back to it. Many of the "lost sheep" of Israel are being found after millennia of wandering and many others grafted in are finding their way home to their Almighty God, YHWH. Halleluyah—Praise you YAH.

It would only be with the defeat of the Nazis at the end of World War II, and the shocking discoveries of the Holocaust with about 6 million Jews dead, that the world community was at last moved to allow the Jews to return fully to their land. The British brokered the final establishment of the Jewish state in 1948, ending the exile that had been going on more than 1,800 years. Now that Israel is re-established, with millions of her people back home, many believers think this circumstance ushers in a series of events counting down to Messiah's return. Only time will tell how ready we are on his return.

God's people seem to be waiting for something or someone to make things better, but ask yourself this question that the great 1st century rabbi Hillel the Elder asked:

If not you, who? If not now, when?

Remember Clement the bishop of Rome, a disciple of the Apostle John? In his Letter to the Corinthians, this earliest church father shared his hope and prayer for all of you:

"Look carefully into the Scriptures, which are the true utterances of the Holy Spirit. Observe that nothing of an unjust or counterfeit character in written in them." (Chapter 45)

"Let us cleave, therefore, to the innocent and righteous, since these are the elect of God. Why are there strifes, and tumults, and divisions, and schisms, and wars among you? Have we not [all] one God and one Christ?...Why do we divide and tear to pieces the members of Christ...Remember the words of our Lord Jesus Christ, how he said, 'Woe to that man [by whom offenses come]! It is better for him that he had never been born than that he should cast a stumbling block before one of my elect...Your schism has subverted [the faith of] many, has discouraged many, has given rise to doubt in many, and has caused grief to us all. And still your sedition continues.'" (Chapter 46)

"Take up the epistle of the blessed Apostle Paul. What did he write to you at the time when the Gospel first began to be preached? But now reflect who those are that have perverted you." (Chapter 47)

"Let us therefore, with all haste, put an end to this [state of things]; and let us fall down before the Lord, and beseech Him with tears, that He would mercifully be reconciled to us, and restore us to our former seemly and holy practice of brotherly love...Let a man be faithful; let him be powerful in the utterance of knowledge; let him be wise in judging of words; let him be pure in all his deeds; yet the more he seems to be superior to

267

others [in these respects], the more humble minded ought he to be, and to seek the common good of all and not merely his own advantage." (Chapter 48)

"Let him who has loved in Christ keep the commandments of Christ." (Chapter 49)

"Blessed are we, beloved, if we keep the commandments of God in the harmony of love; that so through love our sins may be forgiven us…This blessedness comes upon those who have been chosen by God through Jesus Christ our Lord." (Chapter 50)

"You understand, beloved, you understand well the Sacred Scriptures and you have looked very earnestly into the oracles of God. Call then these things to your remembrance." (Chapter 53)

"You see, beloved, that protection is afforded to those that are chastened of the Lord; for since God is good, He corrects us, that we may be admonished by His holy chastisement." (Chapter 56)

"For it is better for you that you should occupy a humble but honorable place in the flock of Christ, than that, being highly exalted, you should be cast out from the hope of His people." (Chapter 57)

We need to take to heart that if Yeshua can be tested and tried, so will we. Let us be cognizant of the fact that satan and his minions know how to use Scripture, so check everything you hear. Regarding the path to salvation, this is what Messiah Yeshua has to say:

Enter through the narrow gate; for the gate is wide and the way is broad that leads to destruction, and there are many who enter through it. For the gate is small and the way is narrow that leads to life, and there are few who find it. (Matthew 7:13-14 NAU)

Study each word and ponder on the message: *many enter* through the wide gate but only *few find* the narrow gate. He did not say few enter it. He is saying you must actively search Scripture and your heart to *find* this narrow gate first, and then you have to do something, i.e., *walk with him* to enter it. This should explain why he also said:

"Not everyone who says to Me, 'Lord, Lord,' will enter the kingdom of heaven, but he who does the will of My Father who is in heaven will enter. "Many will say to Me on that day, 'Lord, Lord, did we not prophesy in Your name, and in Your name cast out demons, and in Your name perform many miracles?' And then I will declare to them, 'I never knew you; DEPART FROM ME, YOU WHO PRACTICE LAWLESSNESS.'
(Matthew 7:21-23 NAU)

"Do not think that I will accuse you before the Father; the one who accuses you is Moses, in whom you have set your hope. For if you believed Moses, you would believe Me, for he wrote about Me. But if you do not believe his writings, how will you believe My words?" (John 5:45-47 NAU).

What the Future Holds

And someone came to Him and said, "Teacher, what good thing shall I do that I may obtain eternal life?" And He said to him, "Why are you asking Me about what is good? There is only One who is good; but if you wish to enter into life, keep the commandments." (Matthew 19:16-17 NAU)

So, while we make efforts to learn from each other, we should all *study,* and not just *read*, the Scripture for ourselves. Examine each word, look at the context, check for translation accuracy and pray for His Guidance. At the end of the day, the responsibility for walking out your salvation lies with you, not with your pastor, church or congregation elders.

Throughout all the times of the Scripture, our Heavenly Father has shown us, repeatedly, how a righteous remnant perseveres even after so many others get cut off for a time due to disobedience. While the remnant continues, Father YHWH has also made provision for those who left Him to return in covenant and into the blessed family He intended for them all along.

Having said that, the issue for today's believers is that many of them look at their faith as a kind of pre-flight checklist that they update in advance of "the rapture." They hope it will take them off the planet while the rest of humanity suffers hardship and death. If so, who will then go looking for that one lost sheep? We, as believers, have succumbed to the many lies told to us, rather than proclaim the Scripture with boldness:

So that we confidently say, "THE LORD IS MY HELPER, I WILL NOT BE AFRAID. WHAT WILL MAN DO TO ME?"
(Hebrews 13:6 NAU)

Paul did not concern himself with what the myriads of people around him thought, whether Jewish or Gentile. Jude called out theological perversion in graphic detail, telling us to go to war against the lies of this world. Peter and John passionately contended against false teachers and their doctrines by name, boldly and publicly, without filter or spin.

Since for all of us our faith came, if we take it back far enough, from the Apostles, let us ask this question: Are we walking in truth, conviction and in the love of Messiah as they once did? Or do we instead rely on the "Torah" of moral relativism and the "Gospel" of situational ethics?

Do we in one breath proclaim disdain at the slaughter of the innocents done by King Manasseh or Herod the Great, only to grant "toleration" to our society murdering more than a million infants a year and calling it a "choice?" Do we deride the sensual

270

perversions of the paganism and homosexuality of the Greco-Roman world, only to turn around in an instant and condone some of those same forbidden practices out of political correctness? Have our tastes and conventions qualified us to be the final editors of Genesis?

Also, if our faith walk seems strange to the generations that have now come of age, maybe it is because we have kicked His Word out of their classrooms or let them embrace a flawed theory about us coming from apes rather than us being the crowning achievement of God Almighty's creative glory. Do we root our understanding in eternal Scripture definitions or base it on the latest academic opinions? What would have happened if Moses had consulted a focus group on whether the Ten Commandments at Mount Sinai are better called the Ten Suggestions, so as not to scare people?

For much of the 20th century and into our current times, we have defined our social progress as a culture in the pursuit of rights for one group or another, whether it be for African Americans, First Nations people, the unborn, women or gays and lesbians. But the sobering fact is that the Scripture offers justice, fairness and protection to everyone; it only "discriminates" on one basis and one basis alone: Are you righteous or wicked? Do you obey or are you rebellious to the Word of God?

And what God says through Scripture, however unpopular, cannot be superseded by the hand of man. As Paul's former teacher, the wise Rabbi Gamaliel counseled:

"So in the present case, I say to you, stay away from these men and let them alone, for if this plan or action is of men, it will be overthrown; but if it is of God, you will not be able to overthrow them; or else you may even be found fighting against God."
(Acts 5:38-39 NAU)

Those who follow God and trust His Word are blessed, treasured and protected, while those who don't are punished, banished or eliminated—not by us, but by Him (Ezekiel 18:4, Romans 6:23).

All of us get the same opportunity in our lives to have all our sins forgiven and become a new creation in Messiah Yeshua. Others may find God's grace perhaps because He chooses to bestow it on them despite who they are, but this is not certain in every case (Exodus 33:19, Romans 9:15). We should not play Russian roulette with the salvation that has been offered to us.

The reality is that we can neither earn, nor pay for, nor deserve grace, and yet the path away from condemnation and judgment, and to eternal life and joy, is right before our feet! The fact is none of us would have eternal life if not for Yeshua, because we all have sinned and come short of the glory of God (Isaiah 53:4-6, Romans 3:23).

Scripture describes as the future of the faith, the return to our Creator and His commandments which never should have been abandoned in the first place:

And the dragon was enraged against the woman; and he went to make war upon the remnant of her seed <u>who keep the Commandments of Elohim and have the testimony of Yeshua.</u> (Revelation 12:17)

<u>Blessed are they who do His (Master YHWH's) Commandments</u> that they may have a right to the tree of life and may enter through the gates into the city. (Revelation 22:14)

We can stay in exile, doubt and grief about our role in this vast Cosmos, or we can decide to come home to Him in obedience. Many of us making that decision today are much like the prodigal son. He realized, only after he left his father's house, that the obedient servants in his father's house were better provided for than he was, because he took his inheritance early and ran away from his obligations. What about you?

Will you back the majority report of the ten spies that the Promised Land is fraught with danger and filled with people too strong to be resisted, or will you stand with a Caleb spirit and say, "We should by all means go up and take that land, for we will surely overcome them?" (Numbers 14:30)

Will you flee into the comfort of false things that will not save you, or stand with Joshua proclaiming, "As for me and my house, we will serve YHWH?" (Joshua 24:15)

Will you take shelter with the 850 prophets of Baal and Asherah who thrive under the protection of Ahab and Jezebel, or bravely walk over to Elijah's side, cheering him on when he says, "Answer me, O YHWH, answer me, that this people may know that You, O YHWH, are Elohim, and that You have turned their heart back again?" (1 Kings 18:37)

Will you feel like so many others that there is nothing to be done about the wickedness in your midst or will you pray a prayer of national repentance as if your life depended on it, as Samuel, David, Hezekiah, Daniel and Nehemiah did?

Will you slay the Philistines of your heart, or become them?

Will you believe that the words of Isaiah, Jeremiah and Ezekiel are not only meant for *those people back then* but for all people today?

And finally, will you be like so many of Yeshua's own followers who later disowned and rejected him or agree with Peter when he asks, "Master to whom shall we go? You have the words of eternal life!" (John 6:68)

You have been *kidnapped from God* because of the sins of your ancestors and held in captivity by ignorance, which is why God Himself said:

My people perish for lack of knowledge. Because you have rejected knowledge, I also will reject you from being My priest. Since you have forgotten the Torah of your Elohim, I also will forget your children. (Hosea 4:6)

Now, however, the time has come to return home to our Heavenly Father, both in this world and in the world to come.

And I saw new heavens and a new earth: for the former heaven and the former earth had passed away: and the sea was no more. And I saw the Set Apart city, the New Jerusalem, descending from Elohim (God) out of heaven, prepared like a bride adorned for her husband.

And I heard a great voice from heaven, which said: "Behold, the tabernacle of Elohim is with men; and He dwells with them: they will be His people; and He will be with them, a Mighty One to them. And every tear will be wiped from their eyes; and there will no more be death, nor mourning, nor wailing; nor will pain be any more; because the former things are passed away." (Revelation 21:1-4)

Where you are now, and where you will be for eternity, is entirely in your hands. In the End of Days, the remnant will be obedient to YHWH our God. I can only pray and hope that we will all be together at that special place, with Him and in Him.

And the Spirit and the bride say, 'Come.' And let him that hears, say, 'Come.' And let him who thirsts, come; and he that is inclined, let him take the living water freely. (Revelation 22:17)

HEAVENLY FATHER,

THANK YOU FOR BEING OUR MIGHTY ELOHIM (GOD),

OUR KING, OUR TEACHER AND OUR GUIDE,

OUR PROTECTOR, OUR PROVIDER, OUR DELIVERER AND
OUR REFUGE.

THANK YOU FOR YOUR LOVE AND YOUR COMPASSION,

FOR YOUR MERCY AND YOUR GRACE UPON OUR LIVES.

PLEASE HOLD US CLOSE TO YOU,

NEVER LEAVE US OR FORSAKE US,

BUT WALK AHEAD OF US AND SHOW US THE WAY,

SO THAT WE WILL NOT STUMBLE OR FALL OR LOSE OUR
WAY.

PLEASE OPEN THE DOORS THAT YOU WANT US TO WALK
THROUGH

AND CLOSE THOSE THAT YOU DON'T,

AND GIVE US THE STRENGTH TO WALK THE RIGHTEOUS
PATH

SO THAT WE TOO, LIKE YOUR SON,

MAY BE OBEDIENT TO YOU AND PLEASING TO YOU.

BLESS US WITH YOUR WISDOM AND UNDERSTANDING,

AND WITH KNOWLEDGE AND DISCERNMENT,

KEEP US SAFE AND PROSPER US.

I PRAY THIS IN YOUR SET APART NAME, FATHER YAHWEH

AND IN THE NAME OF YOUR ONLY BEGOTTEN SON

YESHUA THE MESSIAH

AMEN, AMEN.

FEEDBACK

We encourage you to email us and leave a review, comment or testimony at AJRoth.KFG@gmail.com to share your thoughts and experiences related to this book. Please be civil and polite as we acknowledge that all of you may not agree with everything we have written. You may also leave a review of this book at Amazon.

Additionally, we plan to have a blog at andrewgabrielroth.com and a Facebook page so that you can comment, follow me and receive updates. Also periodically check out my author's page on Amazon.com. I am working on an updated translation of the Apostolic Writings or Renewed Covenant from Aramaic to English, which hopefully will be out by the end of 2021.

Finally, thank you for sharing this important journey as we discussed the history of our Judeo-Christian faith and how we not only got separated from each other but also from our Heavenly Father. We sincerely pray this book will equip you for Messiah's return. This story though is just getting started…

If you are interested to learn more, I teach Scripture weekly at:

onefaithonepeopleministries.com

or write to us at:

One Faith One People Ministries,

P.O. Box 1654, Woodstock, Georgia 30188, USA

Andrew G Roth - Founder and President

Jaye Roth - Co-Founder and VP of Global Outreach